# The Almighty BLACK P STONE NATION

## THE RISE, FALL, AND RESURGENCE OF AN AMERICAN GANG

NATALIE Y. MOORE
AND LANCE WILLIAMS

Lawrence Hill Books

**Library of Congress Cataloging-in-Publication Data**
Moore, Natalie Y.
 The Almighty Black P Stone Nation : the rise, fall, and resurgence of an
American gang / Natalie Y. Moore and Lance Williams.
    p. cm.
 Includes bibliographical references and index.
 ISBN 978-1-55652-845-3 (hardcover)
 ISBN 978-1-61374-491-8 (trade paper)
 1. Gangs—Illinois—Chicago—History. 2. Black P Stone Nation
(Organization—History. 3. African Americans—Illinois—Chicago—History.
I. Williams, Lance. II. Title.
 HV6439.U7C436 2010
 364.106'60977311—dc22

                                                            2010040297

Interior design: Jonathan Hahn

© 2011 by Natalie Y. Moore and Lance Williams
Published by Lawrence Hill Books
An imprint of Chicago Review Press, Incorporated
814 North Franklin Street
Chicago, Illinois 60610
ISBN 978-1-61374-491-8
Printed in the United States of America

*To the Mahone women*
—NATALIE


*To my father, Roy*
—LANCE

# Acknowledgments

THIS PROJECT BEGAN out of sheer curiosity. We started research and are grateful for the staff at the Vivian Harsh Collection at Carter G. Woodson Regional Library, the Chicago History Museum, the University of Chicago Library, the Columbia College Chicago Library, the National Archives (Great Lakes Region), and the Newberry Library. Thanks to all the Stones who generously shared their stories with us.

Chris Pratt came on board as a research assistant at a time when we really needed him, and he proved to be indispensable. I'd be lost without the feedback on drafts, and moral support, from Chana Garcia, Natalie Hopkinson, Adrienne Samuels Gibbs, Ron Stodghill, Jua Mitchell, Prince A. Mhoon, Afi-Odelia Scruggs, Todd Occomy, Mick Dumke, Thomas Fisher Jr., and Christopher M. Singer.

Thanks to Benjamin Talton, Grayson Mitchell, Ethan Michaeli, Aaron Sarver, Tracy Austin, Valerie Mays, Timuel Black, and Diane Luhmann of First Presbyterian for providing connections and/or documents. Lesley Gool graciously assisted with too-many-to-count legal resources. Thanks to Bayo Ojikutu, Yancey Hbrowski, William Jelani Cobb, Ta-Nehisi Coates, Dave Pierini, Patrick Rivers, and the

South Side Community Arts Center Writers Group. Thanks to the Bronzeville Coffeehouse.

My colleagues at WBEZ let me bounce ideas off them and encouraged the project: Julia McEvoy, Cate Cahan, Sally Eisele, Torey Malatia, Steve Edwards, Justin Kaufmann, and Andrew Gill. Thanks to Nancy Day, Jane Saks, and Jen Halperin of Columbia College. Sue Betz and Michelle Schoob—thanks for your keen editing eyes and for believing in us on behalf of Lawrence Hill Press. My family continues to be supportive of my projects, and I thank them. Lance, thanks for the partnership and extra thanks to your family for letting me borrow you.

—NATALIE Y. MOORE

MOST IMPORTANT, I would like to thank my wife and children for their unconditional love and patience, without which I would not have been able to complete this book. And to my parents, Roy and Annette, thanks for always keeping me grounded in a love for my people from the suites to the streets. I would like to give special thanks to John Hagedorn, a friend, colleague, and comrade in the struggle to produce scholarship on street organizations that moves beyond the scope of pathology and criminality. I would also like to thank my colleagues at the Jacob H. Carruthers Center for Inner City Studies at Northeastern Illinois University—Drs. Conrad Worrill, Anderson Thompson, Robert T. Starks, and Zada Johnson—for their support and guidance.

Thanks to Sue Betz and all of the wonderful people at Lawrence Hill Books for giving us this opportunity. And thanks to Michelle Schoob for her editorial support and feedback.

Much thanks to all of the 8-Tray Moes who blessed me to share in all aspects of their lives. It was the years spent on 8-Tray that provided me with the appreciation for true brotherhood and the experience necessary to finish this book. I would like to give a special thanks to all of the Blackstones and their families who welcomed me into the Blackstone family and encouraged me to tell their story.

I've learned a great deal about the Stones over the years from personal experience. Where my personal experience ended, my teachers picked up. To Janis, Lawrence, Red, Khan, Melvin, Joe, Benny, Raheem, Sultan, Duck, Will, Teon, Dr. Russell, and Lew, you have all been excellent teachers—thanks!

I would like to express my gratitude to Natalie, my book partner, for her continued support and patience through the process of researching and writing this book.

—LANCE WILLIAMS

# Contents

# Introduction

THE STORY OF THE Almighty Black P Stone Nation is more than a footnote to Chicago history; the organization is also wrapped in U.S. history. The Stones have been painted as victims of circumstance, as champions of social change, and as brainwashed dupes ready to bomb federal buildings. They have been linked to some of the most violent gangs across the country, including the Vice Lords and the Bloods. The variety of definitions helps generate a sense of mysticism that surrounds the gang. The founders were Eugene "Bull" Hairston, a favorite son of Chicago's black gangsters who saw potential in him, and Jeff Fort, a short, skinny kid from rural Mississippi whose family moved to the South Side of Chicago in the 1950s. Hairston and Fort formed the Blackstone Rangers, the precursor to the P Stone Nation, in the early 1960s on Blackstone Avenue in the Woodlawn neighborhood. The name changed several times during the gang's fifty year history. It started as the Blackstone Rangers, became the Almighty Black P Stone Nation at its peak era, and later changed to the El Rukns. Today the name of the organization is the Black P Stone Nation. The organization has a long and controversial legacy of criminal charges ranging from defrauding the federal government to drug trafficking to conspiracy to commit domestic terrorism.

1

We embarked upon this project because we wanted to write about the conflicting, complicated, and nuanced facets of the organization. One weekday night in 2007, Natalie watched *American Gangster*, the BET series about various black criminal figures and organizations. She saw Lance talk about the Stones on the Jeff Fort episode. The next day she e-mailed him, asking for a list of books about contemporary black street gangs in Chicago. There are none, he replied, and thus our collaboration began on this book.

We are Chicago natives, with deep ties to the city, and we care deeply about urban issues. As a kid in the 1960s and '70s, Lance used to hang out with his father, a reformed Vice Lord. The YMCA hired Mr. Williams to be a gang outreach worker—an "unofficial social worker" with street credibility. The YMCA assigned him to the Stones in Woodlawn. His job included organizing such recreational activities as ball games, picnics, and field trips for members and their girlfriends. He also helped them mediate beefs they had with other street gangs like the Dell Vikings and the Disciples. Lance, who often tagged along, recalls his father telling him about Jeff Fort and the Stones as teenagers putting the organization together. Many of those old Stones remember the young Lance and grew to trust him as he took an academic path studying gangs and youth culture.

Natalie's maternal grandparents moved to Woodlawn from rural Georgia after World War II. Natalie's mother grew up in West Woodlawn, an island of black middle-class homeowners. But the community that reared Jeff Fort had declined over the decades, and some of those scars were always associated with the Stones.

THROUGH THE YEARS the Stones encountered a colorful cast of characters, from white liberal do-gooders to Black Nationalists to community organizers to the Nation of Islam to zealous law enforcement. The Stones' culture also ran counter to mainstream America, and Fort unwittingly guided the mighty Stones into clashes with major federal policies through the decades. At the end of 1968, Bull had been locked up for solicitation of murder, leaving the Stones without their Big Chief. The organization ultimately found itself in the crosshairs of the War on Poverty, the War on Drugs, and the War on Terror.

In the 1960s, President Lyndon B. Johnson's War on Poverty sought to help cities and their underclasses. Urban neighborhoods like Woodlawn received buckets of cash in a program designed to give black youth jobs and opportunities. The Stones were flirting with Black Power and the civil rights movement at the time, but some members were also involved in extortion and violence. The Stones and a rival gang, the Disciples, received nearly a million dollars in federal funding. But at the time the two groups were in constant combat, killing each other and ruining the peace in the neighborhood. Program organizers thought job training could prevent the violence. But the program had adversaries, and the lack of oversight in its implementation allowed it to run amok. Scapegoat Fort went to prison in the early 1970s for defrauding the program.

Upon his release, Fort ushered in the Islamic era of the Stones. In 1977, he officially changed the name of the organization to the El Rukns. Fort evolved into Chief Malik, head of a tight-knit, secretive society of men. Fort insisted that the El Rukns were a religious organization, but law enforcement saw them as a vicious gang entrenched in the drug trade. The so-called War on Drugs raged in the 1980s, and the El Rukns were subjected to newly implemented Reagan-era laws meant to dismantle street organizations. Meanwhile, the Nation of Islam courted an alliance with the El Rukns that continued after Fort went to federal prison again—this time for dealing drugs.

Police and prosecutors never relented in their pursuit of Fort, even while he sat behind bars. Federal investigators wiretapped his phone and listened in on talk that stretched well beyond dealing drugs. They said the El Rukns were plotting terrorist attacks in the United States on behalf of Libya's Colonel Muammar el-Qaddafi. This era long predates the 9/11 attacks and the official declaration of the War on Terror. But today may be an apt time to reexamine the El Rukns; when the U.S. government successfully convicted a group of

El Rukns for plotting with Libyan operatives in 1987, it set the stage for future prosecutors to link U.S. street gangs to terrorists from Arab states. The El Rukn story may serve as a cautionary tale for other street organizations. Their predilection for Islam—and greed, although the two are unrelated—put the organization at risk of falling for FBI traps. Now it's all done in the name of homeland security.

POINTING OUT THE criminal elements of the Blackstone Nation is easy. But there's much more to dissect. Jeff Fort's struggle with identity is one of the factors that contributed to his leadership. Whether he was Jeff, Angel, or Chief Malik, Fort always created a haven for his followers, offering a place to safely express their identity and to commune. He also gave the Stone Nation social capital; they had rules that centered on mission, protocol, and interaction. Fort built a specific organization for and by black males—and the good and bad behavior they exhibited fell within the context of blackness. They weren't foolish enough to mess with white folk lest the police really knock heads. One gang expert in Chicago even likened the activities of black street organizations to Negritude. The Stones certainly weren't an offshoot of this intellectual, French-speaking black movement, but the idea of black identity expressed through socialization and culture in organizations served as a guidepost.

Many sociologists study gangs to examine their extended networks of relationships. Law enforcement officials often view gangs only within the context of organized crime. Our intent isn't to create caricatures or promote black pathology. Nor are we attempting to gloss over the Stones' brutal impact on their community. The history of the Stones is wrapped in the economic and social functions of black Chicago, which is how we approached this project.

As we finished writing this book, we couldn't help but think about modern-day hand-wringing about youth violence in Chicago. Well-meaning educators, politicians, and activists are collectively coming up with solutions. The high-profile death of Derrion Albert, the South Side student whose 2009 beating and death was caught on camera and then posted on YouTube for the world to see, amplified those conversations. Chicago teen killings have been receiving unprecedented national attention these days. But unfortunately this problem is not as new as some observers would like to suggest. The brutality between the Stones and the Disciples—yes, even in the halcyon 1960s, we tell our elders—proved to be shocking.

We unearthed many nuggets about the Stones. This is one of our favorites: an Almighty Black P Stone Nation newspaper from 1970 has a front-page headline blaring "End Police Repression Now." An editorial on page two cried out, "Our leaders are our heroes. They will remain our heroes no matter what the press, politicians, police, courts or jailers do or say about them. We choose and will continue to choose our leaders." The P Stone leaders listed were Bull Hairston, Jeff Fort, and Mickey Cogwell. The editorial admired Marcus Garvey, Martin Luther King Jr., Huey Newton, and Malcolm X. The paper also included articles on the dismal job rate for blacks, quotes from Stokely Carmichael, and bold lettering about the P Stone Nation's opposition to drugs, prostitution, and crime.

Fort used the paper as a clarion call. "Chief Calls for Unity" read the top of the page. The message was for Panthers, Disciples, and Lords—and all black organizations, especially youth groups in Chicago—to move toward black liberation. Fort's message of Stone Love derided the police department's war on gangs as a war on black youth. It hinted that the black officers involved in the gang intelligence unit were Uncle Toms brought in to divide and conquer. No one organization can speak for black folk, Fort wrote, but organizations must come together to operate from a black perspective.

"The sweetest and wildest dream of the fathers and mothers, men and women, sisters and brothers in the Black Chicago community is that we settle our differences and truly come together. Our uniting is also the thing that most feared our oppressors. This is obvious from all of the foul schemes our oppressors have used to keep us divided. If we come together, the rest of the black community will follow," Fort wrote.

He wrote about programs needed to clothe, house, and provide medical care for black people. He criticized the government for spending money on the Vietnam War rather than spending in black communities.

And his final quote at the end of the paper:

To have a nation you must have a people
To have power the people must be united
To have peace you must have truth and understanding
To have these things for stone Black people
You must have a Black Peace Stone Nation.

# 1

# Big Chief and Little Chief

"**T**AKE OFF YOUR hat, nigga."

Normally, Jeff Fort didn't yield to authority. Especially not to the white teachers at Hyde Park High School. They constantly harassed the teenager. When white teachers commanded him to take off his hat, Fort would retort, "Jeff Fort ain't gonna obey."

But the student and his crew did listen to Timuel Black, one of the few black teachers at the high school in the early 1960s. "We were like their daddies," Black says. "They respected us." So when Black stopped Fort in the hallway and ordered him to take off his hat, Fort respectfully removed the cap from his bush-top head.

Fort, the Blackstone Rangers and future P Stone Nation leader, didn't quite fit in this milieu on the South Side of Chicago. Hyde Park High School was an elite place for University of Chicago professors to send their children. Black said the school, located at 62nd and Stony Island, engaged in conspicuous tracking of its white and black students. The administration appeased white parents by creating so-called elite tracks for their students. And white troublemakers stayed in school while any infraction got black kids the boot.

Fort would've been considered a troublemaker. A fearless tough guy, Fort told the jokes but didn't like any turned on him. He was a short, slender teen who carried himself as if he had the physique of a professional bodybuilder. And while the lore around Fort is that he's illiterate and never made it past fourth grade, Black contends that "he could not read at the level he should have been reading, but he could read." And though "he was not by any means a scholar," the pupil had other gifts, leadership qualities that were intangible, difficult to describe. Black said the charisma often ascribed to Fort was obvious in his adolescence. He was not just another rough boy from the neighborhood with low grades.

When Black approached Fort to ask, "Hey, boy, you want to stay in school?" Fort replied, "Yeah, but they are always picking on us."

Fort's hostility and alienation were shared by the peers he organized. Fort—and by extension the Blackstone Rangers—were shaped by the racial struggles in the neighborhood and the burden that came with being a part of the second wave of Southern blacks moving to Chicago. Hyde Park High School is actually in the Woodlawn neighborhood, which is just south of the Hyde Park neighborhood, home to the University of Chicago. The Green Line elevated train runs along 63rd Street, the main drag in Woodlawn, which today is lined with thickly weeded lots and boarded-up buildings, the vestiges of urban blight.

Jeff Fort not fitting in at Hyde Park High School or in Woodlawn had as much to do with black folks as it did with whites. His mother, Annie Fort, had traded Aberdeen, Mississippi, for Chicago in 1956. In addition to this move, several other social, fiscal, and racial policies—official and unofficial—created the unique set of circumstances that led Fort to the gang lifestyle.

The Fort family moved to Chicago during the city's second wave of black migration. After living briefly in an area of the city known as the Black Belt, the family relocated to Woodlawn. The other future Blackstone Ranger leader, Eugene "Bull" Hairston, and his family moved in around the same time. But the Hairstons weren't from the

South; they moved from Columbus, Ohio, to Chicago's "low end," and then to Woodlawn. Like many black families in the late 1950s, the Hairston family got pushed out of a historically black area and relocated to East Woodlawn because their community had to make room for the construction of new public housing.

Families such as the Forts and the Hairstons differed from other families who came to Chicago during the first wave of migration. Black migration to Chicago was distinctly divided into two waves. The first wave, often referred to as the Great Migration, occurred during and right after World War I. African Americans from urban communities down South were met by friends or relatives at the train station on 12th Street when they arrived in Chicago. They moved into an area of the city dubbed the Black Belt, a group of neighborhoods bounded by 16th Street on the north, 39th Street on the south, State Street on the east, and LaSalle Street, running along the Rock Island Railroad tracks, on the west. Their economic and political power grew; the neighborhood's blues and jazz music matured. Black businesses thrived, and black residents voted in this pocket of the South Side. They seamlessly eased into the urban way of life and helped build up the city's black middle class. The black population of Chicago increased by 148.5 percent between 1910 and 1920.

The second wave was a bit different, less sophisticated. Rural Southern blacks were pushed off the land when technological advances after World War II allowed machines to pick cotton faster than people could. In fact, Annie Fort, Jeff's mother, had been a cotton picker. These black Southerners had been deprived of educational opportunities, kept from voting, and subjected to the Ku Klux Klan. They moved to Chicago seeking a better, Northern way of life. The *Chicago Defender*, the city's nationally read black newspaper, encouraged blacks to come to the Promised Land. Once there, they lived in rickety kitchenettes—tiny, cut-up apartments that stacked families on top of one another. Other families moved into newly constructed public housing high-rises that Mayor Richard J. Daley had built to help contain the black population. Public assistance policies didn't encourage men to live in public housing, and therefore mothers ended up raising their children solo.

Some second-wave migrants, like Jeff Fort and his family, felt alienated from the first-wave migrants. "These newcomers had no experience or relationships. They were rural and they were poor and they lived in these cramped-up quarters. Their neighbors were more fortunate, and they didn't have anything to do with them. The young ones began to crowd together; this is the emergence of gangs," Timuel Black says.

## The Community

TO FURTHER UNDERSTAND the forces that led to the formation of the Blackstone Rangers, one must not only understand the tension surrounding the various groups of black migrants but also examine the structure of the neighborhood. And that requires understanding the racial dynamics and segregation in Chicago, and to a lesser extent in Woodlawn itself.

Restrictive racial covenants helped keep Chicago's neighborhoods white from 1916 until 1948. Covenants included language that prohibited blacks from buying or using properties in white areas. If covenants didn't work, some whites resorted to violence. Blacks didn't start moving to Woodlawn in earnest until the mid-twentieth century.

Woodlawn's first residents in the 1850s were of Dutch descent. Two major events came to define the neighborhood. In 1889, Chicago annexed Woodlawn, and in 1893 the World's Columbian Exposition brought twenty thousand new residents. Sprawling, green Jackson Park was created; new apartments, hotels, and stores were built amid the economic bonanza. Sixty-Third Street boasted specialty shops. English, German, and Irish immigrants moved to Woodlawn. In 1915, blacks were 2 percent of the population.

Simultaneously, Chicago's black population grew from fifteen thousand to fifty thousand between 1890 and 1915, and the Black Belt boundaries got pushed farther south, all the way to 47th Street. The University of Chicago, chartered in 1890, purchased real estate beyond its Hyde Park location, and the population expansion of the Black Belt concerned school officials. The university's strategy slyly supported neighborhood organizations that encouraged racial restrictions by contributing to homeowners' associations in Hyde Park, Kenwood, and Woodlawn. Some of these organizations even bragged about their acumen in holding the color line. The Woodlawn Property Owners League covered property just west of the university. A flyer distributed by the Hyde Park and Kenwood Property Owners' Association in 1918 asked, "Shall we sacrifice our property for a third of its value and run like rats from a burning ship, or shall we put up a united front and keep Hyde Park desirable for ourselves?"

In 1937, a *Chicago Defender* editorial condemned Judge Michael Feinberg of the circuit court for upholding a temporary injunction that forced two men who had bought property in Woodlawn to move out of their homes and back into the Black Belt. The editorial also denounced the University of Chicago as the man behind the curtain. "It is well known in Woodlawn that this university is the motive power behind the Restrictive Covenants. In fact, many of the real estate owners in that area refer to the Restrictive Covenants as 'the University of Chicago Agreement to get rid of Negroes.' . . . It is indeed a queer combination, a Jewish judge and a liberal university dedicating themselves to the purpose of maintaining a black ghetto. This judge should be reminded that he is perhaps only a generation away from a Russian or Polish ghetto."

One of those black men who had bought property in Woodlawn was Carl Hansberry, father to playwright Lorraine Hansberry. A college-educated real estate broker, he was vindicated in 1940 when the U.S. Supreme Court repealed restrictive covenants in *Hansberry v. Lee*—but the repeal wasn't enforced. The Hansberry family's experience became inspiration for Lorraine's seminal play *A Raisin in the*

*Sun*, the story of a black family moving from a tenement to a house in a white community. In 1948, the U.S. Supreme Court ruled racial covenants illegal in *Shelley v. Kraemer*. Coupled with the population boom after World War II and a citywide shortage of housing, this moved blacks into Woodlawn. The neighborhood had the city's largest number of apartment conversions as property owners divided buildings into kitchenettes to accommodate the influx. In 1930, Woodlawn had nineteen thousand housing units. By 1960 there were twenty-nine thousand units.

In that year the black population in Woodlawn reached 89 percent. High unemployment, overcrowding, and a decrease in city services marred the neighborhood. Some specialty shops along 63rd turned into taverns.

TODAY, BLACK FAMILIES recall an idyllic life in their neighborhood before it became synonymous with the Stones. Twenty-three-year-old Rudy Nimocks moved to Woodlawn in 1952 with his mother. He joined the Chicago Police Department in 1956 and climbed the ranks, breaking barriers as a black man appointed to high departmental positions. He joined the University of Chicago police force in 1989 and served for twenty years, and he still lives in Woodlawn. Nimocks joined a street crew growing up in the 1940s, but gangs and violence didn't become proliferate in Woodlawn until the 1960s, he says.

Jeff Fort's path didn't surprise Nimocks. "Especially when they come from fragmented families, school dropouts in many cases are psychologically looking for something predictable and orderly. [Gangs] provided that: rules, regulations, strict discipline, standards by which to conduct yourselves," Nimocks says.

Woodlawn is divided into east and west. East of Cottage Grove were mostly apartment buildings. Families who owned two-flat buildings and single-family homes lived west of Cottage Grove. Nearby grocery stores sold milk-fed chicken and sugar, flour, and coffee from barrels. A White Castle was located on 63rd and Evans. Doctors, Pullman porters, dentists, musicians, and postal workers lived in West

Woodlawn. In 1940, the Little Women Club started for seventh- and eighth-grade girls in the neighborhood. A teacher formed a theater group called the Thimble Theater for children. There were Boy Scouts and church youth groups. There were social clubs for teens called the Aristocrats, the Dainty Duchesses, the Nifty Teens, and the Fellows. Lincoln Memorial, the oldest black church in Woodlawn, opened its doors to the Brotherhood of Sleeping Car Porters, the NAACP, and the Chicago Urban League for meetings.

On Friday nights residents could go to the Tivoli Theater on 63rd and Cottage Grove, where Liza Minnelli's father worked as the band manager. Emmett Till, the teenager who was brutally murdered in Mississippi for allegedly whistling at a white woman, was a chubby boy with copper-colored eyes from Woodlawn. Sam Greenlee, author of *The Spook Who Sat by the Door*, grew up in Woodlawn. Other notable residents included the Barrett Sisters, father of gospel music Thomas Dorsey, and at least four Tuskegee Airmen.

One white island remained somewhat intact in Woodlawn amid the demographic shifts—Mount Carmel High School, a popular all-boys Catholic school. The Stones never bothered the students there or wandered onto that turf; after all, they weren't stupid. They knew if they messed with those white boys, the police would handily crush them. Best friends Richard Kolovitz and Dan Brannigan attended Mt. Carmel. They later joined the Chicago Police Department together. Kolovitz is the same age as Jeff Fort and knew of the teen back in the 1960s when he traveled from the Southwest Side of Chicago to attend Mt. Carmel. Kolovitz and Fort's fates intertwined through the next few decades; Kolovitz would spend much of his career chasing Fort and the Stones.

## The Woodlawn Organization

IN THE YEARS to come, many community organizations worked with the Stones. The most politically influential one had worthy roots, and it left an indelible mark on Fort and the Stones.

Legendary organizer Saul Alinsky, whose legacy influenced a young Barack Obama's South Side organizing in the 1980s, fought for the poor around the country. Chicago native Alinsky started off in his hometown by forming the Industrial Areas Foundation. In the 1930s he organized the Back of the Yards neighborhood, a South Side stockyards community chronicled in Upton Sinclair's novel *The Jungle*. Alinsky wanted to expand his organizing beyond white working-class areas in the late 1950s. With racial covenants now illegal, South Side neighborhoods were in flux. Alinsky settled on Englewood, a neighborhood contiguous to Back of the Yards; the organizing had the potential to be powerful. Blacks had started moving into Englewood, a white ethnic community of Norwegians and Germans. The racism was palpable; even though blacks moved into white neighborhoods, the fire department might decide to not respond to a call. However, the Archdiocese of Chicago provided organizational support to Alinsky, and the cardinal had another neighborhood in mind—Woodlawn. The diocese wanted to keep several struggling parishes in that area afloat. They were suffering from white flight, and diocese support was seen as a way to help stabilize the neighborhood. The cardinal offered $150,000, so Woodlawn it was.

Alinsky hired Nicholas Von Hoffman, a young white organizer. Von Hoffman recalled Woodlawn as "a bleak place. But a lot of great people, but it was a bleak world." The organizers didn't want the neighborhood to fall into an irreversible slum. They started the Temporary Woodlawn Organization in 1960; the name changed to The Woodlawn Organization (TWO) once the group decided to stick around longer than originally planned. It became clear that members wielded political capital. Local ministers joined the group. TWO rallied block clubs, churches, and other community organizations. Reverend Arthur Brazier, a black pastor at the Apostolic Church of God, was elected president. At first the battle was waged over paltry local education. Residents weren't as concerned with integration as they were with equity. They took on the conditions at Carnegie Elementary, a school with malcontent teachers, no toilet paper, and a lack of school materials—children performed a strike one day by skipping school. TWO also built alliances with the Woodlawn Businessmen's Association and mustered up support from residents to develop a better neighborhood plan than the one the city had. With help from renowned urban planner Jane Jacobs, TWO battled raggedy landlords. TWO used the spirit of organizing to foster neighborhood pride.

Then TWO took on another adversary.

In *Rules for Radicals: A Pragmatic Primer for Realistic Radicals*, Alinsky's guide for organizing, he discusses how to turn tactics into deliberate acts of power. One of his rules is "pick the target, freeze it, personalize it, and polarize it." Under Alinsky's model, this is a universality that organizers must bear in mind. "In a complex, interrelated urban society, it becomes increasingly difficult to single out who is to blame for any particular evil. There is a constant, and somewhat legitimate, passing of the buck," Alinksy notes. Finding the enemy can be arduous, he says, because the intricacies of urban life put many interlocking institutions—political, metropolitan, corporate—in charge. Therefore, identifying a singular enemy can be a moving target. But Alinsky says that's no excuse. "Obviously, there is no point to tactics unless one has a target upon which to center the attacks."

Woodlawn easily found a target—the University of Chicago. The school unveiled its plan for expansion before the Chicago Land Clearance Commission in July 1960. The university wanted to buy up land in Woodlawn. Residents feared a "Negro removal" redux.

A significant neighborhood of the Black Belt, Bronzeville, had been destroyed by urban renewal, also known as "Negro removal," in the 1950s due to the city's eminent domain policy. Even with such a large, growing black population, Mayor Daley had desperately tried to contain black neighborhoods for a long time. The high-rise public housing projects started going up in the 1950s, and the so-called crown jewel, the Robert Taylor Homes, opened in 1962. Named after Obama advisor Valerie Jarrett's grandfather, the homes were the largest public housing project in the world until the last one came down in 2006. Daley also maintained the color line and exacerbated the city's segregation problems by putting overcrowded black public schools on double shifts instead of building new schools or integrating the adjacent white schools.

Von Hoffman understood the fear of displacement among Woodlawn residents. "At that point, the only people in America who really understood urban renewal was a certain segment of the black population," Von Hoffman said. "People like Saul completely understood what it was about." Brazier said, "Homeowners had already experienced displacement from Lake Meadows, Prairie Shores, and South Commons [apartment complexes built and designed for whites]. Many people in Woodlawn had lived and sold in those areas. None of them believed they received proper money." That stayed fresh on black folks' minds; they also remembered the University of Chicago's ugly support of racist covenants.

The university wanted to expand its south campus by gaining full control of 60th and 61st between Stony Island and Cottage Grove. To help get the word out about these plans, TWO relied on the enormous network of janitors. "People had no telephones and there was no telephone tree. We needed janitors of apartment buildings—one reliable person that you could count on for early mobilization," Von Hoffman said. Daley ignored TWO's call in 1963 for a meeting to discuss the university's expansion, but, unwilling to be snubbed, seven hundred people showed up at city hall for a "visit." Daley loathed Alinsky because he operated outside of the established Chicago Democratic machine politics, which controlled patronage jobs and demanded political loyalty.

It became a political issue as TWO evolved into a powerful force to be reckoned with, and its institutional alliance with the diocese helped. Eventually, a deal with the university was struck in Daley's office and signed in 1963. It said that the university couldn't expand past 61st Street and couldn't convert the grassy Midway Plaisance along 59th Street into a private park. The school also couldn't close off any streets. The government gave money to build a low- to moderate-income housing complex on 63rd and Cottage Grove named Grove Parc.

Against the backdrop of these neighborhood political battles and victories, the Blackstone Rangers began to form. Von Hoffman said Alinsky had a dictum, which was to never organize male adolescents, irrespective of race, because their nature is to be fascists. Alinsky based that belief on his early experiences doing graduate work in criminology at the University of Chicago.

## Early Chicago Gangs

GANG IS OFTEN a loaded word. What defines a gang? Who gets labeled a gang while other groups are called clubs or social organizations? What activities relate to *gangbanging*? Often the label takes on a racial burden. The leaders of the Blackstone Rangers simply followed an example set by other alienated groups decades earlier. They too wanted to flex political power in a city that often succumbed to muscling.

*Ethnic* often means "white" in Chicago. That's not to negate the city's strong black, Mexican, Chinese, Korean, Indian, and Puerto Rican communities. But in the early years of the city's history, English, Irish, German, and Italian immigrant communities formed. The world's largest Polish population outside of Poland is in Chicago. There are Greek, Ukrainian, and Bulgarian neighborhoods. Anton Cermak, a corrupt mayor elected in 1931, and his family emigrated from a small Bohemian village in the late 1800s. They found a thriving Bohemian community in Chicago. Having a governor with a Serbian last name—Rod Blagojevich—seemed unusual to people in other parts of the country when he catapulted to fame as a political punch line in late 2008, but it was hardly a big deal to Chicagoans. These ethnic identities remain strong today in the City of Big Shoulders and play a large role in politics and patronage, and, of course, corruption.

Chicago's first gangs consequently formed along ethnic lines. They were well known for their involvement in bootlegging, extortion, and murder. These gangs were particularly prominent among the Italians, Irish, and Polish and served as farm systems for Chicago's well-established crime syndicate. In Irish communities, politicians and businessmen sponsored gangs and christened them "athletic clubs"—for example, the Hamburg Club, Ragen's Colts, and the Old Rose Athletic Club. These so-called clubs stuffed ballot boxes and intimidated voters. Ragen's Colts, organized by a Democratic alderman, were involved in the 1919 Chicago race riot. They attacked blacks in the Black Belt neighborhood because the community had helped a Republican win a mayoral race, which was perceived as an open attack on the Democratic machine. The riot began when, on a sweltering summer day, a black kid ventured into the white section of a beach on Lake Michigan. As a boy, Mayor Richard J. Daley belonged to the tough Hamburg Club, from the historically Irish-identified Bridgeport neighborhood that's also had a reputation for racism. That gang supposedly participated in the race riot. Other white gangs intimidated blacks who were migrating to the city. The racial strife prompted Mayor Edward Kelly's Commission on Human Relations to establish a juvenile bureau in 1946.

Unlike the white ethnic gangs, the earliest black gangs in Chicago had absolutely no influence on political or economic affairs in the black community. Although very little has been written on black street gangs prior to 1940, it's a fair conclusion that their presence in the black community was limited. However, toward the end of the Great Depression, a few black street gangs emerged as somewhat of an extraordinary occurrence. The most prominent of these groups was the Four Corners, a small group of young toughs who hung out around 35th Street and Indiana Avenue.

The real early black gangsters of Chicago made their money as policy kings, operators of illegal gambling and lottery, in the numbers-running business. The South Side had its share of gambling legends. Sam Young, John "Mushmouth" Johnson, and Robert T.

Motts were among the successful numbers runners. In the Black Belt, residents played policy on nearly every corner; in the Roaring Twenties, half of the black population played the game. Al Capone shifted his greedy eyes toward policy, but the Prohibition gangster stayed away upon the intervention of local politicians. A gentlemen's agreement was struck, and the mob stayed out of the "black lottery" in exchange for controlling the bootleg business on the South Side. Ily Kelly was a policy king along with his brothers Walter and Ross, and was reportedly worth a million dollars. Millionaire brothers Ed, George, and McKissick Jones headed a gambling empire and lived an ornate life. While policy was a vice and not immune to violence, the kings were viewed as Robin Hoods. They contributed to the stability and institutions of the Black Belt through financial support.

After the repeal of Prohibition in 1933, the mob had to find new supplemental revenue streams. That gentlemen's agreement on the South Side swiftly ended. Capone's outfit plotted how to snatch the policy racket from the black millionaires. Ed Jones unwittingly helped. While in jail in Indiana he bragged to a fellow inmate mobster about the lucrative black numbers. That mobster told boss Sam Giancana, who literally executed a takeover plan. Ed Jones got run out of town. Another policy king was murdered. But policy king Teddy Roe had a tough-guy nature and refused to bow down to the Italian mobsters. He talked shit to the mob and escaped a kidnapping. Roe had the only policy wheel, a drum-shaped container from which numbers are drawn, left in Chicago that the mob didn't control. Alas, in 1952 he too was murdered. When the Illinois lottery launched in the 1970s, the policy era came to a close.

Within a few years of the end of the black policy kings' era, the era of the black street gangs began. The end of the system of organized crime that the black policy syndicate had put in place left a huge void in the underground economy in the black community. As a result of Capone's outfit's takeover of policy and vice in the Black Belt, black gangsters lost their ability to control organized crime. By the early 1940s, most black communities, with the exception of a few affluent black neighborhoods, had some black street gang presence. On the South Side, the Deacons were the largest. Their territory encompassed the newly built Ida B. Wells public housing development. Their rivals were the Destroyers, who claimed the area north of Wells, and the 13 Cats, who claimed the area south of the projects. There were also some crews who named themselves after their streets—31st Street Gang, 43rd Street Gang, etc.

While black street gangs on the South Side were still fairly rare, the West Side saw an increase of these groups. In response to the abuse inflicted on black youth by white ethnic gangs in the so-called Jew Town area around 12th Street and Halsted, black youth gangs formed to protect themselves. As more blacks moved into the area, the black street gangs began to imitate the behavior of their white counterparts. The names of some of these early black street gangs on the West Side were the Coons, the Dirty Sheiks, and the Wailing Shebas. These groups gave rise to the 14th Street Clovers and the Imperial Chaplins, who ultimately morphed into the Vice Lords and the Egyptian Cobras.

The Vice Lords and the Egyptian Cobras were influential in the development of the Blackstone Rangers. Leonard Calloway, one of the founders of the Vice Lords, was a first cousin of Eugene "Bull" Hairston, future president of the Blackstone Rangers. Calloway used to live on the South Side prior to his family moving to the West Side. One of the 14th Street Clovers said he used to see a skinny little boy huddled up on Calloway's couch quietly listening to the Vice Lords plan their gang activities. The Clover said that he once asked Calloway, "Man, who is this little dude that is always sitting on your couch listening in on our conversations?" He replied, "Aw, man, that's my little buddy from out South. He gets in trouble with his parents and runs away from home sometimes. I let him spend the night a few nights until things die down at home." The 14th Street Clover said he later found out that the little skinny boy was eleven-year-old Jeff Fort. Although it is hard to know exactly how much Bull and Jeff learned from Calloway, it is highly probable that they learned a few things about founding and leading a street gang from their Vice Lord mentor. The connection between the two groups eventually turned into an alliance called "People." According to Bennie Lee, a Vice Lord leader, the term "People" had its origins in the Vice Lords' adoption of Black Nationalism and Islam. In the mid-1970s, the Vice Lord leadership in the Illinois Department of Corrections interpreted Quranic references to "my people" as meaning the righteous ones of Allah. On the other hand, they interpreted the references to "folks" to mean the ignorant ones. Since their inception, the Stones were in alliance with the Vice Lords, and so were classified as "People" along with a few other gangs that adopted a more nationalist orientation. On the other hand, the Disciples and their affiliates proudly adopted "Folks" as their alliance name. Later, the Egyptian Cobras of the West Side branched out to the South Side and became the largest group within the Black P Stone Nation.

## Bull and Jeff

EUGENE BRUCE HAIRSTON was born to Bruce and Lena Hairston on May 1, 1944, in Columbus, Ohio. His family called him Lil Bruce and he was the little man of the house. The streets transformed him into Bull, and he dropped Lil from his name because, as one Stone says, "wasn't nothing little about him out there in those streets." The family moved to Chicago when he was very young. Bull attended Chicago public schools, but he received his real education from older street hustlers, gamblers, pimps, and drug dealers. They were his first running buddies. Most people who knew Bull before he became a Stone talk about how different he was back then. He was the cliché of what it meant to be young, gifted, and black. To this day, even other black men comment on his looks. One Stone says, "Man, Bull was a good-looking dude and I ain't no faggot!"

Bull loved his family. He had two younger sisters, Janet Marie and Edwina, and two little brothers, Leroy (Baby Bull) and Reginald.

His family at home took precedence over his street family, but he acted as big brother to both. During one of Bull's stints in jail, word got back to him that a Stone named Lefty had tried to force his sister Edwina to have sex with him. Although Stone policy frowned upon a brother performing a hit without the consensus of the ruling body, Bull ordered Lawrence "Slim" Griffin (also known as Lawrence "Killer" Cain), the Stones' main enforcer, to kill Lefty. This was a highly unusual move on Bull's part—he forcefully championed order within the organization. But to Bull, blood family trumped Stone loyalty.

When Jeff Fort found out that Bull had instructed Cain to hit Lefty, he threatened Cain and his family to try to get him to back down from the planned killing. However, Cain was fiercely loyal to Bull. Cain let Jeff know in no uncertain terms that he had no intentions of abandoning the hit. Ultimately, Jeff had to get Bull's mother to intercede, and she convinced Cain to not kill Lefty. Cain said Lena Hairston asked him to let Bull and Jeff work it out between themselves. Lena Hairston and Annie Fort played pivotal roles in Stone leadership. Instructions from mother Hairston and mother Fort were akin to hearing from Bull and Jeff. "Bull's momma and Jeff's momma were fearless," one Stone says. The mothers mediated a lot of conflict within the organization. Retired Chicago police detective Richard Kolovitz observed that the only woman Jeff trusted was his mother. Ditto for Bull.

Jeff "Angel" Fort was one of ten children. He was born to Annie and John Lee Fort on February 20, 1947, in Aberdeen, Mississippi. He had three sisters—Maryam, Kadijah, and Elnora—and six brothers, Johnny, Bennie, Gene, Kaaba, Akaba, and Aki. His family moved to Chicago when he was nine years old. Those who knew Jeff describe him as a moody child with a negative disposition. By age twelve he ran his own little gang of boys, and by fifteen he had been arrested at least nine times. Teachers who had Jeff as a student at Scott Elementary and Flavel Moseley School said Jeff had two sides: he could be an angel one minute but turn into the devil the next. At Scott Elementary he demonstrated extreme, volatile behavior that led to his placement in Moseley, a school that catered to boys with behavioral problems. However, teachers at Moseley described Jeff as being kind and sympathetic. He drew peers to him with his quick-on-his-feet thinking and sharp wit. Some Stones say Jeff was emotional and often demonstrated compassion for those less fortunate than him. But he sometimes lacked confidence in himself and often missed opportunities because he didn't think he was up to the task.

Fast-forward to 1950s Woodlawn, in Chicago. Against the backdrop of the University of Chicago saga, the construction of the largest housing projects in the world, and the racial strife of the city, Fort led a small group of boys who hung out between 64th and 66th on Blackstone Street. In 1959, they were a small clique of about ten juveniles that some called a gang. The community residents accused the boys of snatching purses, stealing, breaking into shops, and fighting gang skirmishes with the Cobras and other South Side gangs. Useni Perkins, a longtime youth worker with the Boys Club, did his first internship with the Woodlawn Boys Club at 62nd and Woodlawn in 1959. Although he didn't work directly with Jeff and his group, he did observe their disruptive behavior inside the Boys Club. Perkins says they were "creating a lot of problems within the agency by being disruptive . . . creating chaos."

It got to the point that Bob Shorter, the club's white director, had to put them out. Perkins speculated that when Jeff and his little group were put out of the Boys Club, they also left with what would eventually become part of their moniker. The club categorized boys by age group, and each group had a different name. Jeff and his boys were in the Rangers age group. After being kicked out of the club, Perkins says they kept the name Rangers. They claimed Blackstone Street and the surrounding area, including Jackson Park, as their turf.

That's how the Blackstone Rangers were born.

Meanwhile, fifteen-year-old Bull led a small clique called the Harper Boys. The Harper Boys' turf ran along Stony Island Avenue and spilled into Jackson Park between 63rd and 67th Streets. They also had about ten guys. Jeff's and Bull's guys would get into it because they occupied the same space around Jackson Park. On one occasion, one of Bull's boys, Carl Robinson, got shot with a zip gun by one of Jeff's people. That shooting intensified the rivalry between the two groups. After a multitude of fights, neither group seemed to be able to dominate the other, so eventually they called a truce and joined forces. Bull and the Harper Boys didn't necessarily agree about using the name Blackstone. Some of the original Harpers say that when the newspapers reported on juvenile petty crimes in the area, they were referred to as the Blackstone Rangers. Not being distinguished in the newspapers is part of what really led to the Harper Boys accepting the new name. Bull and Jeff, the leaders of their respective groups, were recognized as the joint leaders of this newly merged group.

As the Blackstone Rangers developed a reputation for being the toughest group of boys in Woodlawn, older gangsters took notice and incorporated them into organized crime activities in the early 1960s. These South Side men were part of the black syndicates that controlled illicit drug sales, policy, prostitution, gambling, fencing, and a range of other forms of vice. They would use street kids like Bull and Jeff to help them in their criminal enterprises, taking the boys under their wings while grooming them to organize the growing population of street youth in Woodlawn. The older gangsters realized they could get Bull and Jeff to go out and recruit poor boys under seventeen years of age and pay them little to nothing to serve as lookouts, numbers runners, and drug couriers.

The gangsters would also use the boys to collect extortion money and even do hits. The older gangsters knew juveniles could be indicted and prosecuted for major crimes in criminal court, but they couldn't be sent to prison if convicted. At most they would serve two years in the youth commission and then become eligible for proba-tion regardless of the crime they'd committed, even murder. Accord-ing to Red, a former Stone, the older gangsters appointed Bull as the Big Chief and christened Jeff Little Chief. Bull got the position of Big Chief because of his tough street reputation. Bull also hung out with the older gangsters, so he was more streetwise and mature than the average street kid. Jeff received the Little Chief moniker because of his small physical stature. Although Jeff was short and thin, he was fearless and charismatic. He had an incredible rapport with the youngest of the street youth in Woodlawn. The way the older gangsters hooked it up, Bull was given the muscle to go out and recruit neighboring gang leaders to merge their gangs with the Stones. Jeff's job as Little Chief was to go out and recruit the rank and file. Together, Bull and Jeff ran the day-to-day operations of the Stones. But behind the scenes lurked a shadow leadership of older men. This system worked fine for the older gangsters until antipoverty money began to flow into Woodlawn and the Blackstone Rangers' membership swelled.

The federal government began to pour dollars into urban centers throughout America in the mid-1960s. Some of the funds were allocated to faith organizations and social service agencies. With this new money, groups like the Woodlawn Boys Club, the Woodlawn Immanuel Lutheran Church, and The Woodlawn Organization received funding to work with the Blackstone Rangers. The money was used to implement new youth programs and initiatives that ultimately loosened the grip the older gangsters had on the Stones. The older gangsters could not compete with the mainstream institutions for the Stones' loyalty. Most of them had already lost their street muscle to the Italian outfit. They could no longer command the respect of the street youth. Moreover, with the loss of status and power, and the money associated with both, it was easy for the mainstream institutions to flash their new money before the faces of street kids like the Stones in order to get them to come over to their side.

The first newspaper reference to Jeff and Bull was printed in 1965 in the *Chicago Tribune*. Ed Woods, extension director of the Woodlawn Boys Club, and Reverend O. H. Sotnak of the Woodlawn Immanuel Lutheran Church said their new program would help teenage gang boys get a fresh start on life. Three nights a week, 180 boys played basketball, pool, card games, and checkers at the church. Some of the boys even got jobs with help from Woods. The headline said "Teens Given Fresh Start." An accompanying picture shows Woods talking to a smiling dynamic duo—Jeff and Bull.

These clergymen and community workers wanted to find constructive activities to keep young boys off the streets. Woodlawn's population growth brought an influx of boys into the ranks of the Blackstone Rangers. Melvin Lamb grew up in Woodlawn and eventually became a leader in the organization years later during its El Rukn era. Lamb says when he was a child growing up in Woodlawn, all of the boys wanted to be Stones because of the way they dressed. In the early years, the Stones wore white T-shirts with khakis. They sported Converse gym shoes that were equivalent in price and stature then to Air Jordans today. The Stones wore bush-top fades. With the new money they were getting from their affiliation with the antipoverty youth initiatives combined with the cash they already had from extorting protection money from local businesses and taxing independent hustlers, pimps, and operators of gambling houses, the Stones could afford the latest clothes. They stylishly paraded around Woodlawn with matching outfits, and they all had cash in their pockets. Joining the Stones became the dream of most poor black boys in Woodlawn.

Street kids joined the organization at such a rapid rate that Bull and Jeff found themselves at the helm of an intensely dedicated small army. Ultimately Bull and Jeff used their emerging power to cut the few remaining older gangsters out of the action. All of the street game they learned from them would from then on be used exclusively for the benefit of the Stones. By the time the older gangsters realized that they had created a monster, it was too late. The Stones were protected by the various faith organizations and social service agencies that were supposed to be giving them refuge from the streets. But unlike the older gangsters, the faith organizations and social service agencies saw the Stones as a meal ticket. They would do almost anything to remain in the good graces of the Stones, who were their source for millions of dollars of federal antipoverty money.

Bull and Jeff played changing roles in the organization as it dealt with these new power dynamics. Their differing management styles complemented each other. If a military rank were to be used to describe Bull's role in the Blackstone Rangers organization, he would have been the general. One of the Stones describes Bull as "the enforcer, the muscle." He held responsibility for "enforcing a situation to make it right." If the Stones needed to confront a situation, "Bull went out there to grab the mens to help make it happen," according to another Stone. He led the Stones onto the battlefield. Bull also ruled the Main 21, the organization's governing body. He and Jeff provided leadership, but if a problem arose with one of the Mains, Bull regulated.

While Bull's role could be described militarily, Jeff's role was more diplomatic, acting as "Mr. Blackstone Ranger." Jeff personified what it meant to be Blackstone. When something needed to be communicated to the troops, Jeff usually did it. "Angel would sit here and help bring the organization together and make sure when it was time to come together we all sit down and make sure we all have an understanding of, this is the way it's going to go," says one Stone. Jeff served as the public face and spokesman for the organization, both internally and externally, which may explain why he was sometimes perceived to be the sole leader. The Stones knew better. "You know, we always had two leaders and we always will honor and respect both of our leaders," says a Stone. But Jeff articulated the decisions.

Jeff loved attention and Bull enjoyed working behind the scenes. Jeff was the politician, and Bull was the political operative. Their respective leadership roles were greatly influenced by their personalities. Stones say Bull had the ability to deal with all types of men, even killers. "He could look 'em in the eyes and they would get what he was trying to convey to them." The killers respected Bull, and they provided him with the muscle to enforce his law.

Jeff had a more youthful personality than Bull. Jeff surrounded himself with a lot of attentive kids. One Stone says, "Jeff reminded me of a Baptist preacher. He got that charisma, he would come in

and say, 'Man, my brothers, how y'all doing today? I love you, brothers, what can I help you with?'" Jeff interacted with all levels of people inside and outside of the organization. Unlike Bull, Jeff dealt with
everybody, from the high-ranking guys to the lowly members to the
little kids on the streets. One Stone says, "He took time to sit down
with you to talk to you one-on-one. You could tell him whatever was
on your mind." And Jeff was accessible to all youth, regardless of
whether they were Stones. "He was a kind of guy you wanted to learn
something from."

Profound from a young age, Jeff recognized the power in providing
young black males with a sense of identity and belonging. Jeff understood that this way they could be empowered. Moving from Mississippi to Woodlawn taught him how it felt to not fit in and to struggle
with identity. Jeff's vision provided him and boys like him with an
identity—that of a Blackstone Ranger. One of the first things Jeff did
was to organize the boys to put their money together to buy T-shirts
with BLACKSTONE RANGERS printed on them. They wore these shirts
to parties and around the neighborhood to represent their affiliation with the Stones. As time progressed, their outfits became more
prominent and stylish, which raised their status. Many young black
males wanted to be Stones because the red tams and black leather
jackets gave them an identity and a sense of togetherness.

Jeff's experiences as a newcomer in Woodlawn also taught him
what it meant to feel unwanted in your own community. The Boys
Club, his schools, and the residents of Woodlawn provided that lesson. He knew that young black boys like him needed a place to go
where they could feel connected to something. He also knew that by
providing them with a place, he would be able to use these places as
a means for building a power base.

Jeff's former teacher Timuel Black went to Washington, D.C., in
1964 for a civil rights meeting. When he returned, Fort and some
of his friends had stopped attending Hyde Park High School. Black
went to the pool hall on 63rd and Blackstone, hoping he could get the
young men back in the classroom. "C'mon, you guys, let's go back,"

Black told them. "Naw, Mr. Black," Fort said. "They don't want us there. We are gonna take over the whole damn thing."

After Jeff and his little posse were kicked out of the Boys Club, Jeff secured the Woodlawn Immanuel Lutheran Church on East 64th Street for the Stones to use as a hangout in 1965. The following year, Jeff forged a relationship with Reverend John Fry at the First Presbyterian Church on 64th and Kimbark. This relationship led to the Stones using the church as their headquarters for the next several years.

Throughout Stone history, Jeff made it a priority to acquire access to buildings that the Stones could use as places to provide the men with identity, sanctuary, and solace. From pool halls to churches, from apartment buildings to makeshift temples, Jeff made sure he and his members always had a place of their own.

As the Stones solidified as an organization, other groups of young black males were doing the exact same thing, sometimes within the exact same neighborhood boundaries. Egos and territory made for a lethal combination.

# 2

# Birth of the Blackstone Rangers

**T**HE INTENSE RIVALRY between the Blackstone Rangers and the Devil Disciples resembled ethnic and tribal warfare. It was rooted in perceptions of status even though both groups were dirt poor. But those perceptions were merely a mirage to justify a turf war.

Woodlawn Avenue divided the territories with the rigidity of an international border. The Disciple separating line started on Minerva Avenue and ran west all the way through the Englewood neighborhood, the Disciples' birthplace. The original boundaries of the Blackstone Rangers' territory engulfed the rest of Woodlawn and east to Lake Michigan.

Stone territory happened to be in the part of Woodlawn where economic and political institutions thrived. The area incorporated Jackson Park and the lakefront beaches, which were major recreation destinations for all of Woodlawn and other black South Side communities. However, the Stones claimed them as their exclusive province, which of course created animosity from the Disciples, who also wanted to enjoy those outdoor pleasures. Disputes over access to the park and lakefront led to fights among members of the two groups.

There were small groups of Disciples in middle-class West Wood-lawn, and even a couple of Disciple branches (East Side Disciples) east of Cottage Grove; however, the main Disciple territory began in Englewood. Because Englewood was perceived to be a community of working-class and poor folks, the Disciples who dwelled there were perceived to be among the common folk. The Ds willingly adopted that identity while the Stones fashioned themselves as a sophisti-cated and exclusive brotherhood. To this day the Blackstones refer to themselves as "Brothers," and the Disciples refer to themselves as "Folks." The Stones looked down on the Disciples as unsophis-ticated, ignorant, and dirty. *Dirty folks* is a commonly used term to describe gangs of Disciple affiliation. Although gangs affiliated with the Blackstones initiated this as a derogatory label, it is now a popu-lar cultural term used to refer to Disciples by individuals not affili-ated with any gangs. Even the Disciples call themselves "dirty folks" sometimes.

Further exacerbating the enmity between the Ds and the Stones was the late 1960s Chicago Public Schools' decision to change the boundaries for Hyde Park High School. When this change occurred, kids who lived in Disciple territory had to travel into Blackstone turf. The boundary change escalated the violence between the two groups. It also contributed to increased dropout rates among non-gang-affiliated kids who were afraid to go to school because of the warring between the two groups.

Another source of acrimony stemmed from perceived favoritism. The Stones were given preferential treatment by civic and social ser-vice programs that secured federal dollars to work with street youth. A good example of this is the number of early 1960s initiatives imple-mented by the Lutheran Church and the Boys Club. Providing ser-vices to the Stones helped bring in federal aid money that pumped up their budgets, so these groups provided the Stones with sanctuar-ies to organize themselves, technical assistance they needed to grow and develop as an organization, funds to buy material possessions, and affiliations with established institutions and leaders that gave the

Stones credibility. The Disciples didn't get plugged into the antipoverty money until several years later.

But the Disciples had more members—they outnumbered the Stones almost ten to one. And they used their multitude of soldiers to launch a war on the Stones that persists to this day. The Stones were more organized and better armed, but the Disciples had the numbers. Realizing their handicap in the numbers game, the Stones employed a strong-arming strategy that would have impressed a despot.

The Stones waged a "recruitment" campaign that left surrounding gang leaders with little choice but to join up. Stone enforcer Lawrence Cain says Bull and a guy by the name of Pugh (not the well-known Stone Fletcher Pugh) assumed the task of consolidating other gangs in the area. Cain says the majority of the groups joined because "we put pressure on 'em." They would approach the leaders of other gangs and tell them that the Blackstone Rangers wanted them to join their group. As a footnote, the Stone regulators would advise them that this wasn't optional. Joining the Stones was the only way to avoid a showdown. When the gang agreed to join, it would be allowed to keep its identity but had to add Ranger or Stone to its name. And if the organization was big, the leader would be voted in as a Main 21.

Cain recalled using violence when one leader bucked. Edwin "Caboo" Codwell initially led the Kimbark Killers. There were about eight members in the group, which controlled Kimbark Avenue between 63rd and 67th Streets. When the Stones let Caboo know the nonnegotiable option, he rejected them. They responded by shooting him. Cain says they told Caboo, "If you gon' live on Kimbark, you gon' be a Stone." The wounded Caboo eventually acquiesced and became a Main.

The gangs that made up the first wave of Blackstone Rangers came from various blocks in Woodlawn. The primary members consisted of Bull's guys, the Harper Boys. Most of the Harper Boys hung out around Harper Avenue east into Jackson Park and the South Shore neighborhood. Jeff's guys ran from 64th to 67th on Blackstone Avenue. There were also the Gangsters, a group of guys who hung out on 61st and Dorchester. The Conservatives, better known as the Cons, were also in the original group of Blackstone Rangers, as was a small group of guys on 65th and Woodlawn. On Kenwood, the War-lords and the FBIs had early roots with the Rangers, along with the Imperial Lovers, who hailed from Stony Island Avenue.

In 1963, Cornell Steele lorded over a group called the Drexel Casa-novas. Their territory spanned Drexel between 65th and 67th Streets. A group of Stones approached Steele at the 71st Street YMCA about merging his group into the Blackstones. They told him that he could remain the leader of the group, but any decisions regarding killings, narcotics, or prostitution could not be acted on by the Casanovas until they were voted on by the body of the Main 21. The Casano-vas became the Nova Stones, and Steele became a top enforcer for the Stones. His was one of two Rangers branches considered to be in Disciple territory. The other branch in Disciple territory was the Ellis Rebel Stones; they ran Ellis Avenue between 67th Street and 65th Street.

All of this consolidation led to a greater effort—the Stones built themselves into a sweeping coalition of street organizations that was dominated by early members of the Blackstone Rangers. By 1968 there were between four and five thousand Stones among the fif-teen Stone-affiliated groups that were represented in Chicago. The Blackstone Rangers spanned from 23rd Street all the way to 113th Street, east to the lake and west to Cottage Grove Avenue. And some even came from the North Side. Between 1960 and 1976 this coali-tion constantly changed through additions and defections of various groups in the Nation.

## The Main 21

TO IMPOSE ORDER over this labyrinth of members and organizational franchises, Jeff and Bull formed a ruling body called the Main 21, which governed the Blackstone Rangers. Although Main 21 was the name, it was not necessarily a fixed group of twenty-one individuals and did not call for a uniform process for anointment. Usually there were more than twenty-one Stones recognized as Mains. Bull and Jeff were the leaders of the Blackstone Rangers, but they were also considered Mains. The majority of the original Mains of the Blackstone Rangers came from Bull's Harper Boys and Jeff's posse who ran together on Blackstone Street between 64th and 67th. A smaller group in the original Mains consisted of the leaders of the new groups that joined the coalition of Stones. Others were appointed or voted into the Main 21 because they had some special talents that Bull, Jeff, and the Mains felt would strengthen the organization.

Most of the original Mains who came from among the early Blackstone Rangers were Bull's guys who had reputations as street warriors, guys like Lamar "Bop Daddy" Bell, an intelligent street warrior. Bull and Bop were greatly influenced by the Black Power movement. Together, Bull, Bop, Reico Cranshaw, and a few others produced the constitution, or literature, of the Stones. Following the tradition of their first cousins, the Vice Lords, the Stones developed literature that served as the official policy of the organization. Stones were required to live their lives according to the Blackstone creed and codes. The difference between the Vice Lords' and the Blackstones' literature is that the Stones borrowed more elements from the Black Power and Black Nationalist movements. For instance, the Stones adopted the Pan-African colors of red, black, and green as their organizational colors. They adopted the pyramid as their organizational symbol to demonstrate their belief that ancient Egypt, an African civilization, was the first civilization of humanity. The Stones adopted these ideas and symbols because they came into existence right at the time the Black Power and cultural nationalist movements were reaching their peaks. The Vice Lords, on the other hand, formed prior to these movements. The Disciples, who came up at the same time as the Stones, rejected the tenets of Black Power and Black Nationalism because they saw the principles as too closely connected with the Stones, their primary adversaries.

Another one of Bull's guys who played a key role in the organization as a Main 21 was Charles Edward Bey, nicknamed Bear, an intelligent, well-spoken street warrior. Bey served as the highest-ranking
Main 21 after Bull and Jeff, and later, when Bull and Jeff were locked
up, he ran the day-to-day street operations of the organization. Many
recognized Bey as the business manager of the Stones. Some of the
guys loyal to Bull who were also original Main 21 included Andrew
"AD" McChristian, Charles "Bosco" Franklin, and Adam "Leto" Battiste (Bey's brother-in-law).

The second category of Main 21s came from the leaders of some
of the various groups that merged their gangs into the Stones. The
highest-profile person in this category of Main 21s, and one of the
highest-ranking Mains, was Henry "Mickey" Cogwell, probably the
most sophisticated of all of the Mains and the leader of more than
one thousand Cobra Stones, the largest branch of the Blackstone
Rangers. The Cobra Stones' territory covered the south end of the
Robert Taylor Homes, known as "The Hole," and 53rd and Princeton. Mickey also provided protection to many of the taverns in his
area. He ultimately became president of the Bartenders Association
through his strong connection with the Italian syndicate.

Other chiefs who merged their groups into the Stones became
Main 21s. Samuel "Two Mac" Dillard from the Cabrini Green public
housing development and Herbert "Thunder" Stevens of the Four
Corner Stones were two of them. Thunder, along with Black Reuben,
commanded over a thousand Four Corner Stones. Melvin "Lefty"
Bailey ran the Ellis Rebels. Leon "Bo" Young led the Imperial Lovers. Herman "Moose" Holmes was the chief of the Gangster Stones
from 61st and Dorchester. Leonard Sengali and Chester Evans were
originally Black Elephants who merged their group with the Stones.
Sengali eventually became the spokesman for Jeff and the Stones.

The appointed Main 21s who possessed "special talents" included
guys such as Lee "Stone" Jackson and William "Sweet Jones" Throope.
They were promoted because of their expertise in various forms of
vice like drug dealing and prostitution. Their knowledge helped the

Stones generate money by muscling those who controlled the various sectors of the underground economy.

Two older men, George "Watusi" Rose and Paul Martin, were named Mains. Because they were in their thirties, the Stones sought their advice on matters concerning the affairs of the organization. The eccentric Martin frequently wore a clerical collar and professed to be the spiritual leader of the Stones. One Stone says Watusi and Martin thought they would be able to dominate the Mains because they were at least ten years older than their fellow Mains. That invited tension: the younger Mains felt Watusi and Martin often tried to manipulate and dominate them because they were senior. Conversely, Watusi and Martin thought the younger Mains were too cocky and arrogant, which they claimed brought unnecessary heat on the organization.

Also among the original Main 21s were enforcers. Their major role was not to confront the Stones' enemies outside of the organization, although they did that, too. Their primary responsibility was to keep the Mains in check. An individual Main might decide to do something in opposition to Bull, Jeff, or the collective body of the Mains. In those scenarios, Bull would send guys like Cain to check the Main who was acting out of order. The last person a Main wanted to see was Cain. "I'm a shooter, that's what I do," said Cain, referring to those Stone days. He was one of the leaders of the Gangsters on Dorchester, but he also hung out with Bull and the Harper Boys. Bull and Jeff relied heavily on Cain to exact punishment on anyone who deviated from the path that had been established by the organization. Casanova leader Steele also wore an enforcer hat. His set, or branch of the Stones, was right in the middle of the East Side Disciples' territory. Bull's brother Leroy "Baby Bull" Hairston was also an enforcer.

A number of other Main 21s included Bernard "Droop" Green, Cool Johnnie Jones, Robert "Dog" Jackson, Fletcher "Bo Peep" Pugh, George "Porgy" Martin, Theotis "Thee" Clark, Lawrence "Tom Tucker" White, and Sylvester "Hutch" Hutchins. Occasionally this core group would lose members for one reason or another, but new members would join the governing body. Eventually many of the Main 21s were killed or handed down long prison sentences, which caused the body to lose its power and influence within the organization. Those who replaced the original Main 21s didn't have the reputations and characters of the original Mains, so the body itself became marginalized. By 1976 most of the original Mains were a memory and Jeff replaced the body of the Main 21s with a hand-picked group he called the generals.

BY THE MID-1960S the Black Power movement spoke to blacks residing in urban centers. Being down with the movement became popular among urban youth, including the Stones. Bull looked up to Malcolm X, Stokely Carmichael (Kwame Toure), Huey P. Newton, H. Rap Brown, and Bobby Seale. Bull made the Stones who still had chemically processed hair cut their perms out. He encouraged all Stones to wear Afros to reflect a sense of pride in being black. Although most Stones, including Jeff, weren't as pro-black as Bull, they all, to a certain degree, considered themselves Black Nationalists.

The Stones appropriated imagery to complement their combative street reputation. They also sought self-knowledge and understanding of their place as displaced black men in America. A pyramid represented the body and leadership of the Blackstone Rangers. One side of the pyramid had twenty-one stones drawn on it, and each stone represented a Main 21.

The Stones taught members that the pyramid was an ancient symbol left by their African ancestors to remind them of their divinity. In these teachings, the pyramid's base was a simple square with four right triangles like the Egyptian pyramids. When combined, the four ninety-degree angles total 360 degrees. Jeff frequently moralized to the Stones that knowledge allowed their ancient African ancestors to build the greatest civilizations known to humanity. He blamed the transatlantic slave trade for disconnecting black people from the ways of their ancestors. Jeff imparted to the young Stones that it was their duty first to seek knowledge of their history and then to use that knowledge to rebuild an independent nation for all black people, not just Stones. On one occasion a young Stone asked Jeff, "Even the Disciples?" Jeff responded with a coy smile and said, "Yes, my little brother, even the Disciples."

In 1965, Jeff said of their ancestors, "They had kings who ran the governments. And they had princes who were studying on how to run the governments when their daddies died. They would be kings someday but they didn't make it. They were whipped and tied up and shipped to Alabama to work like dogs. So what we gon' do? We gon' have our own governments. The way our daddies did a long time back. They don't let us in they government, we get our own. They not let us in, we be out. We be the out boys for the out peoples. 'Cause we's all princes."

Most people perceived the Stones' symbols scrawled on building walls throughout Woodlawn as simply gang graffiti, but to the Stones the drawings had a deep story. The four sides of the pyramid represented earth, air, fire, and water. One of the Stones recalls Jeff saying that if a person kept his physical, mental, and spiritual self in harmony with the four elements of nature, he could live forever. He says that was why Jeff never used any drugs or alcohol; the leader cherished his body as a temple.

## Martin Luther King Jr. in Chicago

ALTHOUGH THE BLACK POWER movement influenced the development of the Blackstone Rangers, it was not the first activist movement the Stones supported. They first flirted with the civil rights movement. In 1965, the Chicago Freedom Movement represented the alliance of the Southern Christian Leadership Conference (SCLC) and the Coordinating Council of Community Organizations (CCCO). The SCLC, led by Martin Luther King Jr., searched for a location to prove that nonviolent direct action could bring about social change outside of the South. Since the early 1960s, the Chicago CCCO had harnessed anger over racial inequality, especially in the public schools. The northern activism of the group pulled SCLC to Chicago, as did the work of Bernard LaFayette and James Bevel, two veterans of the Southern civil rights movement, on the city's West Side.

The Chicago Freedom Movement declared its intention to eliminate slums in the city. It organized tenants' unions, assumed control of a slum tenement, founded action groups like Operation Breadbasket, and rallied black and white Chicagoans to support its goals. In the early summer of 1966, it turned its attention toward housing discrimination.

On July 10, 1966, over sixty thousand people came to hear King as well as singers Mahalia Jackson, Stevie Wonder, and Peter, Paul and Mary at a citywide rally at Soldier Field. The stadium was packed and the event well under way when hundreds of Blackstone Rangers suddenly marched into the uppermost deck of the stadium. They completely surrounded the venue, carrying a huge banner with a picture of a .50-caliber machine gun. As the Stones filed in, waves of uneasiness washed over the crowd. Sensing that they were about to lose control of the audience, the civil rights leaders quickly moved to restore calm. Reverend Curtis Burrell, who would eventually become the executive director of the nonprofit Kenwood Oakland Community Organization, attended the rally. Burrell said activist Dick Gregory "tried and did bring calm by calling for peace and unity and making a place for our neglected youth." The Blackstone Rangers had officially introduced themselves to the civil rights movement. Burrell said their message rang out loud and clear: "Cut us in or cut it out." The Stones wanted to be included in any decision making on behalf of the black community, especially concerning black youth. Burrell recalled, "All leaders and social activists in the Black Liberation Movement, including the SCLC, now had to give recognition to this new face." These uninvited guests had crashed the party, loudly beating their chests.

Reverend Al Sampson joined the SCLC staff in 1963. He was dispatched to join King and the Chicago Freedom Movement in a yearlong campaign for open housing in 1965. Sampson lived on the West Side with King and his family along with a number of other SCLC staff. One of Sampson's assignments included recruiting the Blackstone Rangers to the Chicago Freedom Movement. With the help of Larry Patterson, a former basketball player and well-known youth outreach worker in Chicago, along with the YMCA's Streets Program run by Ernie Jenkins, Sampson gained access to the Stones. He arranged for the Stones to take SCLC nonviolence workshops, where the Stones learned the seven steps of nonviolence. Sampson also arranged for King to come in and "lay on the pool table with the Stones," that is, play pool with them.

In late July, the Chicago Freedom Movement staged regular marches into all-white neighborhoods on the city's Southwest and Northwest Sides. The Stones and other street organizations participated in these marches, and some served as bodyguards for King. While King marched in the racist Marquette Park neighborhood, white agitators hit him in the head with a brick. Sampson said that later that evening Jeff Fort called a meeting on 16th and Hamlin to discuss the hostile response of the whites. All of the top leadership of all of Chicago's largest gangs showed up—as well as King.

The Stones argued back and forth with King about the pitfalls of nonviolence. They threatened that the next time they participated in a march they were going to come with guns in tow. The Stones told King they refused to be mistreated like he had been. Sampson said never in their wildest dreams had the Stones witnessed the kind of white viciousness that blacks in the South had been dealing with for hundreds of years. Now for the first time the Stones had experienced the venom of some white people. Faced with this reality, the Stones failed to see any value in nonviolent protests.

King listened well that night. He allowed the Stones to vent. After a while, King asked the Stones, "If a building was burning down and you had the ability to save it, what would you do?" The Stones replied, "Muthafucka, don't fuck with us," as they proceeded to curse out the venerable civil rights leader. They said, "Everybody know you use water to put the goddamn fire out, don't play that bullshit with us." They continued to curse him out some more.

King remained cool, and then he asked again, "What did you say you put on the fire?" They responded, "You heard us, muthafucka, you put water on it!"

Sampson said, "Wasn't no sophisticated 'We love Dr. King, so we gon' be nice' type thing going on here. I'm talking about the language of the street thrown at him." King then said, "Water is another option, my brothers, 'cause you don't put out a fire with fire." Then, Sampson said, "He [King] rose to preach . . . and he preached that night." He told the Stones they represented the water of "our people, the sustenance of life."

The next day "the Stones were out there catching bricks with us," even more Stones than had marched the first day. They were able to do three demonstrations in one day and split the police.

On August 26, the Chicago Freedom Movement declared that it would march into first-ring suburb Cicero, the site of a fierce race riot in 1951 and once a base for Al Capone. After that announcement, an agreement was reached that promised positive steps toward opening up housing opportunities in metropolitan Chicago. The Summit Agreement was the culmination of months of organizing and direct action. However, it did not satisfy all activists, some of whom marched on Cicero in September 1966. But after the open-housing marches, the Chicago Freedom Movement lost its focus and momentum. By early 1967, King and the SCLC decided to train their energies on other targets, thus marking the end of this ambitious campaign.

## Black Nationalism and the Black Power Movement

So the Stones gravitated to Black Nationalism and the Black Power movement that was becoming more popular among black youth in northern urban areas. And the Stones found that those ideals meshed nicely with the Blackstone identity. The Stones never completely abandoned the civil rights movement altogether, but they adopted Black Nationalism as a fundamental principle.

The Blackstone Rangers' colors were red, black, and green—colors established by the Marcus Garvey movement of the 1920s and '30s, a strong indication that the Stones were attracted to Black Power. During the early years of Rangers development a vibrant cultural rebirth of Black Nationalism occurred in many large U.S. cities like Chicago. Black people were proudly proclaiming Black Power and self-determination. The Blackstone Rangers were surrounded by many people who celebrated blackness and being African.

In Chicago, singers and musicians like Oscar Brown Jr. and Kelan Phil Cohran introduced many young black people to the Black Power movement, Black Nationalism, and their African heritage. Brown was a singer, songwriter, playwright, poet, and an activist who performed with fellow legends Miles Davis, Aretha Franklin, Nancy Wilson, Max Roach, and Dizzy Gillespie. He earned the title the "High Priest of Hip" and founded the Oscar Brown Jr. H.I.P. Legacy Foundation to continue his work. He said, "I want people to be 'hip.' . . . I want 'hip' to stand for human improvement potential because every human has some potential within them." In a 2005 *ROCTOBER Magazine* interview, Brown explained how his work with the Stones came about:

> I began to audition other actors to do . . . a second show called
> *Summer in the City.* . . . I made contact with the Blackstone
> Rangers, and we began talkin' to them about some alternative
> activity to what they were doin', which was basically gangbangin'
> and terrorizing the neighborhood. . . . The fact that there was this
> gang presence was bad for business and that's one of the reasons
> that I contacted gangs [to ask them] could we do something
> for them that would stop them from steppin' on my hustle! I
> said we'd do a show for 'em, but they said, "Well, we got some

talent, can we be in the show?" We wound up doin' a show called *Opportunity, Please Knock*, which really changed my life, basically, because it let me see that there was this enormous talent in the black community. This is where all the dances came from; this is where all the popular music comes from; so I began to really concentrate on that. *Opportunity, Please Knock* ran for a little while, with those kids being on the *Smothers Brothers Comedy Hour.*

They performed *Opportunity, Please Knock* at First Presbyterian Church on 64th and Kimbark. This type of work that Brown did with the Stones laid the foundation for the organization to be perceived as more than just a gang. Many people began to view the Stones as a youth organization with the potential to save marginalized youth in places like Woodlawn. It also inspired some of the Stones to look at music and the performing arts as vehicles for transforming their lives from youth who demonstrated antisocial behavior into youth who were empowered to bring about social justice in their communities.

Brown produced the full production of *Opportunity, Please Knock* with a little help from the Stones. The shows at First Presbyterian were attended mainly by whites from around the city and suburbs. It was a variety show that included a mix of popular songs of the time, jazz, traditional African drumming, dances, and skits. Women participated in the show, too, including some Rangerettes and others who weren't affiliated with the Stones.

Brown worked primarily with the Imperial Lovers set of the Stones to put on the production. According to one of the Imperial Lovers, they had already had experience putting on performances when they hooked up with Brown. There were a couple of popular singing groups within the Imperial Lovers, and they would put on shows and produce plays. When Brown approached the Stone leadership with the opportunity, they hooked him up with the Imperial Lovers.

A couple of Stones say that eventually some of the Main 21 started coming to the *Opportunity, Please Knock* shows and taking money right out of the cash box. Brown complained to Jeff, but the Mains continued to seize the money, so Brown fell out with the Stones and stopped working on the show.

The cast used some of Brown's industry connections to strike out on their own. They organized a trip to Los Angeles and the Bay Area. Once out on the West Coast, Bull joined the cast. Lamar "Bop Daddy" Bell, a Main 21, was assigned to oversee the cast. Bop's weaknesses were money and women, and his mismanagement forced the cast to downsize. Later the money ran out completely. They ended up stranded in the Bay Area until someone sent them money to go home.

Phil Cohran also worked with the Stones. Cohran is a musician, composer, astronomer, and activist who uses the cultural performing arts to educate and socialize the black community into being conscious of its African heritage. Brother Cohran played the trumpet in Sun Ra's Myth Science Arkestra between 1958 and 1961. After leaving Sun Ra's group, Cohran formed the Artistic Heritage Ensemble (AHE) and later a group of musicians who shared his respect and admiration for tradition, but who knew it so well that they could take it into rarely explored realms of trance and freedom. Musicians from the Chess Records session group—tuba player Aaron Dodd, bassist Louis Satterfield, saxophonist Donald Myrick, trumpet player Charles Handy, drummer Bob Crowder, and guitarist Pete Cosey—joined the ensemble in the summer of 1967, when the group played on the shores of Lake Michigan. That autumn Cohran set up the Affro-Arts Theatre as a permanent home for the kind of events that were taking place on the beach that summer. Cohran on that summer:

> Before that, no one played in the park. We'd have a parade once a year or a band playing for a special group, but no one played in the parks for the general public before this grant we got from a sister named Betty Montgomery. She secured a grant from a wealthy man to have art exhibitions on the lakefront in an old boathouse

that wasn't being used. So they brought together sculptors, writ-ers, poets, dancers, painters and musicians and I had the music. It was next to Lake Shore Drive, so people would drive by and hear this strange music because we weren't playing like other people, and they would hear the thumb piano and the zithers, so they would come back and check us out. At our last performance we had three thousand people, so that place was just run over, and that's where we got established.

The Affro-Arts Theatre opened its doors to Chicago's black com-munity for music, African history, African languages, and African civilization. It sponsored forums pertinent to black liberation such as the Conference on Third World Countries. Many of the Stones participated in these free classes. The theater paid its bills with the money AHE raised by having concerts on Friday, Saturday, and Sun-day evenings. It was through their involvement with Cohran and the theater that the Stones formed a relationship with Sammy Davis Jr. Davis had met Cohran through the Chicago music scene. At the same time, Davis also had ties to Chicago's Italian mob and thereby some of the Stones. The performer happened to be tight with Reico Cranshaw, one of the ranking Stone leaders. According to Cohran, Davis and Lola Falana came to town and promised to perform in the theater to help raise funds. However, he got busy and couldn't per-form, but sent five thousand dollars.

Unfortunately, in 1970 the Affro-Arts Theatre closed its doors. But the Stones' exposure to black cultural nationalism shaped their appreciation of being black. And although everything they did was tempered by their contradictory behavior on the streets, the Stones were experts at living in both worlds. They could eloquently pro-claim the need for black liberation and pride when in the public and without blinking an eye could exercise cold-blooded gangsterism in the streets. Their willingness to get involved in Black National-ist activities distinguished the Stones from all other street gangs before, during, and after their formation. The other gangs viewed

Black Nationalism as radical, so they shied away from it so that they wouldn't bring government attention to the illegal activities they were involved in. The Stones, on the other hand, saw being involved with so-called radical groups as a form of protection from the government. Regardless of how radical these groups were, most of them were still more mainstream than the Stones, and they could be counted on for protection when law enforcement attempted to persecute them.

# 3

# Presbyterian Patrons

REVEREND JOHN FRY moved to Chicago from Philadelphia in June 1965 to be head pastor at First Presbyterian Church in Woodlawn. He quickly surveyed the neighborhood and saw how violence affected the community. The forty-two-year-old minister spent those first few weeks walking up and down the streets and alleys of the neighborhood. He talked to residents. He listened to their gripes about the Rangers. He heard children sing "Mighty, Mighty Blackstone" as they played outside. And Jeff Fort's name reverberated on block after block. The intrepid minister decided to approach the infamous teen.

Fry found Fort at a huge apartment building a couple of blocks away from the church. "I was asking him what he was up to and who these guys [were] that he gathered around and what they were doing," Fry recalls. Fort responded the way anyone would to a strange white man poking around in a black neighborhood. He gave Fry a bunch of bullshit lines about the Stones being just a little boys club innocently meeting in basements. No stranger to urban life, Fry knew Fort's answers were spurious. "He was snowing me," Fry says.

The next time Fry saw Fort, the young man approached him. Fort wanted to know why a church representative was out inspecting the neighborhood. Fry responded that he was new to the city and trying

49

to determine the level of violence and gang activity. "He seemed to buy that," Fry says.

Representatives from the Woodlawn Boys Club approached the church about using its third-floor gym for the Conservative Rangers, part of the Main 21, to use. The request was granted. Like most other branches or sets that became members of the Blackstone Rangers, the Conservative Rangers, or Cons as they were known on the streets, started off as a small, independent street gang. The Woodlawn Boys Club's approach to dealing with the Cons ultimately led to friction between street gangs. Unfortunately many professionals, black and white, who worked for mainstream organizations like the Woodlawn Boys Club did not understand the culture of street gangs. To single out one group and provide them access to structured activities alienated other gangs in the vicinity. The Cons used their access to the church gym as an exclusive right that they felt was solely theirs. Any time other youth attempted to frequent the church gym, the Cons would try to charge them or chase them off. Other gangs felt slighted and ultimately projected their frustration onto the Cons, which led to conflict between the groups. This type of misguided youth programming contributed to the violence between the Stones and the Disciples. Too many times the Stones received resources from mainstream institutions while the Ds had fewer resources available to them. Ultimately the Ds got fed up with constantly being excluded, so they decided to disrupt the Stones' affairs with violence whenever they got a chance.

Fry hired Chuck LaPaglia to do community outreach, and LaPaglia got Fort to come around to the church. "Our purpose in affiliating with these guys was to shut down as much violence as we could; that's what we were about," Fry says. Today the guileless minister lives in the Pacific Northwest. He hadn't spoken publicly about the Stones in decades. "What we did was pound on them all the time to keep their goddamn guns hidden. Don't go shooting people." At the time, violence between the Stones and the Disciples was as sure as sunrise, he says.

Fry says he and LaPaglia were convinced that Jeff and Bull could do much, much more with the power they wielded. And they tried to guide the boys without shoving religion in their faces or telling them exactly what to do. Fry had hopes for the Stones to become "more like a community organization than a fucking street gang."

To some, the leaders of First Presbyterian were nothing but a bunch of misguided liberals who enabled a gang to blithely carry on its nefarious activity. The police sneered at the church's outreach efforts and didn't flinch at doing raids at the church or deriding the ministers. False rumors circulated about Stone activity in the church, that there were cultlike sacrifices of women at the altar or that the church ran a honeymoon club for couples to spend a conjugal night in the gym. The alliance between the Stones and the church was quite controversial and seemingly odd. The church leaders felt they had to do something, anything, to try to quell the fierce violence between the Stones and the Disciples. People were dying, and their Christian duty wouldn't allow them to ignore the devastation. In the coming decades, the Stones would repeatedly find themselves with religious allies and leanings. Some criticized the religion as a mask, but the Stones' connection with First Presbyterian signaled the beginning of a somewhat formalized spiritual influence. That doesn't mean the Stones were praying on their knees or visiting people on the sick-and-shut-in list. They had parties in the gym, charging fifty cents for the sounds of Motown and cups brimming with Wild Irish Rose. "I knew they were drinking," Fry says. "What do you expect them to do? They're going to be kids, after all. It didn't bother me that they were drinking in the church." It kept them off the streets.

Make no mistake—Fry didn't run a missionary operation. He says some of the congregation expected the Rangers "would be just like really nice kids and would probably start coming to church. They had to be disabused of these fantasies." But Fry says an urban Christian mission compelled him to open up the church's doors.

Meanwhile, the War on Poverty was under way during the 1960s, and policy makers and politicians alike struggled with a "Negro youth problem." The problems and solutions differed. The police didn't engage with young people; instead they took a hostile street approach. The gangs wouldn't control their behavior. There weren't enough jobs or educational opportunities for young black males. In the wake of this debate, government, nonprofits, and foundations began funding initiatives. Perhaps the charisma of Jeff Fort or the raw potential of the Stones persuaded the philanthropic community to dispense its dollars into the organization. And that, too, became another contentious solution as the community scratched its head over what to do with the Stones.

Fry often preached to the community about Woodlawn in his sermons. In one mid-1960s sermon, he described the Rangers as a largely positive group. The Rangers, Fry says, were acting out of discontent with the conditions of Woodlawn, which is partly why they had stayed at odds with the police and society. "It is in terms of the breakdown of Democracy that I want to talk a moment about the Blackstone Rangers, about whom I presume even residents of Lake Forest [a wealthy Chicago suburb] have heard. The Blackstone Rangers are an organization of very poor boys who have grown up in Woodlawn mostly, but also very poor boys who live all over the South and West sides. Their answer to the chaos and violence and banality of life in an antidemocracy has been to create a large organization capable of producing some genuine order and some safety from this exceedingly hostile environment," Fry proclaimed.

Fry says his objective was to reduce teenage violence. He hoped by helping the Stones establish relationships with other South Side institutions and introducing the Stones to political, social, and economic opportunities, this could happen.

Although Fry and Fort denied Fry's influence on the Stones, others in the community were suspicious. Reverend Curtis Burrell, former executive director of the Kenwood Oakland Community Organization, said he observed on many occasions LaPaglia and Ann Swierbacher of First Presbyterian accompanying Fort to community meetings. He said, "They [LaPaglia and Swierbacher] would be over in the corner with Jeff whispering at these meetings." Burrell believed they told Jeff what to do. This led to a widely held belief among many in the black community that the Stones never acted on their own. Many believe that Fry and his staff actually controlled the Stones. Back then, Fort described his relationship to the church as one of respect for LaPaglia and Fry. "People . . . get it in their head that Reverend Fry is controlling us, but nobody is controlling us at all. The way we look at it is that God Himself is controlling us and guiding us in the proper way."

## First Presbyterian Church

IN 2008, FIRST PRESBYTERIAN celebrated its 175th anniversary. The church's roots are spread across Chicago. During the mid-1800s, early congregants met downtown in the newly incorporated city. The church didn't hesitate to engage in current affairs. In October 1845, the church rocked the presbytery with a resolution denouncing slavery, calling it a "heinous sin against God." Women of the congregation raised money to improve the lives of immigrants. Church members participated in protests against alcohol and city corruption. First Presbyterian grew and recruited big philanthropic names such as Marshall Field to its board. By the early twentieth century First Pres had moved around to various locations on the South Side, and it finally settled in its current home at 64th and Kimbark in 1928. It's a beautiful white building with the facade of a cathedral. As the demographics of Woodlawn began to change in the 1950s and African Americans moved into the neighborhood, the church stayed put and built a multiethnic character instead of participating in white flight. The church picked a white man and a black man to co-pastor: Charles T. Leber and Ulysses B. Blakeley. The church had a host of troubles, including declining membership and the threat of the University of Chicago inching its way into Woodlawn. The pastors challenged the university's expansion and worked with community organizer Saul

Alinsky as well as The Woodlawn Organization. First Presbyterian put a Head Start in the church, worked with at-risk young women, and offered job training for adults. Bringing the Blackstone Rangers into the fold meshed with the church's community outreach goals.

Harold Walker came on board as associate pastor in 1965. The white Alabaman began his pastorate in east Mississippi and came to Chicago for a better divinity education. Turns out he had lived in the next county over in Mississippi from where Jeff's family had previously lived. He learned that Annie Fort had worked on a cotton farm and picked up the family to move to Chicago for a better life. As associate pastor, Walker tended to the sick and buried the dead. He knew of Fry's work with the Stones and the Alinsky model he followed.

"I didn't know whether to agree with him [Fry] or not but I didn't have a better solution," Walker says. "I didn't see any clear alternatives. John's argument always made sense: get to grassroots, where people are, try to see what it is to make them do what they're doing." But Walker didn't give Fry an amen corner. "John and I would argue. I thought there was violence going on. I thought the Stones were doing some arm-twisting with businesses, extortion, and I know there was enforced intimidation to young people to get them to join the Stones. That was one of the big problems. And Jeff and Gene [Bull]—they had the ability to scare people."

For the most part the Stones moved in and out of the church freely. A church staffer was always supposed to be on-site when the boys were present; even if the Stones were on the third floor partying, the First Pres person would chaperone remotely from the pastor's study by reading or just camping out. There were instructions that encouraged popping into the dance from time to time to check in and to remain with police if they came in the building for a search or raid.

If there were problems with the Stones, the church went to Fort. Walker mentioned to Fort once that an electric typewriter had disappeared. It showed up a couple of days later. Mary Lou Todd, a retired church secretary, said the women were preparing for an upcoming church dinner and someone stole all of the chicken. The next day the chicken reappeared. Todd said every year Head Start hosted a Christmas party for two to three hundred neighborhood children. And each year a Stone dressed up as Santa, delivering gifts and jokes to classes. "Angel" Jeff knew how to put on an endearing demeanor around those who weren't Stones. He didn't yell, and he typically walked around First Pres as mild mannered as Clark Kent. In spring 1966, First Presbyterian held an Easter Week Job Project with the Rangers to provide work-training experience, and each Ranger earned $1.75 an hour. They painted classrooms and performed other upkeep of the church. Some of the guys also went to other homes and churches throughout the city to do work. In a memo to the church staff, Fry wrote that First Presbyterian was a clearinghouse for community relations problems with the Rangers. If citizens from the area called with a Stones problem, staffers were instructed to take down the particulars. "Our role is not to solve the problem. Our role is to understand it clearly so that it can later be presented to the Rangers." Fry says there was nothing formal about the relationship between the church and the Stones. Sometimes they sat around in Fry's office. Fry learned that many had quit school in third grade, didn't know their fathers, and dealt with mothers who made their living in the streets. The Stones became each others' brothers. Fry says that context informed how the church interacted with the youth.

"We couldn't invite them and say, 'Now I'm your boss and I'll counsel and tell you how fucked up you are,'" Fry reflects. "None of that would've worked two seconds. They were smart guys." But the minister also criticized Christian apathy in a 1960s sermon, preaching, "Do you know what? I am sick of Christian responsibility. I have found secular responsibility much more responsible and Christian irresponsibility much too inviting. I do not believe in Christian responsibility." But Fry obviously had some sway with the Stones, and when Black Power diverged from the civil rights movement, the minister happily provided guidance about the politics of the era. Civil rights leader Reverend James Bevel met with the Stones at the church and showed a film about riots in Watts to reveal the futility of rioting.

The church gave annual reports to the congregation about its relationship to the Stones. In January 1967, the affiliation was described
as a nonstop dialogue between staffers and the Rangers. "We have
sought to take the lead in dramatizing the paucity of recreational and
vocational training resources for Woodlawn youth. By opening our
building for full use we have been meeting a small part of the whole
problem," the report said. "We have sought to protect the Ranger
vision from any crippling, emasculating, destructive efforts on the
part of the general community to wipe out the Rangers or 'break
their back.'"

Fry's four basic principles on community organizing were: confront violence at its roots, identify with the group as partners in a
conflicted world, represent true Christianity through identifying
with the unfamiliar, and resist public opinion that dismisses the
poorest of ghetto people.

ANOTHER INFLUENTIAL PASTOR in Woodlawn connected with the
Stones was Bishop Arthur Brazier, who has been at Apostolic Church
of God in Woodlawn since the early 1960s, when he was a reverend.
Brazier also served as president of The Woodlawn Organization. Taverns and blight were neighbors to the church, and people nicknamed
the area Baby Skid Row. Stretches of 63rd Street teemed with unsa-
vory business owners. But another enemy lurked, one Brazier hadn't
anticipated. The Stones and the East Side Disciples fought in the
area with the intensity of gladiators. Quite fittingly, parents at one of
the local elementary schools dubbed the playground Little Vietnam.
Tension between adults and youth ballooned.

"We tried to avoid the word *gang*—it was so negative. We called
them youth groups," Brazier says. "The expansion and rise of these
two groups caught us by surprise." By 1966, TWO understood that
it needed to figure out a way to get rid of these toxic turf battles
that ultimately led to shootings. "I was being bombarded in the late
'60s—parents asking me to call the mayor and encourage the mayor
to call out the National Guard." Meanwhile, absenteeism soared at

Hyde Park High School, especially when the Disciples had to cross Woodlawn Avenue to get to school. The violence was territorial. Drugs hadn't infiltrated enough into urban communities to cause such bedlam so the friction wasn't about selling on someone else's drug turf. The daily Chicago newspapers often ran articles about neighborhood gang attacks and youth being locked up in connection to attacks.

Like Reverend Fry, Reverend Brazier resolved that he needed to engage the boys on the street. He approached Bull and Mickey Cogwell about getting a grant to minimize violence. They consented. The reverend also needed Woodlawn participation. At a TWO meeting in December 1966, Brazier, black man to black community, explained:

> Washington people say that there is not one successful program with the gangs in the country and they don't want to throw any more money down the rathole of traditional agency-run programs. We have the missing ingredient: self-determination. Our programs will be administered by the community, by TWO. And it will utilize the unique aspects and advantages of the existing gang structure. Many fear this. They say it won't work. We think it will.

In spring 1967, TWO received funding from the Office of Equal Opportunity (OEO), a government agency started by President Lyndon B. Johnson for his War on Poverty. The controlling Chicago mayor Richard J. Daley had previously started his own community action agency when the War on Poverty launched. In keeping with the Democratic machine, Daley put his black loyalists in place to run the programs. He didn't like Washington putting its fingerprints on the city. But back then TWO represented black political opposition to the powerful mayor, and TWO operated its OEO dollars without the mayor's input or blessing. TWO received $927,000 to provide education and job training to the Rangers and Disciples. Washington embraced the prospect. Sargent Shriver, then head of the War on

Poverty, predicted that TWO would put the Rangers and East Side Disciples to work, and the city would see armed fighting between the two groups come to an end. Fry called it the most stirring idea to come out of the War on Poverty.

As the Stones wrestled with defining themselves, they wrote an open letter to Mayor Daley in response to negative publicity the youth had been receiving. They pledged to create a new image of usefulness: open a nonprofit to help the community; start a school for the young "emphasizing ladies and gentlemen-type personalities, and a community of self pride"; refrain from violence and profanity; "disarm ourselves and rely on police protection from gangs who still have revenge and warfare on their minds"; and work with Operation Breadbasket, the NAACP, churches, etc. They also wrote letters to get grants, characterizing themselves as poor boys who needed a chance, whether opening a restaurant or creating recreational space. Money from the Ford Foundation followed.

First Presbyterian belonged to TWO, and Fry was down with Brazier's plan. He said so in a sermon. Fry preached about Brazier: "The president of that organization is no honky preacher, who fiddles with his glasses. . . . And he is about the finest black man and maddest black man in this country. . . . Jesus Christ chooses to speak through a black man, and Jesus Christ told me to keep my white mouth cool. Blessed by the name of Jesus Christ forever. Amen."

With the OEO money, Brazier set up two schools, one for the East Side Disciples and the other for the Stones. He got the education department at the Xerox Corporation to draw up the curriculum. The Chicago Urban League helped with finding jobs. Brazier hired an auditor to monitor the books. One of the goals was to pick out boys who had dropped out of school but had potential, give them instruction, and have youth, in turn, work with their peers. They all got paid and received carfare. Local public schools disapproved because they thought TWO encouraged the boys to drop out so they could tout their own program. Jeff Fort earned six thousand dollars a year.

Brazier says now that it was a mistake to have the young gang leaders acting as teachers right away. "My view is in the first year or two we should've had professionals—then gradually go into youth teaching. We went too fast, too far early on." Brazier insists that guys were getting off the street and in some cases getting jobs. Some of them were hired by the University of Chicago, Argonne National Laboratories, and agricultural factory International Harvester. He says no one expected the program to be a roaring success in year one. Brazier pleaded with Fort that this program could make young men more responsible in the community. But not long after the program commenced, police arrested Fort for murder and he sat in jail, unable to work on the program. His case eventually got discharged, but it was too late for the OEO program's credibility. Fort's stature as the Stones' leader and his arrest record became linked to the program, and that provided fodder to critics. The lack of adult supervision contributed to fraud: the trainees falsely signed checks and routinely didn't show up to the programming. Enemies of the OEO program and the Stones would soon get their chance to be heard. And Fort would pay a huge price for his involvement, brought up before a huge audience in Washington, D.C., by a Senate committee. Those with any kind of affiliation with the Stones or the job-training program found themselves on the defense, too. The OEO program ended in 1968. Brazier stands by his intentions and the War on Poverty. "It did a lot of good. The war in Vietnam did more to hurt the War on Poverty."

## Police Contact

AN IMPLAUSIBLE ALLIANCE occurred in July 1966. Stones leaders and Third District police officials joined forces temporarily so both sides could ostensibly keep their turf. On the West Side, melees supposedly derived from a revolutionary group stirring up trouble. Rumors circulated that the group had control over major West Side and

South Side gangs. Police commander William Griffin said as soon as he heard about the rioting he sought out the Stones. The chaos had threatened to ooze into Woodlawn. Lamar "Bop" Bell and Fort met with Griffin and agreed to work with officers to prevent rioting. "We don't want a riot," Fort told the *Chicago Daily Defender*. "We're trying to get people not to riot. We know we can't win fighting the police and National Guard. For the last three days, we've been working with the police trying to keep down incidents that might lead to a riot."

The truce didn't last long. A few months later, police arrested Fort, Bull, Bell, and Bernard Green along with forty-three other boys for an outbreak that led to attacks on police with bottles and gunfire. A police car had rolled up to a large crowd standing on the corner of 63rd Place. According to reports, as the squad car passed, the crowd threw bottles and shot at the officers. Police returned fire; twenty-four police cars arrived. After the arrests, police promised extra uniformed police in the area.

Chicago police thought very little of any outreach to the gangs. They scoffed at government grants and considered them a waste. They blamed Fry for coddling the Stones with his open-door policy. Police officer Rich Kolovitz, who worked in the gang unit, believes Fry and LaPaglia helped the Stones become what they were—and he's not referring to community involvement.

"He [Fry] provided them with a place to meet during the bad weather, during the rain, a place where they could hide guns, a place where they could start hiding weapons. As they progressed, as it evolved from just kids on the corner to a street gang," Kolovitz says.

Even the Stones admit that Fry tolerated their criminal behavior. Says one Stone, "See, we always thought a preacher don't let nobody have guns. Man, he down there with us, we shooting machine guns in the basement of the church and this that and the other. I say, man, I used to think, well, maybe he was one of them jack-leg preachers. But he was right there with us. When we be runnin' in that church, been done shot somebody. Comin' in the door with a shotgun, he be like, oh! He go back into his office. We on the second floor, we sittin' down having meetings, we got guns and everything laying around in there. He come in there [and say] 'Pardon me, Jeff, I need to talk to you.'"

Police eyes locked on the Stones, Vice Lords, and Disciples. In 1967 the department reported 150 gang-related killings in Chicago, an all-time high. The same year the police created the Gang Intelligence Unit (GIU). Before the unit came along, the gang problem was decentralized; district commanders individually collected stats. The top brass found this ineffective, and they put GIU into the department's criminal investigation division. Led by Lieutenant Ed Buckney, it initially comprised fifteen investigators. This organization allowed information and enforcement to be centralized in one unit. Buckney later became the ninth black captain in the history of the Chicago Police Department.

The unit was aggressive, and that partly stemmed from Woodlawn residents demanding a respite from the violence. But many also didn't understand why the police didn't try to engage with the youth. "When people don't feel they have a voice or interest in being served, they find another way," reflected First Presbyterian's Harold Walker. "The strategy of police is to put violent people in jail. It's absurd because then you put everybody in jail. Find alternatives to violence." Reverend Brazier, too, thought little of the GIU. He said they were negative and unhelpful and would make sweeps in the training centers, hunting for Stones.

One of the criticisms against the GIU was that middle-class black cops had no interest in helping black youth—or about as much interest as average white folk. But police refuted that accusation. "That's totally unfair," Buckney told a reporter in the mid-1980s. "What middle class? We're going back to the '60s. The black middle class, what there was, was made up of professional people, which the police weren't a part of. If you go out there and talk to any police officers from any era, we were just poor guys that happened to get lucky enough to come out of the army and get on at the police department. But that's totally untrue that officers were from the middle class."

Law enforcement felt a reason to be forceful; in 1967, officials reported 115 Woodlawn shooting incidents in which the victims or offenders were under seventeen. The principal of a local elementary school, the one nicknamed Little Vietnam, said he discovered that children had to pay $0.25 a day or $1.25 a week to the Rangers to get to school because they had to cross through territory controlled by the Rangers. Buckney said in a mid-1980s interview, "Jeff and the Main 21, they did very little of the dirty work. They usually put the twelve-, thirteen-, fourteen-year-olds up to do the shooting and those kinds of things. Because it was very unlikely that they would go to jail."

The role of First Presbyterian caught the attention of the denomination's in-house magazine. *Presbyterian Life* published a profile of the Stone–First Pres relationship in 1968. "The best thing that could possibly happen would be for Reverend Fry to get transferred and for First Presbyterian Church to forget about the Blackstone Rangers," Buckney said. "It would be best if *Presbyterian Life* and all the other magazines would just forget the Blackstone Rangers. Printing all these things about them just makes them heroes and makes matters worse." From Buckney's point of view, the church and social agencies could do nothing for the gangs. He didn't believe in organizing youth fellowship. He saw nothing redeeming in the Stones. The only thing to be done was to let the police handle the problem and break up the gangs.

Third District police commander William Griffin complained in the late 1960s that the Woodlawn clergy refused to cooperate with authorities. "I don't know what he [Fry] is trying to achieve. I don't know if Reverend Fry is trying to establish his own little empire, if Reverend Fry is power-mad or what," Griffin said. Fry said he had lunch with an official from the Third District. Fry said the man told him how useful he could be if he pointed out some of the guys on the streets. The minister responded by telling the officer about a confrontation he had witnessed: officers had entered an apartment building in Woodlawn and thrown women and kids down the stairs. "If you arrest those cops and put them to the judge, then maybe I would finger," Fry told the officer. The officer got up and left.

One notorious story about First Presbyterian is often repeated whenever the church is mentioned. That story says that ministers allowed the Stones to keep a cache of weapons in the church. Reverend Walker said that was partially true. In 1966, Fry and LaPaglia negotiated a deal where some Stones and Disciples turned in their weapons. On July 4, a big pile of pistols and weapons was surrendered with the caveat that the weapons wouldn't be used in investigations of any crime. The pastors locked the weapons in a safe on the second floor as agents from the U.S. Treasury Department watched. A seventy-something-year-old church secretary did an inventory and passed out copies. The agreement had transpired because the Stones said they didn't trust Chicago police. Supposedly no one had the combination to the lock on the safe. Several months later the press got tipped about the weapons; the episode led to a police raid on the church and discovery of the weapons. And that led to bomb threats and condemnation of First Presbyterian.

After the church raid, Fry preached the following: "One hundred and twenty-seven were in the church that night, playing ball and meeting with agency representatives about jobs and housing. They were searched, and cuffed, all were held by swaggering, verbally nasty policemen with carbines and magnum pistols at the ready. For almost two hours, these 127 boys suffered the invasion of what they have come to consider some kind of haven from violence. Without one word of rebuttal, one response. They maintained their fabulous cool, and when the police finally left the gym where they were being detained at gunpoint they together shouted 'Blackstone!'"

Fry remained undaunted. He found an imaginative method to combat the police.


## Fighting Back

IN FALL 1968, the Black P Stone Legal Defense Project launched out of First Presbyterian with the purpose of giving legal representation to those who needed it. Up until this time, the public defender's office usually represented the Stones. The church viewed the office as overburdened and insufficiently equipped to command fair trials. The legal defense project also provided bail money; accused Stones previously had sat in jail for months until trial time. By 1970 the project had handled 207 cases; 53 were pending. Of 178 cases carried to completion, 100 were won and the defendants discharged, 24 received probation, and 19 received fines. Of the cases discharged, 4 percent were discharged at the hearing stage—that signaled harassment to the church. Of the 78 cases lost, 33 were plea agreements to lesser charges with the state's attorneys.

Here are some examples of cases from the church:

Lee Jackson and Melvin Bailey worked at the Southmoor Hotel on 67th and Stony Island. Jackson was a security guard and accused a man of having stolen clothes from a tenant. Jackson and Bailey held on to the clothes. The man returned with the police. He told the officer that the two robbed him at knifepoint. The next day the state's attorney asked the arresting officer about the case. He called the case bullshit and said he only pinched the two because they were Main 21 members. Charges were dropped.

Allen Christmas and Lofton James were accused of attempted murder during a fight at a dance at DuSable High School. Bail was set at $20,000. The private attorney's investigation found a high school coach who chaperoned at the dance. He verified that Christmas and James were trying to stop the fight. Charges were dropped.

Leonard Sengali, a Stone who worked for the Kenwood Oakland Community Organization, was driving back from an Operation Breadbasket meeting. Four squad cars surrounded him for an alleged traffic violation. Police searched his car and found suspicious-looking leaves. They arrested Sengali for marijuana possession, negligent driving, and resisting arrest. The marijuana turned out to be grass—the kind on your lawn. He was found not guilty on all counts.

A detailed legal defense report from the church listed violations from police and state's attorneys. It saved the biggest screed for the Gang Intelligence Unit. It listed illegal search and seizures, harassment, beatings, intimidation, property damage, and character assassination. The report said GIU head Buckney went to Washington, D.C., to try to prevent the OEO federal grant. The legal defense project report complained of raids at the church, a YMCA, Chicago Theological Seminary's cooperative housing, and the Black Disciples Center.

The congregation of First Presbyterian didn't fund the legal defense project. The church found a millionaire patron from Denver. Charles F. Kettering, grandson of the General Motors inventor, bankrolled it through the Kettering Foundation. Apparently Kettering had fostered a relationship with Bull and often visited him in the Illinois state penitentiary when he was locked up for solicitation of murder. The foundation sent checks in the tens of thousands, which in turn went to pay for private attorneys when any of the Stones got caught up in a legal predicament.

In an undated *Chicago Today* article, the Gang Intelligence Unit tried to dissuade Kettering from patronizing the Stones. Officers told him the money encouraged gangsterism. Eventually the checks stopped. On August 18, 1970, the Kettering Foundation ended its support of the Ranger Defense Program. Charles Kettering wrote a letter to Fort via Fort's attorney. In the letter, Kettering reiterated that his purpose had been to reduce police harassment in hopes that it would trickle down to the GIU in order to have the unit reevaluate its policies. But negative publicity regarding the fund and the alleged violence carried out by the Stones undermined Kettering's efforts. He wrote to Jeff, "Wish I could discuss all of this with you in person, but you're a hard guy to track down."

In closing, Jeff, let me say again what I said or asked you the last time I came to Chicago. The Rangers came to be as a means to achieve some positive and constructive social or community objectives. You and Bull had a dream and the Rangers were a way of achieving it. This was many years ago. But now I think you must ask yourself the question if the Black P Stone Nation is still the best way of achieving what it is you want to achieve in behalf of the young people of Chicago. . . . Given the balance of power, and the way things are going there, you might conclude that at this point the very presence of the Black P Stone Nation is doing the South Side and/or the Stones and/or the city of Chicago more harm than good.

In all, the Kettering Foundation had contributed approximately $260,000 by the time the defense project ended.

In 1968, concern about the relationship between the Stones and First Presbyterian left more than the police anxious and angry. Brazier said that in the beginning the church did try to do some good with the Stones. But there were unintended consequences. "Two things stuck in my mind," Brazier recalls. One time he talked to Fry in Fry's office and the minister had a huge graph on the wall with the names of all the Stones in jail, their charges, and how long they'd be there. "I thought that was weird for a church," Brazier says. "Secondly, I was trying to get a grant to clean buildings in Woodlawn that had been marked by graffiti that the Blackstone Rangers were doing. I asked him if he would use his influence to have Stones cease doing graffiti. He turned me down flat; said he wouldn't do it. He said he was more concerned about landlords cleaning up their buildings."

Community organizer Nicholas Von Hoffman, who'd done community work in Woodlawn earlier in the decade, says the ministers at First Pres were romantic goofballs. "You have to be very realistic and it's no world for ministers or social work types. They were all imbeciles; they came from the wrong world." Von Hoffman says their intentions were good but they ended up encouraging bad behavior. "This was strictly the road to hell paved with good intentions."

Reverend Jerry Wise first came to First Presbyterian in the 1970s and disagrees. "Usually they'll say these guys were fuzzy-headed liberals, naive, particularly to the race thing. . . . John Fry was a World War II veteran. He wasn't a fool." Wise said it's easy to stand back forty years later and second-guess.

The presbytery passed a resolution officially commending First Presbyterian's work with the Rangers. But in winter 1968 the Presbytery of Chicago worried about the Stones' connection to the church. A Presbyterian minister who chaired a special committee on police relations met with local police. Officers pressed for Fry to be removed from First Presbyterian. In 1969 the Presbytery of Chicago presented a report of its own internal investigation of the church. First Presbyterian had requested the investigation. Dozens of interviews were conducted, but the police declined to participate. The committee looked into rumors of extortion, weapons, and narcotics and into whether Fry and LaPaglia had used a female church staffer to control Fort through sex.

The report vindicated Fry of any wrongdoing. It concluded that the relationship between the church and the Stones was positive.

# 4

# 1968

THE STONES CELEBRATED 1968 with a bang by hosting a big New Year's Eve bash at First Presbyterian Church. It was a Sunday night and the temperature was subzero. They sang "hey, hey, hey" to Stevie Wonder's "I Was Made to Love Her." Three Stones—Theodore "Teddy" Williams, Thomas, and Felix—and Adell McChristian burst out the doors of the church into the bitter cold night to get some wine from the liquor store on 63rd Street, a block north and around the corner from the church. McChristian wasn't a Stone but they made him come along because he was old enough to buy the wine. Just as the guys walked up the street, somebody across the street hollered "Blackstone!" It was too dark to see exactly who the two guys and a girl were and too cold to go check them out. The Stones slowed down slightly. They had to be cautious; sometimes Disciples would sneak up on their rivals by acting like they were Stones and then shoot. Because of the frigid weather, they yelled back "Blackstone!" and kept moving. Suddenly gunshots rang out. The Stones took off quickly to get to the liquor store for cover. Teddy, the youngest, got spooked. When he heard the shooting, he halted. He was only sixteen and didn't have a lot of experience on the streets. Once he got himself together to run, it was too late. The shooter caught him in the back. Thomas, seventeen, tried to go back to help, but the shooter caught him in the thigh.

The shooting brought a stillness over Woodlawn, apart from an Aretha Franklin record blaring from the church. "R-e-s-p-e-c-t" echoed in the cold night air while Teddy's body lay in a quickly freezing pool of blood in front of the liquor store. Felix managed to help Thomas make it to his house on 61st and Kimbark. McChristian ran nonstop all the way to his house on 78th and Woodlawn.

THE DAY AFTER TEDDY'S MURDER, comedian and civil rights activist Dick Gregory held a press conference to announce the end of his forty-day fast in protest of the Vietnam War. He announced a plan to run for U.S. president as a write-in candidate. Gregory also said that he planned to organize massive protests leading up to and through the Democratic National Convention to be held that August in Chicago. Gregory, who lived in Chicago at the time, wanted to force the city to enact a stronger fair housing ordinance and take other steps to address civil rights issues. Gregory's plan included recruiting the Vice Lords, the Blackstone Rangers, and the Disciples to participate in these protests.

These kinds of announcements by black leaders, ones that encouraged alliances between gangs and Black Nationalists—not the escalating violence between the Stones and Disciples—scared the shit out of the feds.

THE YEAR 1968 was pivotal in U.S. history and for the Blackstone Rangers. Television news covered people protesting the Vietnam War and marching for civil rights and a wide range of radical groups vandalizing government and corporate buildings.

And while it was never their intention, the Stones got caught up in 1968. To the Stones, their only enemies were the Disciples. To the government, the Stones were a perceived threat to local and national security. The Stones had a history of social activism and well-known associations with Black Nationalist leaders. These leaders recognized the Stones as potential allies, troops, and sometimes fodder. The Stones had already demonstrated their willingness to commit violence.

And while the world watched the year of protest in America, few people outside of Woodlawn, with the exception of FBI agents, paid any attention to the killing of members of the Blackstones and the Disciples. The FBI could not have cared less about the astounding violence that put young black men to death. The FBI's only concern was that the civil rights and Black Nationalist movements would gain momentum and politicize these gangs. By no means did the FBI want the Stones to be politicized to form an "interlocking director-ate" with other youth gangs to carry out revolutionary acts against the government. As America was losing the wars in Vietnam and on poverty, the country seemed vulnerable to a potential uprising from groups like the Stones. The feds worried about the Stones' real and imaginary relationships with the Black Panthers, the Nation of Islam, and the Republic of New Afrika. Consequently, the FBI began to intensify its surveillance of the Stones. Agents placed informants in and around the organization to report on its every move. And to ensure the Stones' destabilization, the FBI implemented a misinfor-mation campaign. They would pull gang members off the streets and warn them that the FBI had intelligence indicating that opposing gangs had planned attacks against them. There was also evidence that the FBI sent letters to gang leaders warning them that their oppo-sition had hits out on their lives. The FBI's strategy was to create friction between the Stones and the Disciples and other groups that sought to form alliances. And while the Stones' battle with external enemies was intense, its biggest challenge was the possibility of los-ing their founding leader, Eugene "Bull" Hairston. He was put on trial for solicitation of murder on May 31, 1968. The outcome would forever change the leadership and spirit of the Blackstone Rangers.

THE MURDER OF THEODORE "TEDDY" WILLIAMS kicked off a bloody war between the Stones and Disciples. Teddy and Thomas worked for The Woodlawn Organization's job-training program funded by the federal Office of Equal Opportunity (OEO). They made forty-five dollars a week, a nice piece of a change for a young cat from the 'hood. The cold-blooded hit was going to have a severe effect on the truce and the lucrative job program. Although one of the program's goals was to provide armistice between the Stones and the Ds, no one expected the truce to last one day after Teddy's death. It happened on a holiday week when the training wasn't in session, so there was at least a brief time for tempers to cool. Program directors Reverend Arthur Brazier and Leon Finney instructed their people to talk the Stones down before the Monday morning session.

The stakes were high.

The job training already operated under a cloud of suspicion. Temporarily suspending the program because of the threat of an all-out gang war would provide critics with just enough ammunition needed to shut it down. Brazier, Finney, and the TWO program staff took action. Much was said about how the "white man" wanted to see this program fail and how it fell upon the leaders of the Stones and the Disciples to prove the "white man" wrong. Now more than ever the Stones and Disciples needed to put their intense rivalry—rooted in competition for resources—aside. The gang chiefs were preached to and pleaded with. They needed to understand that their biggest threat was not one another but the "white man." Brazier and Finney told the chiefs that they knew it would be hard, but they had to find a way to forget past differences. If they couldn't, they would face a real threat to their actual existence.

A great deal of tension simmered those first few days, but things moved as well as could be expected. If they could just get through Thursday without a bloodbath, they might make it. Friday was payday and no one wanted the money jeopardized. That makes what happened so surprising. To this day no one knows why seventeen-year-old Bernard, a Stone, walked into the TWO job-training center on 866 East 63rd and shot eighteen-year-old Disciple Joseph Evans in the face. Evans survived, and Bernard bizarrely explained that he shot Evans by accident.

The shooting prompted OEO regional director Allen Beals to send a telegram to Brazier. Beals said he could not believe that such an incident could happen, and he blamed TWO for mismanaging the program. Beals accused TWO of not maintaining proper standards of conduct for enrollment and of having a subprofessional staff. He insisted that weapons and violence would not be tolerated in this federal project. He said TWO could lose its funding.

The shooting impelled the police to search First Presbyterian, where TWO operated another job-training center. Police found a homemade bomb, a sawed-off rifle, and several rounds of ammunition in the basement of the church. Reverend John Fry says that he didn't know anything about the weapons and ammunition; he believed that someone had planted the artillery.

## Juvenile Hit Men

THE BLACKSTONE RANGERS leadership had learned a tactic from the older gangsters who had used juveniles in their operations. In 1968, the Cook County state's attorney's office recognized a pattern of juveniles under seventeen involved in shootings. In the first two weeks of the year, forty-seven incidents involved teen gang shootings. State's attorney John Stamos called for new state statutes covering the prosecution of juveniles. Stamos also launched a major investigation to determine if a number of those recent shootings had been ordered by older Blackstone Rangers.

On September 12, 1967, Leo McClure, thirty-three, was murdered. Two other men, thirty-six-year-old Dorocher Berrien and thirty-four-year-old Theodore Newsome, were wounded as the trio of drug peddlers sat in a car on 62nd and Kenwood. According to the state's attorney's office, fourteen-year-old Marvin Martin, the self-proclaimed president of the junior Conservative Rangers, testified that thirteen-year-old Dennis Jackson did the shooting. Marvin said he was standing on the corner of 62nd and Kenwood with Dennis, his thirteen-year-old brother Sanders, and another young man when Paul Martin approached them. Martin, thirty-four, was a high-ranking member of the Stones. Marvin Martin (no relation) said Paul pointed to the car sitting on the corner and said, "There's the car, hit it." Marvin accused Dennis of shooting six times into the car as he shouted, "You messin' with the chief." Marvin said after the shooting the boys ran back to his house. According to Marvin, later in the day Bull asked the group of boys if they had handled the situation, and Dennis said, "Yeah, I shot each one of them twice." Dennis then asked Bull for money. Marvin said Bull gave Dennis a five-dollar bill and a one-dollar bill. He told Dennis to keep a dollar and give a dollar each to the other boys. When Dennis asked Bull why he had been asked to shoot the men, Bull said the men in the car were selling narcotics on Stones' turf without their permission.

The Cook County state's attorney's office charged twenty-three-year-old Eugene "Bull" Hairston and Paul Martin each with two counts of attempted murder and three counts of solicitation of murder. Paul Martin got a fast trial. Bull's trial lasted for months.

Paul Martin regarded himself as the spiritual leader of the Stones. Throughout his weeklong trial, he wore a Roman collar and clutched a Bible. On January 26, the jury deliberated for an hour and fifty-five minutes and found him not guilty of all charges.

## FBI Surveillance

MILDRED STEGALL, PRESIDENT JOHNSON'S personal staff assistant, called the FBI on February 13 to relay a message. The White House had concerns about the Blackstone Rangers and had been informed that the organization had worked out an agreement with other gangs in the area. According to the White House, each gang had staked out a particular area of Chicago, creating a system of "interlocking directorates" in which the gangs planned to cause mayhem.

Cartha D. "Deke" DeLoach, one of FBI director J. Edgar Hoover's most trusted lieutenants, handled this matter for the FBI. DeLoach assigned this case to W. C. Sullivan, director of the FBI Domestic Intelligence Division. The FBI knew all about the Stones. It had files on the organization dating back to 1966, the same year some members had acted as security for Martin Luther King Jr.'s Chicago visit. The division immediately reviewed its bureau files and contacted the Chicago office to determine if the White House's concern had merit. An inquiry to the FBI's Chicago office failed to divulge any information to substantiate the allegation. In fact, FBI sources in Chicago thought it implausible that these "undisciplined" youths would consent to influence or take direction from another gang. The FBI consulted Chicago police, but the department said it had no information signaling the Stones, or any youth gang for that matter, attempted to cooperate through "interlocking directorates" to "bring havoc" to Chicago. Within two days of the White House inquiry, the FBI reported that its sources considered such gang activity highly unlikely and such cooperation ran counter to traditional gang activities and intergang hostility. Agents forwarded the report to the U.S. attorney general's office.

Nonetheless, the FBI intensified its surveillance on the Stones. Officials knew about the leadership—Main 21—and membership, which they estimated to be fifteen hundred youth. Through informants who worked directly with the Stones (and the Stones themselves), the FBI believed the organization to be in a state of disarray because of the intermittent incarcerations of Fort, Hairston, and a few other Mains. The Stones suffered from internal friction, which made it difficult to formulate a plan for citywide gang cooperation for any purpose. FBI informants perceived the Stones to have the capacity only to try to protect their own strictly defined gang area in Woodlawn. Moreover, Stone violence was only directed at other gangs and not at the community—white or black. Although the FBI

worried about the potential for the Stones to be politicized, it had
no evidence that more than a few Stones listened to Black Nationalists. Ultimately, the FBI informants communicated that the TWO
training program was enough to subdue the Stones who didn't want
to risk the grant money.

ON THE EVENING of Valentine's Day, Nick Dorenzo and his friend
Paul Hawkins were strolling east on 62nd Street in Woodlawn. At the
same time, Donald Blanton and his buddies were hanging out in the
area trying to find something to get into. They had just crossed 63rd
Street and were headed north on Dorchester. When Dorenzo arrived
at 62nd, he saw Blanton and his boys. Dorenzo was an instructor for
the TWO program and a Disciples leader. He wasn't sure if Blanton
and his boys were Stones. They looked kind of young so he yelled
"Mighty Eastside Disciples" to scare them off in case they were.
They didn't budge. He panicked. Groups of young gangbangers were
known for jumping people they outnumbered. He pulled his gun
out, hoping that would make them run, but they seemed to be more
perplexed by his actions than scared. He definitely had no plans to
shoot them; he had too much to lose with his $5,200-a-year job. But
he also didn't want to take the chance of getting jumped by a bunch
of wild-ass little dudes. He figured since he had pulled his pistol out,
maybe he could fire some shots in their direction to scare them off.
Just as he fired, two fourteen-year-old girls, Demetria Wormley and
Dorothy Profit, walked through a lot on 62nd and Dorchester. They
had just left Jackson Park and were headed home. They both got hit
by bullets fired from Dorenzo's pistol. Demetria was shot in the back
of the neck and killed; Dorothy was shot in the hand. Donald took
a bullet in the shoulder; he and Dorothy survived. Dorenzo knew he
was finished. After the shooting, he walked slowly back to his house
on 64th and University to wait for the police to come and get him.
They did the next day.

Yet again the spotlight shone on TWO in the worst way. Brazier
attacked the press for trying to discredit the program by reporting

only on students and instructors involved in crime. He complained that the newspapers deliberately tried to sabotage the program, so he denied reporters access to the program facilities.

The OEO set up several guidelines to improve the program: they hired more professionals to supervise the educational programs and discontinued the payment of fees to gang members for recruiting others to participate in the program. Upon receiving the new guidelines, Brazier called a press conference to announce that TWO was considering dropping the program "because some of the requirements are unclear."

Meanwhile, Fort had just gotten out of jail. He had spent the first few months of 1968 locked up in the county jail fighting a murder case from the previous year. To this point, he had not been able to benefit from the TWO money. One of the Stones says, "When he first came out, he said . . . 'Out of every check, I'm gon give everybody twenty-five dollars and take the rest.'" All of the Stones had to give Fort their checks, which would then be taken to FairFax, a neighborhood convenient store. The store cashed the checks and Fort gave twenty-five of the forty- or forty-five-dollar check back to each Stone. No Stones objected because they had had their way with the money prior to Fort's release. Now it was time to give back to the Nation. One Stone recalled, "A lot of that money was used for bond money, guns and stuff."

Continued violence between the Stones and the Disciples brought down a ton of heat on the Stones. The cops snatched Stones off the streets every day. The newspapers criticized the Stones. The OEO felt pressure to shut the program down because of all this drama. On March 4, the Stones and the Disciples decided to call a truce as a PR move to prevent them from losing their OEO money. So what occurred the following day doesn't make sense. On March 5, the Chicago office of the FBI claimed to have received an anonymous call notifying them that the Stones were planning a disturbance near 51st and Lake Shore Drive in a few days. The anonymous caller also told the FBI that the Stones planned to bomb a police district on 48th and Wabash within the next three weeks. The caller claimed that the Stones had a cache of guns stashed at the St. Regis Apartments on 40th and Ellis and expected the delivery of a bazooka on March 5.

The FBI immediately notified the police, although the FBI didn't trust the department because of territorial friction. Using FBI intelligence, the police searched the St. Regis Apartments and found nothing. To ensure that the police weren't withholding evidence, the FBI called in two of its Stone informants. One confirmed that there had been a plan to cause a disturbance on 51st and Lake Shore Drive but it never went down. However, the informant said that he didn't know anything about any guns being stored at the St. Regis Apartments. The second informant believed that the Stone plan to bomb the police district was just a rumor. He told the FBI that the Stones tried to stay low-key to avoid negative attention to TWO so the money could stay in their pockets. Also, he doubted the Stones would do anything that might derail Bull's upcoming trial. Despite having only information from an anonymous caller that had been debunked by the police and two of its own informants, the FBI sent memorandums to the Secret Service and the military.

The following week, the FBI found what it needed to substantiate the alleged Stone plan to wage an armed attack against the United States. The source was a *Chicago Tribune* article titled "Negro Gang Leader Tells Arms Offer." The article reported on a six-hour recorded interview conducted by the Chicago police with George "Watusi" Rose, a ranking Main 21 member. In the interview, Watusi said that a group of white communists offered the Stones hand grenades and automatic rifles in the event of a riot. The offer included money and automatic weapons mounted on jeeps that could be transported to any riot area in the city via semitrailers. Watusi said the Stones rejected the offer because they didn't trust white people. Plus the Stones knew that the government would come down on them hard if they were caught conspiring with white communists. A group of Black Nationalists offered the Stones hand grenades and sniperscopes. This time the Stones agreed, Watusi said, because they trusted the black brothers more than the whites. During the Detroit riots in summer 1967, a group of Black Nationalists had approached the Stones about inciting riots in Chicago. He said they also wanted to disrupt the city during the upcoming Democratic National Convention.

When asked about Stone allegiance to the Black Nationalist movement, Watusi said the Stones were in the early stages of a black syndicate as opposed to supporting Black Nationalists. He said the Stones stockpiled all of their weapons in a central location so that no one of its branches had more weapons than any other. They routinely moved the weapons cache around to avoid its capture in a raid. If a Main 21 decided that one of the branches needed some weapons, he would have the weapons distributed to the location and returned when finished.

On March 15, a second source who represented an organization that collected intelligence information regarding youth gangs in Chicago, probably a GIU officer, said that information in the newspaper article regarding the Stones receiving mounted 105-millimeter guns seemed credible. This same source also said he couldn't surmise whether the rumor that the Stones had been offered money and weapons from white communists was true or not. On March 19, a third source, also probably with the GIU, advised that the information in the newspaper article was a figment of Watusi's imagination. He said Watusi had been marked for death by the Stones and therefore gave information that he believed the police wanted to hear in exchange for protection.

In regards to the Stones' ability or inclination to partner with other gangs or Black Nationalists to carry out an armed struggle against the United States, the FBI's confidential sources in Chicago and the Chicago police department believed that the Blackstone Rangers were too disorganized at the time to accomplish such a feat. They felt that the destabilization of the Stones' top leadership caused chaos. The sources said they had heard no information or indication that the Stones or any other youth gang was attempting to organize other gangs for the purposes of violence.

The FBI's confidential sources felt that the main objective of the Stones was to protect their territory, and as a result most gang violence was not directed at the community, black or white. These sources indicated that the Stones as a whole were not Black Nationalists in their worldview; however, some individual Stones espoused the Black Nationalist ideology. Finally, one of the major problems the FBI had with verifying Watusi's story was that he had fled Chicago with his family out of fear for their lives. After the interview, the Chicago Police Department lost contact with him and didn't know his whereabouts. The interview recordings were forwarded to Mayor Daley and a U.S. Senate commission.

## Stone Reaction to King's Death

THE FBI TOILED on with its mission to link the Stones to an armed struggle against the United States. Regardless of what was being said about the Blackstone Rangers' inability or unwillingness to involve themselves in an armed struggle, the FBI remained unconvinced. There was too much at risk, especially in urban areas where social and political unrest verged on explosion. On March 28, Martin Luther King Jr. led a march in Memphis that turned violent. A sixteen-year-old black boy was killed, 60 people were injured, and over 150 were arrested. If this could happen during a so-called nonviolent march, what would happen if a group like the Stones—which had demonstrated its readiness to perform violence—was involved? Three days after the march in Memphis, President Johnson announced steps to limit the war in Vietnam and his decision not to seek reelection. Civil unrest, Johnson's seeming surrender in Vietnam, and his unwillingness to run for reelection made the United States appear weak in the eyes of the FBI. The agency worried that this weakness would embolden militant groups to make their move against the country.

King's assassination on the balcony of the Lorraine Motel in Memphis put the FBI's concern to the test. Just as the FBI feared,

King's death sparked rioting all across America. Chicago, Baltimore, Boston, Detroit, Kansas City, Newark, Washington, D.C., and many other cities went up in flames as angry black protesters chanted, "burn, baby, burn." Presidential candidate Robert Kennedy, upon hearing of the murder just before he planned to give a speech in Indianapolis, instead delivered a eulogy in which he pleaded with the audience to "tame the savageness of man and make gentle the life of this world."

But two days later a shoot-out between Black Panthers and Oakland police resulted in several arrests and deaths, including sixteen-year-old Panther Lil Bobby Hutton. Johnson signed the Civil Rights Act of 1968 within a week of King's death in an attempt to bring a halt to the black rebellions. But it would not be enough.

In Chicago, over sixteen thousand federal troops, federalized Illinois National Guards, and Chicago police patrolled the streets. The federal soldiers arrived in Chicago within two days of King's murder. The stores along Madison Avenue on the West Side had been fire-bombed and looted. As people drove around, they had to go through blockades set up by the National Guard. At one of the checkpoints, people were ordered to get out of their cars to be searched. The guardsmen confiscated from children toy guns that looked too much like real guns.

On the South Side, eighteen hundred federal soldiers set up a camp at 63rd Street in Jackson Park. Each soldier carried his own ammunition and an M-14 rifle fixed with a bayonet. The soldiers were ordered to shoot to protect their lives and on orders from an officer. They patrolled the major streets in Woodlawn. Blockades were set up at intersections along 63rd to protect the stores, banks, and businesses. Woodlawn, along with many other black communities in Chicago, had become a police state. While the West Side burned with an orange haze, the Main 21 met at First Presbyterian to talk about the spread of violence in the community. Reverend Fry made the point that rioting would only harm Woodlawn. Whether Fry's words made the difference or their own moral compass prevailed, the Stones worked to maintain order in the community. They held a peaceful demonstration instead. About two thousand guys stood up on the Midway at the University of Chicago. "All of those people in Hyde Park messed their pants. But it showed a presence and a strength," said Reverend Harold Walker, who ministered at the church.

The *Chicago Daily Defender* reported on one thousand Blackstone Rangers meeting over the weekend and pledging to react nonviolently to King's death. The youth ranged in ages from twelve to early twenties. Fort said that all Rangers loved and honored King. "In his memory," Fort told the newspaper, "we will do all we can to preserve peace in our community. He believed in nonviolence and we want to follow in his path." The Main 21 backed Fort.

Wadsworth Upper Grade Center, at 62nd and University, held an assembly to pay tribute to the slain leader. Just as the assembly began, several hundred Blackstone Rangers marched into the school. Principal Yakir Korey thought the Stones were coming in to cause trouble. Instead, members of the Blackstones asked him for an all-male assembly. Korey granted the request, and the Blackstones urged the boys not to harm the school or the businesses in the community.

Still, some people believed that Fort and the Stones used this "peace in the community" kick to extort local businesses in a protection racket. A group of merchants claimed they were approached by members of the Blackstones and asked to pay one hundred dollars for a placard that read "DO NOT Touch—Black P Stones—Jeff." The signs had two eyes on them indicating that the Stones were watching. The merchants feared that if they didn't pay the Stones, their businesses would be vandalized. The placards appeared in store windows along East 55th and 53rd Streets and Stony Island between 67th and 69th Streets. Two prominent businessmen, Marshall Stern, president of the Woodlawn Businessmen's Association, and Sam Friedman, president of the Jackson Park Businessmen's Association, said that although they knew of merchants who were solicited for "protection money by young thugs after the recent disturbances," they believed the Rangers had nothing to do with the extortion racket. Stern credited the Stones for their efforts to "cool things down" and said the signs posted on stores by Blackstone members were a positive step in preventing disorder. The police didn't buy it. They vowed to investigate the reported extortion racket.

## The Poor People's Campaign

JUST A LITTLE over a month after King's assassination, the Southern Christian Leadership Conference (SCLC) decided to continue his Poor People's Campaign. The SCLC led twenty-five hundred people to Washington, D.C., to occupy Resurrection City, a shantytown campsite near the Lincoln Memorial. Jesse Jackson was elected Resurrection City manager, and the Blackstone Rangers were invited. After only five days at Resurrection City, some of the Stones got restless. Dan Brown, a junior member of the Blackstone Rangers, recalls "getting a little bored."

The *Chicago Daily Defender* reported that march leaders had a tough time controlling the various street youth organizations that they had invited from different parts of the country. Fights broke out. The SCLC's Reverend James Bevel was dispatched to deal with the Stones. He had some familiarity with them from when he first went to Chicago with King in 1966. Once he had all of the Stones and other youth organizations from other cities together, Bevels challenged them. "You want to cut and shoot people, then you're like Stokely and Rap," Bevels shouted at the gangbangers. "THEY ARE WHITE PEOPLE," referring to Stokely, H. Rap Brown, and the Black Panther Party. "They think violence, and violence is what white people are hung up on."

The youth sat stunned by his words. They had always seen the Black Panthers as the direct opposite of white people. To them, leaders of the civil rights movement acted white. Calling a young street warrior whitey was like accusing him of raping his mother. No street guy wanted to be associated with being white; that was the squarest thing out. Bevel's tactic worked. The Stones cooled down for a while. But eventually their disruptive behavior—buying whiskey and threatening to burn down the shantytown—got the Stones sent home.

## Hit on David Barksdale

**WHILE KING'S DEATH** brought widespread disturbances to many black communities in Chicago, it brought unprecedented peace between the Blackstone Rangers and the Disciples. A month went by with no shootings or killings. Jeff Fort, now acting as the sole leader of the Rangers because of Bull's trial, and Disciples leader David Barksdale agreed to a peace talk on May 8 in the Cook County jail with superintendent Winston Moore. Despite the calm, Moore sensed a need to invite the leaders to talk about ending violence on the South Side. Moore said, "Nothing was accomplished." Events after the meeting make the timing of Moore's request curious. Bull's murder trial happened in the same building and at the same time as the meeting. As three Stones, including twenty-year-old Bernard Green, walked out of the criminal courts building, ten Disciples confronted them. Insults were exchanged and a brief fight broke out between Green and twenty-year-old Disciple Orthell Champion. Neither Fort nor Barksdale witnessed the fight. But that same day, GIU detectives Richard Peck, Sidney Clark, and Donald Foulkes provoked the two groups. GIU detectives had a reputation for whipping up beefs between the Stones and the Ds; the persistent conflicts helped them justify cracking down on the two groups. As the detectives rode in their squad car, they saw Barksdale and two other Disciples in an automobile on 65th and University. The officers pulled them over and asked Barksdale if it was true that he had worked Fort over at the county jail meeting. According to the detectives, Barksdale told them that there "was an order out to the Blackstone Rangers to kill me." Barksdale told the officers to follow him.

Although anything west of Woodlawn Avenue fell into Disciple territory, the Ellis Rebel Stones were one of two Blackstone sets over the border, and their presence drove David Barksdale and the Ds crazy. Ellis Rebels had to be on constant lookout for Ds running raids on them. Barksdale knew this, so he knew full well that when he led GIU detectives Richard Peck, Sidney Clark, and Donald Foulkes to 65th and Ellis he would be attacked—everybody knew his car. He wanted the GIU detectives to witness it and catch the culprits. His plan worked like a charm.

The detectives arrested Melvin "Lefty" Bailey, a nineteen-year-old Rebel Stone leader, in a gangway at 6512 South Ellis as he threw away a .45-caliber automatic. On the porch at 6524 South Ellis, the detectives caught a Main 21, Andrew McChristian, trying to unjam his .25-caliber automatic. They were accused of shooting up Barksdale's car as he drove onto the block.

After the detectives arrested Bailey and McChristian, they took them back to Barksdale's bullet-riddled car to rub it in. The Ds escaped without a scratch. While the detectives had Bailey and McChristian at David's car, Edward Dinkins, a Stone, approached the detectives and told Peck that he couldn't arrest Bailey and McChristian. According to the detectives, Barksdale identified Dinkins as one of the assailants, so the detectives arrested him along with the other two. All were charged with three counts of attempted murder, armed violence, and unlawful use of weapons.

The so-called hit on Barksdale ushered in a wave of rumors about an oncoming war between the Stones and the Disciples. A rash of unexplained shootings also occurred in Woodlawn.

A Chicago FBI informant advised the FBI on May 10 that, as a result of the Rangers' attempted murder of Barksdale, the probability of violence between the two gangs would increase in intensity. Based on this unsubstantiated intelligence, the FBI warned the police to be on alert for a gang war between the Stones and the Disciples to go down in Hyde Park over the weekend. But nothing happened.

Three days later the same warning came, only this time the "rumble" was to go down in the Englewood neighborhood. Again, nothing happened.

But the Stones had other problems.

The jury for Bull's murder solicitation trial was still being selected in May. One of the shooting victims, Dorocher Berrien, refused to cooperate. According to prosecutor Nicholas Motherway, Berrien's life had been threatened. Judge Lois Wexler put Berrien on the witness stand anyway, and he reluctantly testified. Berrien said he hadn't seen Bull or the young Sanders Martin on the day and time of the shooting. Bull testified on his own behalf at the trial and said he didn't have any knowledge of the shootings. He said that at the time of the shooting he was at First Presbyterian setting up a training school. Bull said the money given to Dennis Jackson wasn't for murder but for his work as an usher in the *Opportunity, Please Knock* performances. No evidence incriminated Bull, and a jury had found Paul Martin not guilty on the same evidence. Bull, however, was convicted of solicitation of murder. The jury cleared him on the murder and attempted murder charges. Bull received a fifteen-year sentence but ended up serving seven. He wouldn't see the street again until 1975. Now Little Chief Fort ran the Stones alone.

With Bull locked up and Jeff taking over the day-to-day leadership, the way the Stones operated began to change. Together, Bull and Jeff had complemented each other. Bull was more mature, conservative, and influenced by Black Nationalism. He made the Stones stop processing their hair and instead wear Afros. Bull hated narcotics and dope peddlers, but he loved to smoke marijuana. Jeff was younger, wilder, and flashier. Strangely, he didn't smoke, drink, or curse. Jeff appealed to the younger guys while Bull had the deep loyalty and respect of the older Stones. Bull had virtually handpicked the Main 21. He was their sole leader and they were his trusted advisors. Bull led based on the consensus of the Main 21. Authoritarian Jeff, on the other hand, had little respect for consensus and surrounded himself with a small group of killers (most of whom were not Main 21s) and his trusted advisor, John Fry. Fort required loyalty and could be unconditionally deadly when he found followers disloyal, especially those in leadership positions.

With Bull off the streets, Jeff's leadership style slowly began to take over. Over time the Main 21 became less influential. And in response the Mains became more renegade in their behavior. They tried things with Jeff that they would never have tried with Bull. Because the Mains were older, more street savvy, and accustomed and willing to do violence, Jeff couldn't do much to control them.

## Falling Out

**ALTHOUGH A RUNNING FEUD** had been going on between the Mains and the Imperials for years, it finally came to a head in October 1968, shortly after Bull got locked up. The Imperials had a center on 63rd and Stony Island where they hung out, played pool, threw parties, and kept a stash of weed. The Mains had a habit of coming to the Imperials' spot and taking it over. They refused to pay to get into parties, hogged the pool table, and some of them smoked the Imperials' weed without paying for it. The Imperials complained to their leader, Bo. Bo was a Main, but he wasn't particularly tight with Jeff and his inner circle. After Bo brought the problem to Jeff several times, Jeff decided to call a meeting between the Mains and the Imperials. The meeting went down in the courtyard of a building across the street from the Imperial Lovers' spot. Jeff, the Mains, and all the members of the Imperial Lovers were present. As Jeff addressed the group, an Imperial Lover named Freddy whispered to the other Imperial Lovers, "Man, these niggas is out of pocket" (meaning that what Jeff and the Mains were talking about was bogus). Hearing his comment, Edward Bey, one of the highest-ranking Mains and also known for being an enforcer, said to Freddy, "Nigga, shut up, you disrespecting the Chief while he's talkin'." Jeff went on, and again Freddy whispered, "Man, these niggas are wrong." Bey, hearing this comment, flew into a rage, flipped over the table, and charged at Freddy. But before Bey could get his hands on him, Freddy pulled a pistol out and fired twice at Bey. He missed. The rest of the Imperials pulled their guns out. Jeff, shocked at the Imperials' behavior, looked at Bo, the Imperials' chief, and said, "Bo, man, what's up, what's all of this?" But it was too late; the meeting had been turned out by the Imperials. Jeff and the Mains, recognizing they were outgunned, slowly backed out of the courtyard with the Imperials' guns pointed at them.

The next few days in Woodlawn were tense. Everybody was strapped. The Imperials perched on rooftops expecting the Mains to come at them hard. During the standoff, other branches of the Stones, including the Golden Rangers, the Outlaw Rangers, and the Conservative Rangers, told the Imperials they stood with them. Like the Imperials, they were tired of Jeff and the Mains trying to run over them.

Sensing that there was about to be a civil war within the Blackstone Rangers, Jeff quickly reached out to Bo to try to resolve the beef between the Mains and the Imperials. Jeff told Bo that he planned to have Freddy shot for shooting at Bey. This, Jeff argued, would satisfy the Mains and would prevent a full-fledged war within the organization. Bo said, "Naw, Chief, I can't let that happen." Bo argued that Bey was wrong for attacking Freddy and that Freddy had a right to protect himself. Jeff said, "Man, I can't let a nigga shoot at a Main and get away with it. I got to have the nigga shot, Bo!" Bo replied, "Hell naw, Chief, I can't let you shoot my man." Jeff said, "OK, Bo, we'll just shoot him in the foot." Bo said, "Come on, Chief, I can't let you just shoot the dude in the foot. Look, Chief. Since you just got to shoot somebody, shoot me in the foot and it'll be over." Jeff, totally against the idea of shooting Bo, answered, "Bo, you my man, you know I can't shoot you." So after some back and forth they finally agreed to let Bey and Freddy go into a room together and fight. Bo knew that Bey, a topflight boxer, would destroy Freddy, but it was the best deal he could get. It was better than Freddy getting shot or the whole organization going to war. Bo was right; Bey banged up Freddy pretty bad. But it didn't resolve the problem.

With the falling-out between the Mains and the Imperial Lovers, and some of the other branches in Woodlawn taking the Imperials' side, Jeff realized he didn't have the full support of all the branches. Nor did all of the Mains support him. Bull would be locked up for the next seven years and would not be there to keep things in order. Jeff understood that those who were more loyal to Bull than to him would never fully support him. Jeff began to slowly assert himself as the sole leader of the organization by changing its name from the Blackstone Rangers to the Black P Stone Nation. Jeff had always been known as the Black Prince. Bull called himself King and had given Jeff the title of Prince. The Black P in the new name really represented Black Prince. The Black P Stone Nation became the post-Bull name of the Blackstone Rangers. Bull's role in the Stones began to wane as early as late 1967 when he was forced to spend much of his time fighting his solicitation of murder case. The first sighting of the use of the name Black P Stone Nation occurred in early 1968. Almighty seems to have been added a little later. By 1970, the Almighty Black P Stone Nation had become the common name for the organization.

## The FBI's Propaganda Campaign

**THE FBI WAS** officially desperate. Agents did whatever they could to link murders of black youth to the Stones. With no hard evidence, they began to associate a rash of shootings with so-called gang violence.

In a memo on gang violence dated May 10, 1968, an unidentified male was shot in the back while standing in front of his residence. An "unknown male Negro youth" shot him. The victim was not seriously hurt. The FBI referred to another shooting as gang-related because another "unknown male Negro youth" was shot in the thumb. Two days later, according to FBI files, an unidentified person with an unidentified residence was shot in the stomach while walking on the street near his residence. On the same day, two separate and apparently unrelated shootings involving black youth had occurred. It appears that being young, black, and male was all it took to be labeled a gang member by the police.

Perhaps this desperation stemmed from a file that provided intelligence from an informant indicating there were 5,679 members of the Blackstone Rangers. At the time there were only five thousand Chicago police officers. The internal memo said the Stones consisted of a number of smaller groups that met nightly except on Sundays. A president, who maintained the records, headed each group of about two hundred. The source told the FBI that the purpose of the group was to fight white people. Anybody with common sense knew that was a lie. If the Stones had attacked white people, they would have been handily shut down. With one exception—a botched attempted robbery of a University of Chicago student—the Stones had only attacked black people.

Nevertheless, the FBI used bogus intelligence like that to justify its surveillance of the Stones. To heighten the concern among local and federal law enforcement agencies, the FBI implemented a campaign leading up to the Democratic National Convention that would cast the Blackstone Rangers as an emerging black militant group intent on carrying out violence. The FBI began by reporting to the U.S. attorney general, the Secret Service, and the Region I 113th Military Intelligence Group that the Blackstone Rangers were using the Pleasant Valley Farm, operated by the social justice nonprofit Community Renewal Society of Chicago, for military training. The memo had no evidence to substantiate such a claim, but the FBI forwarded the report nonetheless.

Some Stones did visit the farm from May 14 to May 16. They played basketball, fished, and helped build a facility. Farm supervisors reported that the Rangers acted appropriately, and that their quarters were spick and span when they left.

The *Chicago Tribune* reported on June 12 that Chicago police accused the Stones of receiving weapons from Tom Collins. Collins had been convicted of illegally shipping guns to Chicago without a federal license, and now he was accused of selling twenty-eight thousand dollars' worth of guns to the Stones since the beginning of 1968. Collins had received five hundred weapons from McHenry County, where Pleasant Valley Farm was located. When the *Chicago Daily Defender* asked Fort if he had purchased the guns, he said, "Man, what would I want with $1,000 worth of guns? . . . The detectives are trying to build me up to an Al Capone [so] they can knock me off."

But on June 28, the FBI got what it wanted. The Chicago police arrested three individuals, whose names were redacted in the report, for having unregistered weapons and charged them with unlawful use of weapons among other charges. They recovered three .22-caliber rifles, a 3.48-caliber Winchester, and a twelve-gauge Winchester shotgun. No evidence presented in the report proved these individuals were Stones. Still, the FBI forwarded the report to the military and the Secret Service.

Leading up to the Democratic National Convention, the FBI issued a barrage of intelligence reports on the Stones to local and federal law enforcement. On July 19, a report claimed that the Stones and a group of "black militants" from Chicago were in the rural area of Hopkins Park, Illinois, conducting target practice. Hopkins Park, approximately forty miles south of Chicago, was an extremely poor area that held the largest population of black farmers outside the South. Even within this report, the FBI admitted their claims were unsubstantiated.

Three days later the FBI issued another memorandum titled "Racial Tensions, Harvey, Illinois." The memo reported on rumors of the Stones attempting to consolidate all black youth gangs in Harvey into the Black P Stone Nation. It noted that entertainer Sammy Davis Jr. had helped organize the Blackstones to keep peace in the area so that his business investments in the Harvey–Dixmoor area would be protected. Davis co-owned a number of lounges, liquor stores, and other businesses in the area. The memo noted that several businesses in the suburb complained about black youth soliciting contributions for the Stones. Threats had allegedly been made when their requests were turned down.

The FBI continued rolling out memos. Another one a few days later reported that several carloads of Stones planned to travel to Chicago Heights, an impoverished, predominately black town south of Chicago, to assist a group of "militants" in an attack against police. Nothing happened.

Understanding the dynamics of what the United States was facing at the time explains why the FBI was so afraid of a growing spirit of militancy. The FBI's paranoia partly stemmed from incidents such as the one that had occurred in Ohio in July. Black militants led by Fred Ahmed Evans engaged in a fierce gunfight with police in the Glenville Shootout of Cleveland. The FBI fretted that the Stones might join the "black militants" in their fight against America. The propaganda war that the feds waged against the Stones attempted to cast them as radical black militants who were on the verge of waging a revolution against America. Their goal was to make the Blackstone Rangers appear to be a threat to national security in order to justify their incarceration.

The FBI's culminating act against the Stones occurred on July 23. FBI director Hoover wrote the following letter, "Youth Gang Violence Chicago, Illinois Racial Matters" to the FBI special agent in charge in Chicago:

> The youth gang problem in your area is acute. It is difficult to say whether youth gangs such as the Blackstone Rangers or Disciples are interested in racial militancy or merely exploiting the racial situation for the impetus it gives their programs for extortion in the ghettos. The Bureau feels that this area of your work needs further in-depth probing to determine the youth gangs' involvement in racial matters. Accordingly, if you have not already done so, you should open cases on youth gangs in your area such as those mentioned above as well as their leaders to resolve the extent that these gangs and their leaders may be involved in racial militancy. These investigations should receive your prompt attention and the results should be submitted in form suitable for dissemination.

Just nine days after Hoover's call to "open cases" on groups like the Stones, the Chicago police department's Gang Intelligence Unit conveniently found a do-it-yourself bomb—a half-foot galvanized pipe, cupped at both ends with a hole in the center for placing a fuse—and a bag of black powder in a poolroom frequented by the Stones on East 67th Street. Police arrested one Stone, whose name was redacted in the memo. He was charged under the explosive section of the unlawful use of weapons statute. The Stone denied knowing about the explosive.

With less than two weeks until the Democratic National Convention (DNC), the FBI scrambled to link the Stones to a violent plan of disruption. The FBI's strategy had relied on snitches, informants, and local law enforcement agencies for information. Now the FBI dispatched its own agents to conduct interviews and snatch Stones off the streets. The FBI under Hoover's leadership felt motivated to go after the Blackstone Rangers because they were one of the largest black youth organizations in America. Their potential to be politicized by the more black militant factions of the Black Power movement was great. If Hoover felt threatened by Dr. King and his nonviolent movement, imagine his feelings about one of America's largest street gangs, who had already demonstrated their willingness to do violence? The feds felt the Stones were a threat to America in general and the DNC immediately. Hoover and the FBI used many illegal and unethical methods to cast American citizens, criminal and noncriminal alike, as subversives who were threats to national security.

Based on these interviews, the FBI concluded that on August 1 hundreds of Stones had met at First Presbyterian. The FBI claimed its sources said Fort told the Stones about plans under way for them to disrupt the convention by killing Vice President Hubert Humphrey and Senator Eugene McCarthy. One source added Stone nemesis Senator John McClellan to the hit list. This same source professed that the Stones planned to attack various Chicago police stations with firearms and explosive devices during the convention. Supposedly numerous rifles, revolvers, and hand grenades were displayed at the meeting. The same source said any members caught leaking this information would be killed.

Some of the FBI sources were questionable. In reading the files, there's a sense that some of the sources simply told the FBI what they wanted to hear. Others, for whatever reasons, wanted to see the FBI handle the Stones. And although the FBI had multiple sources that repeated the so-called Stone convention plans, multiple sources also disputed these claims. In fact, according to the police, the Stones met on August 3, not August 1. The FBI informants claimed the Rangers wanted to disrupt the national convention out of anger toward Mayor Daley, who opposed them getting the OEO funding. But when the FBI interviewed leaders and members of the Stones about all of this—and there were many arrested and interrogated—they all denied having any knowledge of plans to disrupt the convention or plots to assassinate government officials. Police even gave Fort two polygraph tests; both were inconclusive.

Mayor Daley opened the Democratic National Convention on August 26. While the convention moved toward nominating Humphrey for president, police enforced an 11:00 P.M. curfew. On that Monday night, demonstrations were widespread but generally peaceful. Two days later, Chicago police famously took action against crowds of demonstrators without provocation. The police beat some marchers unconscious and sent at least 100 to emergency rooms while arresting 175. Daley clumsily tried to explain the police action the next day at a press conference. "The policeman isn't there to create disorder," Daley said. "The policeman is there to preserve disorder."

The months of investigating dubious claims proved a waste for the FBI. For all the effort the agency spent to connect the Stones to a wicked plot at the convention, not one Stone showed up to cause disorder.

But back in Woodlawn the Stones faced a different—major—disorder. The *Chicago Tribune* had reported that the Blackstone Rangers and the Disciples had a mass meeting on July 20 to pledge to bring peace to the Woodlawn community. About two hundred Stones and Disciples had gathered on the Midway of the University of Chicago near 59th and Dorchester. Bull told a reporter that he, as the leader of the Stones, and Jeff Fort, as the number two man, wanted to meet with David Barksdale, the president of the Disciples. Bull said, "We had a talk about keeping peace and agreed not to fight each other anymore." The meeting lasted thirty minutes, concluding with the two groups holding a "unity march" through the Woodlawn community to the Parkman Elementary School at 245 West 51st Street.

However, less than three weeks after Bull was locked up, the Blackstone Rangers and the Disciples had entered into another full-fledged war—sparked by the Stones' killing of Booker Ransom, a nineteen-year-old Disciple. An FBI memorandum reported that Ransom was standing with a group of Disciples on the corner of 65th and University at approximately 11:50 P.M. when a red 1964 Chevrolet turned the corner. According to the report and an interview with one of the victims, LeRoy Hairston, Bull's younger brother, opened fire from the passenger seat. Hairston fired six or seven shots from an automatic pistol, killing Ransom and superficially wounding another Disciple.

In retaliation, a group of Disciple hit men crept into "the hole," the most notorious section of the infamous Robert Taylor Homes public housing development. Located at the development's southern end, between 52nd and 54th and State Street, "the hole" consisted of three high-rise buildings; even the police considered it impenetrable. It was a stronghold for the Cobra Stones, the largest set of the Almighty Black P Stone Nation, and the chief was Henry "Mickey" Cogwell—a high-ranking member after Bull and Fort in the Blackstone Rangers. The Disciple hit team entered the open area at approximately 1:15 A.M., waiting for the first Cobra Stones to exit the building. At about 4:30 A.M., three Cobra Stones came out of the 5247 building and the Disciples opened fire. One Cobra Stone returned fire but was hit in the shoulder while another was shot in the thigh.

When police arrived, they found eighteen-year-old Jerome "Pony Soldier" Cogwell lying near the elevator on the ground floor, shot once in the head. He was Mickey's brother. The six Disciples were nowhere to be found. Pony Soldier was rushed to Billings Hospital at the University of Chicago, where he died a few hours later on the operating table. Fort showed up at the hospital demanding proper treatment for the fallen Stone. Thirty-five to fifty Rangers also came to the hospital to show support but later left quietly.

The murders of Ransom and Pony Soldier set off a wave of violence unprecedented in the history of black Chicago. The Blackstone Rangers and the Disciples waged intensive recruiting drives to bolster their numbers to fight this war. Elementary and high schools were favored recruiting grounds. The *Chicago Daily Defender* reported that gunmen invaded Parker High School on 68th and Stewart on the first day of school and shot and wounded three students. Parker High School had Disciples, Gangsters, and Cobra Stones. Shootings and beatings also occurred at DuSable High School during the first week of school.

By the third week of school, the relatively quiet South Side summer was now a distant memory. Twelve boys had been killed and forty-two others had been wounded in gang shootings since school opened. Some shootings happened right in the hallways. By the end of the first month of school, gang violence had killed forty-five Chicagoans. Hundreds more, mostly young black males, had been wounded, beaten, or maimed.

## The Stones and the Panthers

WITH ALL OF THE VIOLENCE going on in the black community, the Black Panthers thought that by forming some type of alliance with the street gangs they might be able to steer them away from killing each other. The Black Panthers saw potential in the Stones and wanted to foster their community leanings, not their predilection for street violence.

The first sign of the Blackstone Rangers and the Black Panther Party hooking up occurred in October 1968. The *Chicago Tribune* reported on a rally for Black Panther Party Defense Minister Huey P. Newton held at the Senate Theater on West Madison Street on Chicago's West Side. Newton was serving a two- to fifteen-year sentence for manslaughter in the death of an Oakland policeman. At that point, no official chapter of the Black Panthers existed in Chicago, but undercover police agents observed thirty members of the Panthers at the meeting. Dressed in their uniform of black berets and black leather jackets, they marched in military fashion to their seats. About two hundred people attended the rally. Blackstone leadership attended, along with the Egyptian Cobras and the Vice Lords. During the rally, Black Nationalist speakers and street youth organizations called for unification among the groups. One speaker described the street youth organizations as the "warriors that are needed." According to Oakland police, Panther leaders there indicated to several sources that they had been working hard to recruit the Blackstone Rangers. They said the Panthers wanted to try to pick up a gang already in existence that would be willing to adhere to the principles of the Panthers.

The Black Panthers rehearsed their military stance the night before. They wanted to impress the Stones. They also wanted to build a black political coalition that would shake up the Chicago Democratic machine. Deep down, they knew such an alliance would spook the establishment. It turned out the FBI fretted even more. On a January weekday morning in 1969, the leadership of the Black Panther Party headed to a meeting with the Stones in Woodlawn. "I think Jeff was trying to recruit us into the Blackstone Rangers," says Bobby Rush, a former Panther and current Chicago Democratic congressman. "Our goal was to try to get Jeff more political." Several Panthers pulled up to the building. They got out of the car carrying guns and marched down the street in a military formation. When police got word about a squadron of young black men carrying guns down the street, it didn't take long for them to show up. Mortified by the scene, officers arrested some Panthers before they could stash their weapons. So the Panthers and the Stones didn't meet. Undeterred, Rush and Fred Hampton returned that night with several male and female Panthers to First Presbyterian. Fort made sure he presented his own show. Stones met the Panthers at the church door.

As the Panthers walked up the stairs, men with walkie-talkies communicated at each level. Stones wore red berets; Panthers wore black ones. "When we got to the gymnasium, Jeff greeted us. We shook hands and everything," Rush says. "I remember Jeff saying, 'When you came in, you demonstrated your weaponry, and we wanted to show you a few things we've got here.'" They convened at an eight-foot table. Fort sat at the head. Hampton and Rush sat on either side. Fort picked up the walkie-talkie and instructed someone to bring out the machine gun. The room was pitch black except for a little light shining on the gun. Rush says mutual respect existed between the organizations. "We weren't trying to recruit the Stones into an apparatus. We wanted to build a coalition. I think they wanted us to become an affiliated organization," Rush says. The Panthers wanted to influence the Stones into a political organization that performed community activities like establishing free clinics.

Rush believes a coalition would have resulted in the city's first black mayor long before Harold Washington's 1983 victory. Rush muses that this would-be coalition could've been a political threat, "a threat that could've had national and international implications. We would've been quite successful. They [the establishment] had to tear that potential asunder or destroy the basic fabric of it." The meeting lasted about an hour. The last thing said was that the groups would keep talking and have a subsequent meeting. Rush says Fort was receptive.

No follow-up meetings ever happened. Police killed Hampton in December 1969 as he slept in his West Side home. The Stones made sure they paid their respects at the funeral. "I recall right in the middle of [civil rights leader Ralph] Abernathy's speech, I heard a shuffle. I looked toward the rear of the church and Jeff came in," Rush recalls. Two thousand Stones walked in wearing red berets and dark sunglasses. They spoke not a word but marched around the church, then marched right back out.

Years later, it was revealed that the FBI had sent anonymous letters to Fort and Hampton written by a "concerned black brother" who penned to both men that the one was trying to kill the other. Fort never believed the letter to be authentic. According to the Stones, Fort was actually amused by it. He knew all along that the feds had sent the letter. Conventional street wisdom is that street brothers don't send one another letters warning them that someone has a hit out on them. The letter, however, does speak volumes about the degree to which the feds were willing to use unethical, illegal tactics to cause dissension between the two groups.

The Panthers were a political organization that was not opposed to advocating violence in the struggle for black liberation. The Stones were less political than the Panthers but had demonstrated a greater capacity to be involved in violence. One former police officer, a founding member of the Afro-American Patrolman's League, says that the feds saw the Panthers as the head and the Stones as the body of a potentially uncontrollable black militant organization. He says the feds "would have gone to hell and back" to stop the head from hooking up with the body.

The Panthers and the Stones never hooked up, but it wasn't because of the letters. The Panthers came to view the Stones as counterrevolutionaries who weren't willing to discipline themselves to become a force for black liberation. The Stones, on the other hand, viewed the Panthers as political idealists and pseudo-revolutionaries. The leadership of both groups had respect for each other, but neither had any intention of allowing their organization to become incorporated into the other.

# 5

# Things Fall Apart

**H**E WOULD GIVE only his name.

On July 9, 1968, Jeff Fort spent a mere fifteen minutes before a Senate hearing. Senator John McClellan, a powerful Arkansas Democrat, chaired the subcommittee tasked to investigate whether government and private foundation money had financed criminal activity by Chicago street gangs. After asking his name, the senator asked Fort where he lived. Fort's attorney interrupted; his client wouldn't answer any more questions. The lawyer wanted an opportunity to cross-examine all witnesses who had previously testified about Fort. The Blackstone Ranger leader also wanted to confront his accusers.

"This is not a court," McClellan said. "We cannot deprive your client of his freedoms. We are here to investigate. Your client was a center chief in an antipoverty project, drawing $6,000 a year in federal funds, and we are investigating that program."

The $927,000 War on Poverty grant bestowed upon The Woodlawn Organization a year earlier had caught the attention of Congress. The subcommittee targeted Fort, the Stones, and the Disciples. For the senators, Fort symbolized the failing of Lyndon B. Johnson's Great Society: wasted money poured into the inner city by liberals.

"I'm sorry, Mr. Chairman," said Marshall Patner, Fort's attorney. "I cannot permit my client to answer without the right to cross-examine other witnesses." Another senator warned that walking out of the hearing could lead to federal jail time, but Patner didn't back down.

"If you advise your client to place himself in contempt of Congress, that is up to you," McClellan said. He again asked Fort his place of residence. "I'm sorry, we cannot answer that question," said Patner, and he and Fort got up and left the room at the Capitol. McClellan shouted after them, "Under these circumstances, as far as I know, both of you are in contempt!"

Outside the courtroom, Fort told reporters, "This is an unfair thing. This is what they've been doing to black people all the time, you dig?"

THE FBI HAD already turned up the heat on the Stones with its 1968 campaign. The War on Poverty struggled against sharp criticism about whether it made any measurable impact. Now another federal body put the program under the spotlight.

And the Stones were grappling with their own tenuous relationships. The ramifications of the OEO dollars were just beginning to be felt. The $927,000 grant afforded an opening for enemies of the program—and the Stones—to bare their contempt. It became an effective weapon to try to shut down gangs because Stone guilt was predetermined before the gavel pounded on day one of the Senate hearings. Chicago police had long complained in the press about gangs and conducted raids throughout Woodlawn. But the McClellan hearings took the condemnation to another level—the gangs were accused of bribery and blackmail. The policy debate about how to work with disaffected youth garnered a national audience as Chicago police and antipoverty liberals explained their perspectives. Fort had been arrested dozens of times, and fined, but he hadn't served real jail time. A Congressional hearing seemed an unlikely place for Fort's critics to lambaste him and destroy the Stones' credibility.

The Blackstones also vacillated between a flirtation with Black Power and their attraction to the criminal elements of the streets.

Chicago police didn't relent in their mission to destroy the Stones. Community and foundation support waned as the Stones kept getting arrested and garnering negative publicity. Fort had myriad basics to juggle: police run-ins, court appearances, running the organization, and doing community work.

Within the Blackstone Nation of about five thousand, internal conflict had brewed when Bull got locked up for solicitation of murder. Although Bull and Jeff had spent brief stints in county jail during the early history of the Stones, neither had been off the streets for over two years at a time. Bull would be gone for the next seven years. In early 1970, major conflict erupted within the group's leadership. The sources of internal conflict revolved around essentially two factors. First, Jeff had a hard time controlling the Main 21. Second, although Bull had always been fiercely opposed to narcotics, Jeff had given the go-ahead for the Stones to get involved with selling heroin. The Stones' new interaction with heroin caused the Mains to begin to beef with each other over the profits, and, of course, many of them started to use the drug.

## The McClellan Hearing

WHEN REVEREND ARTHUR BRAZIER received the OEO dollars on behalf of The Woodlawn Organization, he hired an auditing firm to monitor the federal money on a monthly basis. Brazier said he knew there needed to be oversight given the hostility toward the OEO program. The auditing firm provided the minister with a quarterly report. Brazier also tried to put in his own safeguards. His staff passed the checks out each week to the Stone and Disciple participants. "We thought that was good control," Brazier says.

The feds became aware of fraud—participants collecting checks without actually doing any job training—from two sources. The Chicago Police Department first reported to the FBI in 1968 that the Stones were involved in a check kickback scheme and check-signing fraud. One of the prerequisites for being placed on the payroll of the job-training program was to "donate" a percentage of the check to the Blackstone leaders. The police passed this information to the FBI who passed it on to the McClellan committee. The second tip to the feds came from FBI Stone informants. Stones who caught cases passed the goings-on directly to the FBI to work off time.

In early 1968, Brazier discovered that the auditing firm did a miserable job. Three staffers from the U.S. General Accountability Office, the investigative arm of Congress, showed up at Brazier's office asking for all of the OEO records. Brazier refused. A couple of months later some staffers from McClellan's subcommittee returned with subpoenas. "I said I didn't have anything," Brazier recalls. The men went away. But Brazier later gave them copies of records and checks. As Brazier copied the checks to give to the government, he turned them over and realized that some signatures looked the same. "I didn't have to be a handwriting expert," Brazier says, the forgery was obvious. The minister shipped several file cabinets' worth of records to Washington. The fraud that the GAO discovered dovetailed with ongoing Senate investigations of other cities.

"Riots, Civil and Criminal Disorders" was the name of the permanent subcommittee performing investigations for the Senate. Years earlier this same subcommittee had investigated the Teamsters, bringing to light the secrets of the organized crime syndicate and the union's role. Now the subcommittee peered in on cities— from Houston to Detroit to Newark—to examine the tumultuous racial uprisings and discord of the 1960s. For the Chicago hearings, held in late June 1968, the Senate focused on the Stones and the Disciples.

Experts eagerly explained their theories about how the $927,000 went toward subsidizing murders carried out by the Stones and the Disciples. The premise was that if gang members committed crimes, this money helped them. Chairman McClellan didn't hide his bias. In his opening statements, the senator remarked that the money had "strengthened and perpetuated" the two "South Side Negro gangs."

He added that the OEO program had little if any success. Senators were perplexed about why Reverend Fry welcomed the Stones into his Presbyterian church. Many who testified said the church aided the Stones in illegal activity such as buying weapons. The hearings gave critics a public opportunity to articulate their scorn. But there were also McClellan critics. When well-known attorney Abner Mikva campaigned for an Illinois congressional seat in 1968, he said McClellan violated ethics standards. "Senator McClellan's credentials in the area of help for the poor hardly recommend him for the job of evaluating the TWO program," Mikva said. A long-serving Southern senator, McClellan had spoken out against McCarthyism, yet often opposed civil rights legislation.

George "Watusi" Rose, the former Stone leader, testified that the gang collected five to eight thousand dollars a week from jobs provided by the grant and used the cash to buy arms and marijuana. The wares were stored in the basement of one of the job-training centers. Rose also said that Fry encouraged the Stones to engage in extortion. Charles LaPaglia of First Presbyterian called Rose a tool of police harassment. He said Rose had been dismissed from the Rangers in September 1967 because Rose attempted to take over the leadership from Bull, who was in jail. "If there was a criminal element in the Rangers, Rose was it," LaPaglia testified. Still, a parade of Stone detractors flew to Washington, D.C., to testify.

"The program has no guidelines and no purpose," testified Winston Moore, superintendent of the Cook County jail in Chicago. "It was a payoff program . . . an attempt to bribe Woodlawn kids not to riot. They were told if they didn't do anything and didn't riot, you'll get all this money." Moore wasn't involved in the program, but he did have prior interaction with the Stones and Disciples in the jail. Congress used him as simply another heckler of the program.

Moore labeled the gangs the black mafia. "If they meant to train these kids to go into organized crime, then it was very effective. These gangs are just set up for selling dope, for prostitution, extortion, and any other thing that will make you a buck." He also slammed the philosophy behind the program. "To give complete control to these gang leaders is an insult to the Negro community. I don't think the OEO would do this in a white area." Moore intimated that black gangs wouldn't be given money if they lived around whites.

Moore testified that Disciples leader David Barksdale had called him up to gleefully inform him about the OEO money. The two knew each other and were friendly from Moore's days working at the Illinois Youth Commission. Moore said Barksdale informed him that he no longer needed his help in getting a job because of the TWO money. "I told him [Barksdale] that even the poverty people couldn't be that stupid. I just couldn't believe it."

"Neither could I," interrupted McClellan. Moore also said that a woman from TWO had approached him and offered ten thousand dollars a year to work with the gangs. Moore declined, and he said Barksdale later called him pleading for help because no members had gotten jobs yet. Moore testified that he visited the job centers and in his estimation found that the program served no purpose. "We're fooling ourselves when we say you can work with gang members. You need programs for the youth of an entire community, and to work through these gangs only dignifies the leaders and gives them more stature." Moore accused students in the OEO program of giving a twenty-five- to forty-five-dollar kickback a week to gang leaders. They used the money to buy guns, he said.

The University of Chicago had participated in writing the initial proposal for the OEO grant. John Walsh, a subcommittee investigator, reported to the Senate committee that the university had received nearly sixty-four thousand dollars to evaluate the program; by the time of the hearing, however, it had done virtually nothing. When the feds went to the university to determine what had happened to the money, Josel Berger of the university's public relations staff told them that he could not find the contract in the files. Irving Spergel, a University of Chicago professor, had been named a project director of the evaluation study and was responsible for writing the program evaluation report. Spergel had nothing to say about all of this. However, a University of Chicago spokesman said that Spergel would return twenty thousand in unused funds.

Cook County state's attorney Robert Karton blamed the Stones for the crime in Woodlawn. Staggering, he called it. "We don't have enough policemen to protect everybody," Karton said. He said the Chicago Police Department needed to triple or quadruple the Gang Intelligence Unit.

The subcommittee also got to hear from Chicago police. The GIU's Ed Buckney talked about the city's gang problem and conveyed police boundaries of support. "The Chicago Police Department, for example, will stand behind any program which is well planned, well conceived, and designed to help the youth of the community," Buckney said. "But we will also state emphatically that if anyone comes up with a program to the detriment of our community we will see that they are prosecuted to the fullest extent of the law. That is what we intend to do."

Third District commander William Griffin gave damning testimony about the OEO money. He said officers would get statements from arrested youth who were trainees in the program. "It is not uncommon to hear remarks alluding to the fact that they are learning nothing at the center and their only purpose in enrolling is to receive the $45 payment. On one occasion, a sixteen-year-old youth remarked to me that the only thing he learned in the centers was to steal, cheat, and be slick."

McClellan took a sympathetic tone with Griffin. The chairman asked questions that allowed the police commander to rail against allegations of police brutality in Woodlawn and accusations of being prejudiced against Negroes. (Griffin himself was a "Negro.") Naturally Griffin used the limelight to complain about Fry's uncooperativeness with the police department and to pan his work with the Stones. McClellan happily backed him up.

"He [Fry] seems to have kind of a hatred for Mayor Daley and the police of Chicago. He goes on to say that you folks are conducting yourself to make insurrection obligatory for honorable men," McClellan said. He continued reading from a letter that Fry had written about the thuggery of the police department. McClellan looked up at Griffin and said, "You don't look much like a thug to me."

Race and class certainly played a role in the conditions in Wood-lawn. But the police issue with teens wasn't a straight black-white issue, which gave the department some credibility, at least at the Senate hearing. A black man headed the gang unit and the black commander boasted of an integrated police department. Griffin testified that 35 percent of the police officers in the Woodlawn area were black and that the squad cars were integrated.

The police department was still miffed that Fort had beat a murder charge that put him in jail from October 1967 until March 1968. "It has become virtually impossible to convict the leaders of the teen gangs. A typical illustration is Jeff Fort, leader of the Blackstone Rangers," Griffin said. The commander said there were witnesses to the shooting. "Because of threats to kill all the children and the mother, four units of the police department combined to give round-the-clock protection to this family including taking the children to school and bringing them back again."

Griffin said that he had seen Fort and Disciple leader Barksdale driving Mustangs, Cadillacs, and Buicks while wearing fine threads. The commander insinuated that federal government money bank-rolled this flashiness.

"Recent indications have been that other street gangs have, or will make attempts to get on the bandwagon. To be acknowledged they must also establish a reputation comparable to that of the Rangers and Disciples. Is it possible that the qualifications for such grants be the ability of gang structures to control the crime rate? My answer to the above inquiries is a definite and emphatic 'no' with any emphasis that might be implied," Griffin concluded in his testimony.

The Senate then brought in a Chicago mother. Annabelle Martin testified that she saw guns, drugs, and liquor at First Presbyterian. Eight of her nine sons were in the gang; her youngest son wasn't old enough. She said she went to Fry seeking help in getting her four-teen- and fifteen-year-old sons an attorney after police arrested them for a murder—the Bull Hairston case. Martin testified that her sons were involved at Bull's behest but that they hadn't done the actual shootings. Fry connected her with an attorney, she said, who advised her sons to leave town. The attorney instructed that Fry would give her train money for the family to go stay with her relatives in Mississippi. But Martin didn't leave. According to Martin, the attorney then offered her money to have her sons change their testimony to pin the murder on another gang leader. She refused. Fry denied this. Martin testified that her sons had to pay twenty-five cents a week in gang membership dues. She said food for the family was sacrificed and that her sons stole from her to come up with the money.

When it was time for Fry to testify, he saw an opportunity to clear his name and First Presbyterian's reputation. The reverend came with a prepared statement: "First, I categorically deny the allegation that I encouraged Blackstone Rangers to practice extortion of any person, including South Side merchants." He defended the legal defense fund the church ran for the Stones. "The Chicago police apparently disagree with our intention to assure fair and full trials for Blackstone Rangers, and have conducted a vigorous multifaceted campaign designed to make us abandon our program. . . . The police have sought to create the impression that many individual shootings on the South Side were somehow related to the First Presbyterian church."

Fry said the ministry consisted of more than legal support. The church supported the Stones' refusal to go along with a racist system. "We have found that the Blackstone Rangers are an organization of great influence and promise. They are not a gang. They are a community organization. They organized originally in order to survive in a very hostile and violent environment. They quickly came to substantial size and prominence. They are determined to use their numerical strength, and to hold themselves together for the single purpose of maintaining hope for full justice, real equality, and freedom in fact, and in the hearts of all black brothers."

As for the allegations of drugs, guns, and sex, Fry told the subcommittee: "I am here to tell you that the outrageous allegations made before this committee have not deterred us for ten seconds. We shall maintain our friendship with and support of the Blackstone Rangers. I do not know what inspired the malicious set of false allegations which have been presented to this committee. But I hereby call them lies."

Fry declared that male youth organizations were capable of participating in civic life and "are not in fact so-called criminals who deserve to be killed or put in jail as some policemen have, I am told, callously testified before you." Fry explained that one hundred boys had jobs from the OEO program.

McClellan didn't buy Fry's version of the Stones.

McClellan: "When you had them in session, did you ever have them bow their heads and pray for them?"
Fry: "I have not, sir."
McClellan: "You did not. What did you do in these meetings? You didn't have any prayer meetings, you didn't pray for them, you didn't have religious services, you didn't counsel them about their way of life, and so forth. What did you do?"
Fry: "I discussed their legal situation."

McClellan inquired how many Stone converts were now members of the church. Fry responded, "We maintain an open-door policy to all, which includes the Rangers. There have, on numerous occasions, been Rangers who attend not only our worship services but various church functions, family night dinners, discussions, and things of this kind."

Unsatisfied, McClellan pressed again on the number of converts. Fry said, "None have joined the church and I could not say how many have come to view life in a way consonant, fully consonant, with the Christian faith."

McClellan found another way to discredit the church's work with the Stones. The scuttlebutt had always been that Fort couldn't read. He turned his questioning toward Fort's IQ. McClellan said, "My information is that it averages from forty-eight, I believe, to fifty-eight. You are an educated man. What does that signify to you with respect to his intellect?"

Fry responded that the tests exhibited cultural bias. McClellan urged Fry to say Fort didn't know how to write his name. Fry rejected the bait.

A few weeks later, at McClellan's urging, the full Senate unanimously voted to cite Jeff Fort for contempt because he had refused to answer any questions during the hearing. On July 31, antipoverty officials shut off OEO money to Woodlawn. According to Nicholas Lemann's *The Promised Land,* the new head of OEO, Bertrand Harding, who had replaced Sargent Shriver, sent a memo to President Johnson:

> As I indicated to you on the phone, I have been delaying final action on this application in order to be sure that whatever I did was consistent with Mayor Daley's views. He has, however, refused to render an opinion. My best judgment at this time is that, in spite of the changes proposed in the project, we will not re-fund. Most of the evidence I have now indicates that the project was one of those experiences that just didn't work out.

Daley, who had never wanted Washington on his turf, bore no political liability from the botched program.

A day after the money stopped, twenty-one-year-old Jeff Fort was indicted for contempt for not answering the questions at the McClellan hearing. Fort was released on a one-thousand-dollar bond and also freed on a five-thousand-dollar bond for a charge of aggravated battery involving a postal employee.


## Social Programs and the Stones

THE STONES MAINTAINED but had highs and lows.

Carol Adams, a graduate sociology student at the University of Chicago in 1968, was offered two jobs: one at Northeastern Illinois University's Center for Inner City Studies, the other at Kenwood

Oakland Community Organization (KOCO), a nonprofit that served the neighborhoods in its name. Adams took the former job and her activist friend Willeva Lindsey went to KOCO and the Community Renewal Society (CRS). They worked with and researched the Stones, eventually becoming honorary Stones.

"They thought we were righteously committed," says Adams, who is now head of the DuSable Museum of African American History in Chicago. There was no formal ceremony, but the Stones appreciated them as sisters who cared about the community. Adams took Sengali and a group of Stones to Oakland, home of the Black Panther Party. "The trip was surreal," Lindsey says. "Once outside of Chicago, they were extremely uncomfortable. They said, 'This ain't shit.' They were big in this [Chicago] community. Nobody recognized them there [Oakland]. Their red hats captured no attention."

The Stones benefited from Toward Responsible Freedom, a $3.5 million program sponsored by the social justice CRS and doled out through KOCO. The donations came from a steel company, a telephone company foundation, and the Sears-Roebuck Foundation. The grant was also supposed to help the Stones open up and operate a restaurant called Black People's Stone Place and foster black economic empowerment. Fort and Charles Edward Bey, another gang leader, were hired on October 1 to work with the program. Fort received nine thousand dollars a year to organize youth, and Bey accepted eight thousand a year.

Fort's boss was Mennonite reverend Curtis Burrell, president of KOCO. Burrell had served time in federal, state, and county penitentiaries on drug charges. After his release he enrolled in Goshen College Biblical Seminary in Indiana and became pastor of the Woodlawn Mennonite church. "I served a lot of time in a lot of places," Burrell told the *Chicago Tribune*. "But I became a Christian in prison and now I am a sinner who is saved." Mayor Daley had also appointed him to a Model Cities planning council.

The Chicago Police Department despised the outpouring of philanthropic dollars. In November, the police brass decided to increase the Gang Intelligence Unit from thirty-eight officers to about two hundred. Edward Buckney, head of the unit, lashed out at the private foundation money. "I am opposed to gang leaders being paid high salaries for doing nothing and for being hired for no other reason than that they are gang leaders," he said. "I fail to see where an illiterate can contribute to his community."

That was always the paradox of Jeff Fort.

TODAY DR. CONRAD WORRILL is the coordinator of the Inner City Studies Program at Northeastern Illinois University and the director of its Jacob H. Carruthers Center for Inner City Studies. In 1968, he served as youth director of the Sears YMCA on the city's West Side. A coalition asked if they could have meetings to discuss the dearth of black men in the construction industry. Among those in attendance were Jesse Jackson, Vice Lord Bobby Gore, and KOCO's Burrell. They mulled over the exclusion of black men in the city's big construction trade school. At one meeting, Fort and Stone Leonard Sengali showed up. Fort wore sunglasses, and when he entered the room everyone quieted.

"Jeff was low-key charisma," Worrill says. "Jeff Fort was not a speaker. He could speak but he had another kind of aura. He walked with power. He had a swagger."

At that meeting the men planned a protest to shut down a construction site for a new expressway set to run through the South Side. They showed up at the construction site with a bunch of Stones in tow. Police arrested many of them, but that didn't deter the Stones. "To me, it was a proud day in the black community the day those brothers walked down the Dan Ryan [Expressway]. They felt like warriors and not enemies of the community," Carol Adams says. Out of that demonstration grew the LSD initiative, a collective of the Lords, the Stones, and the Disciples. The leadership of the three major street gangs wanted to address the disparities in the hiring of blacks in the construction trades. Although the institutionalized racism in the construction trades proved to be too deeply rooted for LSD to overcome, it did spawn a number of organizations that worked to increase the hiring of blacks in the construction trades. One of the organizations, the Coalition for United Community Action, still stands today. CUCA still works to increase the hiring and contract letting of blacks in the construction industry.

## 1969

A NEW YEAR, 1969, looked like it might be promising, but that feeling of optimism didn't last. An Illinois politician invited Fort to attend the 1969 inauguration of President Richard Nixon. Fort didn't go, but he sent Mickey Cogwell in his place. Meanwhile, Fort and his boys were charged with mob action for a disturbance at a high school. Fort said they were there to quiet gang violence in the neighborhood; the police saw it otherwise. The Stones challenged the establishment by suing Mayor Daley; James Conlisk, superintendent of police; GIU captain Ed Buckney; and Edward Hanrahan, state's attorney of Cook County. Fort and Bey complained that the prosecutions were only for the sake of harassment and intimidation. The plaintiffs sought an injunction against further harassment.

Their complaint said the Rangers were engaging in a peaceful protest march down the parkway on Garfield Boulevard under the supervision and with the permission of the local police. The complaint alleged that the youth were engaged in peaceful discussions with the principal of Forrestville High School at his invitation. GIU officers arrived and arrested the youth. The complaint described the only incident as a minor scuffle in which a student's glasses were accidentally knocked off and one lens broken. The suit was thrown out.

FORT REMAINED ENTANGLED in legal battles. In June 1969, a court sentenced him to six months in a state prison farm after a jury found him guilty of battery. And the Gang Intelligence Unit continued to knock Stone heads after officer James Alfano was killed in Woodlawn in 1970. The previous year, police officer Richard Peck had been shot in the chest on 63rd and Woodlawn. Police identified the shooter as a Stone. The Main 21 had taken over the Southmoor Hotel in Wood-lawn to have their meetings and were accused of strong-arming the tenants.

The contradictory sides of Jeff Fort blazed on. In a *Defender* letter to the editor, someone saw the best in Fort. "Jeff Fort has the power to stop the street gangs. God has sent me a message that Jeff Fort is going to be converted, he might even become a preacher. Some day he will preach to all of the gang members and convert them so they will stop killing our brothers. The Lord is upon Jeff Fort."

Maybe the nationalistic leanings of the Stones appealed to the reader. The P Stone Nation worked with groups to fight extortion-ists targeting black businesses, marched with civil rights leader Julian Bond in a racially torn downstate Illinois town, and fought for pro-gramming in a public housing development. They conducted voter registration drives with the idea of using Mayor Richard J. Daley as a political model. Democrat Daley had grown up in an ethnic Irish part of Chicago, and he had been a member of a youth club—the Hamburg Club. Many members had gone on to become part of the Democratic machine. The Stone Nation saw a similar path. "Natu-rally, we'd like to see Jeff Fort as a South Side alderman, or even as mayor for that matter," one Stone said.

But that activism didn't counteract a growing problem in Wood-lawn. The violence, threats, and intimidation the Stones imposed on the black community began to take their toll, and the community reached a boiling point. Angry sentiment started in 1968 with the killing of fourteen-year-old Demetria Wormley, who had been caught in crossfire between the Stones and the Disciples. The same year, five-year-old Melvin Whitehead was shot in the head while watching TV in his house. Stones had shot into his house trying to get his four-teen-year-old Disciple brother. Parents were afraid to send their kids to schools, which had turned into gang recruitment centers. Between the Stone and Disciple feuding and the recruitment campaigns, kids were being beaten and shot going to and from school. Even class-rooms and hallways inside the schools were dangerous.

Woodlawn residents were afraid that if they complained, espe-cially to the police, the Stones would retaliate. Others wanted to give the Stones the benefit of the doubt for their youthful reckless-ness. Their antisocial behavior no doubt resulted from marginaliza-tion and institutional racism. The Stones did do some community outreach, and they had kept Woodlawn cool during the riots after King's assassination. They had participated in marches and protests for social justice.

But many of the pro-black Blackstone sympathizers, most of whom were professional organizers who lived in safe communities but worked with the Stones, could afford to sympathize because they didn't live and raise their children amid the violence. The tenor of the era was Black Power and unity. It wasn't cool for black people to criticize other blacks even when they were damaging the community.

In this atmosphere of solidarity, various groups and individuals tried to help the Stones help themselves for the betterment of the community. Churches in the area tried to help. Warner Saunders and Useni Perkins of the Boys Club tried to help them. Reverend Jesse Jackson attempted to get them involved with SCLC's Poor People's Campaign. Fred Hampton and Bobby Rush of the Black Panther Party tried to politicize them. Reverend Arthur Brazier and Leon Finney tried to offer them job training. Oscar Brown Jr., the famous cultural entertainer, tried to provide them with a platform to display their talent within the entertainment industry. Sammy Davis Jr. gave them money and went into business with them. The list goes on. With each collaboration, each partnership, the Stones accused the groups and individuals of trying to get over. The Stones fell out with each and every group, leaving with threats and intimidation.

The Stones were involved in extorting businesses and shaking down community organizations that had grants to work with youth, because they saw that money as theirs. They perceived themselves as the gatekeepers of all things related to poor black youth, especially

when related to money. They threatened and tried to intimidate anyone who criticized or disagreed with them. But the violence, once
confined to the youth who had adopted the gangbanging lifestyle in
places like Woodlawn and the projects, now affected the larger black
community of innocent victims.

The *Chicago Daily Defender* reported that a South Shore group of
two hundred parents and youths gathered at Parkside Elementary
School to protest the death of Nate Jones, a twenty-year-old victim
of gang violence. A witness to the shooting identified "Kingfish," a
known Stone, as the killer. State senator Richard Newhouse led the
speakers and called for "an end to these vultures and vipers," referring to the Blackstone Rangers, "who have done a worse job on us
than the Ku Klux Klan could have done—raping our women, stealing from us, killing our children." Newhouse called for "one hundred thousand people, who are strong enough to get rid of this thing,
because this thing has got to stop."

The protest against the Stones reached its height with Burrell's
campaign against the gang. Burrell said that in 1968 CRS arranged
a meeting with KOCO and Fort on a Sunday afternoon at the Chicago Theological Seminary on the campus of the University of Chicago. Fort and some of his people came to the meeting, and they
all agreed to cooperate under the direction of KOCO. Fort declared
that his desire was to work with the youth. KOCO hired him as a
youth director.

Burrell said that a KOCO board member warned that working
with Fort and the Blackstones would be a big mistake. That board
member didn't want to take a chance, so he returned to his hometown of Detroit. Burrell said with the new funding and the addition
of the Blackstone participation, KOCO "swole up as a person on
steroids."

Burrell faced criticism for the alliance. Daddy-O Daylie, a popular
black radio personality, had a program on the black station WVON.
While interviewing Burrell on his show he called him the "gangster
preacher." Burrell's assessment of the Stones is that they were pawns

in a grand scheme to run black people off the land. According to Burrell, white people empowered the Stones with antipoverty money so that they would buy guns that they would use to terrorize black people into fleeing their communities. He said the Stones didn't know any better. Burrell said the Stones came out of a social milieu of brokenness as black people; no men in the family, just women, welfare. He said he wanted to prevent black people from getting pushed off the land, the lakefront. He said Kenwood-Oakland was the most prime real estate in Chicago.

As KOCO continued its efforts to work together with the community, the number of office and organizing staff who were part of the Stone Nation increased. Leonard Sengali, the spokesman for Fort and the Black P Stone Nation, became the chief organizer. Several girlfriends became secretaries and office assistants. Burrell said the quality of teamwork disintegrated. His frustration began to grow. But some consequential work was done. KOCO arranged for a plastic industry company based in suburban Downers Grove to train blacks in the neighborhood.

Then, one afternoon when Burrell entered the KOCO office, an eerie silence hung in the air, and new faces stared at him. A gunshot rang out from the basement. No one was shot; it was just an act of intimidation. Soon Chester Evans, a Stone Main 21, appeared. Evans told Burrell that "Chief" was on the way and wanted to talk to him and Blood and several other staff members. Blood was Thomas "Blood" Mickles, a KOCO board member. Soon Fort came in and allegedly said, "Hi, Rev, I want the three of you to ride with us to the forest preserve out in Palos Heights and have a talk." Burrell said they had commandeered the vehicle used to transport the work crew to Downers Grove. He refused to go, and that ended it. The Stones didn't press the issue. They didn't need to. They were seasoned intimidators who knew the limits of most black people. After that incident, Burrell said, some of his professional staff ran away. Tony Stateger, their economic developer, went to Washington to work with the Nixon Poverty Program.

Burrell said he felt threatened and intimidated in his small office space. He had heard that the Blackstones were conducting extracurricular activities of extortion and intimidation outside the KOCO parameters. He said there was an effort to extort money from people like Daddy-O Daylie. Burrell complained to Jeff about the growing discord and the lack of cooperation between him and the staff, a large part being Jeff's people. He said he and Jeff had a private meeting at his house, along with some of the Main 21s. At the meeting, Burrell recalled, Jeff told those in the room, "Listen, me and the Rev here, we like this. Everybody know Zorro. I'm Zorro, but the Rev here is Don Diego, Zorro in disguise." Although Jeff's words were meant to impress upon the Mains that he wanted things to work out between them and KOCO, the instruction went unheeded. Nothing changed.

In his frustration, Burrell paid a ministerial visit to Reverend Jesse Jackson, who was convalescing at St. Joseph Hospital in the suburbs. He said Jackson told him of the threats that he and his family were getting from the Stones. The Stones were "leaning on him for eighty thousand dollars." Meanwhile, one of the Stone leaders said that Jackson owed the Stones eighty thousand as payment for their involvement in the 1969 Black Expo. The Black Expo was an annual convention organized by Jackson and Operation Breadbasket. It was the largest gathering of black businesses, entrepreneurs, and entertainers of its time. Tens of thousands of black people from all over America converged on Chicago's International Amphitheater to attend this five-day trade fair. The Stones were hired to provide security for the event, including personal security for entertainers like the Jackson Five.

Burrell returned to the KOCO office with a plan and script in mind. He wrote on the office blackboard: "Attention all KOCO staff, as of Friday noon, you may pick up your checks because this office will be temporarily closed for the purpose of inventory and re-evaluation. Signed, Chairman, Rev. Curtis E. Reverend Burrell, Jr." Next he went to the *Chicago Daily Defender* to let it be known that he had fired the staff and all of the Stones. He also appeared at

Operation Breadbasket at the Capital Theater on 79th and Halsted. Burrell said that he intentionally didn't consult with the KOCO board of directors before firing the Stones and shutting down the office because he knew the Stones would threaten and intimidate him.

A Stone staffer confronted Burrell, saying, "All right, Reverend Burrell, I want you to sign my vacation check and I don't care about this so-and-so job." Burrell refused and said, "Brother, you stay on vacation, you only come twice a month, on the first and the fifteenth to pick up your check." The Stone cussed him out and blocked the doorway to Burrell's office. Burrell had prepared for this moment. He opened his Samsonite briefcase where he had a loaded nine-millimeter Browning automatic. Burrell pulled it out, looked the Stone in the eye, and told him, "Move, let me pass." When he refused, Burrell pointed the gun down at the floor and fired three shots.

Burrell hurried to the hospital to tell Jackson what had happened. He knew Jackson would be hiding out from his recent confrontation with the Stones. Jackson chuckled, picked up the phone, and called W. L. Lillard of the Lillard Security Agency on the West Side. Burrell said Jackson told Lillard, "Reverend Burrell fired the Stones and just had to shoot his way out of his office. He needs your services."

A couple of KOCO board directors agreed to pay for the security. Lillard escorted Burrell to 26th and California, the office of Cook County state's attorney Edward Hanrahan. Hanrahan had recently been involved in the villainous killing of Black Panthers Fred Hampton and Mark Clark on the West Side. Lillard let Hanrahan know that conflict had ignited between Burrell and the Stones. Burrell said he immediately went to the Chicago news media, including TV, radio, local newspapers, and *Jet* magazine. Jackson allowed him to speak at Operation Breadbasket to get his side of the story out. The Stones, according to Burrell, didn't use the media to communicate. They allegedly communicated by throwing a firebomb at the KOCO office door and firing thirteen bullets through the front window of his home. He said he got his family out of town to a place of safety.

He responded by announcing an invitation to the community to walk with him in what he called the Walk Against Fear.

According to the *Chicago Tribune*, Burrell led the walk on Sunday, June 23. His group of twelve to twenty people began their walk from KOCO's headquarters on 47th and Lake Park and walked ten blocks north. In his group were reporters Charles Armstrong and Lu Palmer, his bodyguards, and a few brave souls. Across the street, on the east side of Lake Park, stood Jeff Fort and his larger group. A group of 150, mostly youth, followed Burrell's group shouting, "Traitor," "Nigger," and "Reverend Burrell, you're crazy." Some in the group of Stones carried placards that read NARCOTICS DESTROYS THE MIND: REVEREND BURRELL DESTROYS YOUTH, WHAT CLOUD IS REVEREND BURRELL ON? and REVEREND BURRELL WANTS MONEY TO PAY OFF NARCOTICS PUSHERS. These references to drugs were intended to assassinate the character of Burrell, a self-confessed recovering heroin addict.

Burrell said the Stones invited him to First Presbyterian. Accompanying him were his bodyguards and about two hundred grassroots community black men. He said the Stones didn't display any armed hostility or verbal threats. They wanted to listen to him. Burrell asked for the Stones to cease terrorizing the community. He said his comments caused Lamar "Bop" Bell, a Main 21, to ask him how they could trust him. He responded that trust wasn't the issue, but them doing the right thing. Burrell didn't think, in that moment, they welcomed his appeal.

Burrell hired Reverend John Barber, a former Operation Breadbasket staffer, to be education director of KOCO. On the day he invited Barber to the Mennonite Church, the church he pastored, to discuss Barber's new salary, shots were fired through the windows. Twenty youth surrounded the church. A Burrell bodyguard cracked the heavy oak church door and dashed out in a counterattack, wounding an assailant. The following day, July 29, Barber held a press conference ordering a war against "criminal elements in the Black P Stone Nation." Barber warned the gang leaders to abandon their attempts to control the black community. This may have been the strongest statement to date made against the Stones by a leader of a black group. "We are telling them this morning that the Stones are not going to run it, black men are going to run it." ("Stones Run It" was a popular slogan the Stones used to project their control and dominion over their territories. The Stones had spray-painted it all over walls throughout their territories.)

The day after the press conference, the church was destroyed by arson.

Burrell ended up testifying at the McClellan hearing. He reported to the subcommittee everything that the Stones had done to him and KOCO, including the shots fired into his house and church, the firebomb thrown at KOCO, the threats and intimidation that had occurred at KOCO, and the burning down of his church. Burrell flew to Colorado to meet with Stone patron Charles Kettering, whose foundation had been funding the Blackstone Rangers. He said they appealed to Kettering to shift some of those funds to rebuild the church since his money had helped the forces responsible for burning it down. He said Kettering refused.

## Decline

FOR THE FIRST TIME in their history, the Stones were being challenged by neither Disciples nor law enforcement. On August 5, 1970, Fort held a press conference at First Presbyterian Church to denounce Reverends Burrell and Barber for testifying before the U.S. Senate hearing. Fort also called the Black Men Moving group a "vigilante group out to kill black leaders such as me."

During the press conference Fort wore a large floppy hat and sunglasses. Eight young Stones surrounded him wearing red military combat hats bearing the insignia of a twenty-one-stone pyramid. Two bodyguards flanked him. On the stage, the curtains had a large pyramid that had ALMIGHTY on top and BLACK P STONE on the bottom.

Fort accused the two ministers of going to Washington to seek the aid of a "white racist who has no love or liking for black people and knows nothing about the situation in the black community." Fort also called Senator McClellan "a racist worse than Chicago's Mayor Daley and State's Attorney Edward Hanrahan." Fort said he still had respect for Burrell and Barber, but he just couldn't understand why they went to a racist. Fort added that civil rights leader Reverend Ralph Abernathy assured him that he would come to Chicago soon to mediate the dispute.

Fort said that he called the news conference to make sure people were aware of the "seriousness of the situation," which he described as youth arming themselves for possible attacks by an "army of black men," referring to the Black Men Moving group, headed by Barber. Fort called Barber a "crazy fool and an animal" and accused him of trying to kill Leonard Sengali, the Stones' spokesman. Fort warned, "I said before that there would be no killing without killing." If the Black Men Moving group thought that they were going to come at the Almighty Blackstone P Stone Nation, they had better be ready for the Stones to come back at them. He called Barber's group Philistines to suggest the army was moving in. Fort coolly added, "I'll wait until Abernathy gets here to decide which way I'll go." Then he said with full confidence, "Because my army's already organized and theirs is just getting together."

The same day, Abernathy, the president of the SCLC, announced that he would send a team to look into the conflicts between Barber and Burrell and the Blackstone Rangers. The SCLC held a meeting but no solution materialized. KOCO fired Burrell for violating the organization's constitution by acting undemocratically when he fired the Stones. Fort was rehired as a youth coordinator under the new leadership.

In September 1970, Fort failed to appear in court on charges of attempted murder, aggravated kidnapping, and aiding the escape of someone accused of murdering a police officer. Chicago police caught Fort in New York in October; they said he had tried to flee to Algeria. Fort got sent to Cook County jail. After three mistrials, caused by a prejudiced jury, underdeveloped indictments, and a hung jury, respectively, the charges were dropped. It was clear that the police had trumped up charges against Fort to try to get him on something. The jurors and the judge didn't go for it. During the same period, a federal grand jury began hearing testimony into the charges that the Stones had defrauded the government of $927,000.

In December, Fort quit his job as KOCO youth coordinator. Burrell surmised that Fort resigned because of unfavorable publicity. Fort and about fifty Rangers were arrested for mob action and disorderly conduct because of a march he led on the Midway Plaisance near the University of Chicago. The police gang unit said about nine hundred gang members were on the Midway. They were rallying to rename a street after Jerome "Pony Soldier" Cogwell, a Ranger leader killed by a rival gang member. In contrast to the police's observation, other onlookers described the rally as peaceful. That same month a jury found Fort guilty of contempt for not answering the questions before Congress.

While Jeff fought a number of cases, including the charges trumped up against him by the Chicago police, his leadership was weakened by his inability to tend to the day-to-day affairs of the Stones. The Main 21, the core of the Blackstone leadership, was always as strong if not stronger than Bull and Jeff. Many of the Main 21 were mature men who had run their own groups, and they were accustomed to violence. Some already controlled whole communities, while others were firmly established as the top players in their respected areas of vice. They were guys like Mickey Cogwell, the leader of the Cobra Stones, who controlled a large section of the Robert Taylor public housing high-rise development. Some say the Cobra Stones were over one thousand strong, the largest set in the Black P Stone Nation. Mains like Lee Stone and Troope knew the drug game inside and out. Later there were Mains like Black Reuben, leader of the Four Corner Rangers, and Thunder, Steven El. Black Reuben once slapped Larry Hoover, the leader of the Gangster Disciples, and lived to tell about it. There were guys within the body of the Main 21 who were stone-cold killers. Controlling these men was a monumental if not impossible task.

Even when Bull ran the streets with Jeff, they did not have complete control over the Mains. The Mains often did their own thing within their respective gangs. Nevertheless, if a Main needed to be regulated, Bull did it. He had convinced most of them to incorporate their smaller sets into what would make up the Almighty Black P Stone Nation. A source close to the Stones said Jeff had a very tough time controlling the Mains because he "was suspicious . . . he was insecure . . . he was intimidated by his size." The older, stronger, more mature Main 21s intimidated twenty-year-old Jeff.

Some of the Main 21 who were more loyal to Bull began to question Jeff's leadership. Although everyone knew that Bull and Jeff shared in the leadership of the organization, the Mains gave a little more deference to Bull. For instance, Lawrence Cain, one of the Main 21 enforcers, said that he and Jeff once had an altercation over Cain's bond money. According to Cain, there was an understanding among Bull, Jeff, and the Mains that all Mains were to be bonded out of jail immediately when they caught cases. Cain got locked up and needed to be bailed out, but Jeff refused to get him out. So when Cain finally got out in September 1969, he said, "I start moving against everything he [Jeff] was doing. All the stores Jeff had his arms around, I was going in moving on 'em." Cain said he also didn't respect the Stone–KOCO alliance. Jeff couldn't handle Cain because Cain was the organization's chief muscle; he had the nickname Killer Cain. Moreover, he helped lead the Gangster Stones, so Jeff knew that if he moved against Cain he might find himself in a battle with other Gangster Stones who might be more loyal to Cain than to him.

Cain went as far as to take some guns from a couple of the Stones' stashes. When Jeff found out, he gave Moose, a Main 21, a gun and ordered him to go shoot Cain. Instead, Moose, a Gangster Stone, went to Cain and gave him the gun and told him what Jeff had ordered him to do. Shortly afterward, Jeff came over to Kimbark Avenue where Cain was hanging out with a group of Stones. Jeff was with his brother and Lee Stone, another Main. When they got out of the car, Cain said to Skeet (Daniel Felton), "Shoot that stud." Cain said Skeet fired three shots at Jeff while Jeff just stood there. Jeff then jumped in his Mustang and took off. For several weeks both Jeff and Cain laid low.

The *Chicago Tribune* reported that Jeff feared for his life. The article said Jeff had been seen alone, which was unheard of because he was usually "accompanied by a dozen or more gang lieutenants" as he moved around Woodlawn. After the beef with Cain, observers spotted Jeff all alone in the Woodlawn Boys Club. Eventually, Jeff and Cain squashed the beef when Jeff called a meeting at First Presbyterian to deal with the situation. About four hundred Stones showed up; some came to support Jeff, and others were there for Cain. Jeff approached Cain and asked him what the problem was. Cain said, "Ain't no problem, I just didn't appreciate you sending Moose to hit me." He told Jeff, "If you had a problem with me you should have come directly to me." Jeff didn't pursue the matter any further, but much tension remained between the two.

Jeff's decision to sanction the Stones' involvement in selling heroin also contributed to their unraveling. Jeff was found guilty of battery for beating a postal worker, and while he was locked up in the county jail he learned that William Throope, a Main 21, was out on the streets making a killing in the heroin game. The Mains knew they weren't supposed to sell heroin, but there wasn't anybody on the street to stop them. Jeff figured that since all this heroin had been dumped into the community and others were getting rich by peddling it, he might as well get something out of it. So he sent word to Throope that he would sanction him selling heroin as long as he cut Jeff and the Stones in. Jeff made it clear that one of the first things he wanted was eighty thousand dollars to pay his bond.

Throope got his supply from a West Side guy named Lonnie Branch. Branch was hooked up with the Italian outfit. He supplied Throope and the Stones with a five-gallon container of raw dope every week. Throope cut, mixed, packaged, and distributed it to the other Mains to sell on the streets. Throope was supposed to be collecting Jeff's bond money from the proceeds. Although he made small weekly payments to Jeff's main girlfriend, he didn't cough up the eighty grand needed. Some of the Mains who were close to Throope saw him with large sums of money that exceeded the bond amount. When Jeff questioned what was going on, the Mains could only tell him that Throope said he had it. The Mains warned Throope about messing up the money, but he assured them that he had everything under control. Finally Jeff summoned Throope and some of the Mains to visit him at the county jail to discuss the money. Everybody showed up but Throope.

On August 1, 1971, the *Chicago Tribune* reported that the police were looking for Stone enforcer Cain for the shooting of William Throope. Throope's female companion had been killed in a shooting, and Throope was critically wounded. According to the Chicago police, Throope identified Cain. However, two months later, Throope refused to identify Cain in court, and Cain walked.

After Throope was shot, Charles Edward Bey assumed his position as the third-ranking leader of the Stones. But by early 1971 the Stone leadership had declined, and the police felt pretty good that the year would see the downfall of the Stones. Fort was now locked up for jumping bond, so he was off the street. The government and foundation money had stopped. Even the GIU unit started to downsize as police saw the gang's power wane. Many of the Mains were incapacitated by their heroin addictions. Only Cain could halfway control the Mains. But Cain got into it with Bey and ended up shooting him eight times. Miraculously, Bey survived.

In April 1971, Fort and twenty-two other Stones were indicted for defrauding the U.S. government. Here was the logic: TWO required the trainees to sign time and attendance sheets at the centers on arrival and departure at both sessions on each day. As center chief, Fort was responsible for collecting these sheets at the end of each week and returning them to TWO staffers. Stipend checks payable to the trainees were based on the time and attendance sheet data. The checks were forwarded to the centers for the chief and his staff to distribute to the trainees each Friday afternoon. Attached to each check was a receipt to be signed by the trainee/payee, collected by the staff, and returned to TWO.

During the trial, the government presented testimony from train-ees who identified hundreds of forged signatures. One of the youth instructors identified more than twelve hundred instances when he signed trainees' names on time and attendance sheets on the orders of Fort and others. He said he would take entire sheets home and arbitrarily fill in the remaining blanks. Someone else testified that Fort and others instructed him to maintain a separate dock list in which he recorded accurate attendance figures for the purpose of determining the weekly kickback amount per trainee. Fort and the others argued in their defense that there wasn't enough evidence against them, and that Fort had been in jail for a chunk of the time the program ran.

But in 1972, Fort and four others—Fletcher Pugh, Mickey Cog-well, Charles Edward Bey, and Robert Jackson—were sentenced to federal prison for conspiracy to defraud and forgery. Adam Battiste pled guilty to forty-nine counts of conspiracy. Fort was still in the county jail for jumping bail during his New York trip. The judge made the prison term concurrent with the state prison sentence. Fort said he wanted to complete his education. "You've already got a PhD in Woodlawn," the judge said. "This is a real turning point in your life."

"I know that," Fort replied.

People have always asked why no Disciples were charged for any of this, especially since David Barksdale and the Disciple leaders were involved in the same kickback scheme the Stones were involved in. It may be as simple as the fact that the Disciples didn't have the same political beef with the feds the Stones did. The theory is that the feds perceived the Stones to be a potential threat to national security; the Disciples never expressed any political consciousness. Therefore the Stones were targeted, not the Disciples.

Brazier doesn't look fondly on those Stone Woodlawn days. No one from TWO who helped manage the OEO money went to trial or jail for fraud. When asked if Fort was a scapegoat, Brazier said no. "Nothing we did was contrary to the law. Jeff and others did deserve to go to jail. I saw the checks. It was the same handwriting." Brazier said TWO tried to do the right thing but you "can't stop people from doing wrong."

WITH BULL AND JEFF locked up and Throope and Bey shot, the only person on the outside to impose law on the organization was Cain. The *Chicago Daily Defender* reported on March 13, 1973, that Bey had identified Cain as his shooter. Cain received a sentence for fourteen years to life for a double murder that he and Chester Evans, another Main, committed back in 1969. They had killed two drug dealers who were selling out of an apartment hotel on 46th Street. By 1973, virtually all of the original Main 21s of significance were either incarcerated, had been driven out of the Main 21 body for one reason or another, or were dead. With the exception of Mickey Cogwell, there were no original Main 21s out on the street to lead a body more than five thousand strong.

AMID THIS CHAOS, an important relationship ended. In 1971, an attorney called and tipped Reverend Fry about a warrant issued for his arrest. "I took this very seriously. If I ever got into their jail, I'd be dead in two seconds," Fry recalled, although he added that whatever had been in that warrant was bullshit. He gathered his family with swiftness and left at 5:00 A.M. to head out west. Fry never returned to work in Chicago. An adult son sold the house for him.

Fry resigned from First Presbyterian a few days before those couple dozen Stones were indicted for illegally taking money from the OEO program. But Fry's departure didn't foreclose on the church's relationship with the Stones—not immediately.

Jeff Doane came to First Presbyterian in 1972 to work on urban ministry. He jokes that he probably looked like a public assistance lawyer with his lean figure and strawberry blond hair. "Whatever one wants to say about gang life, there was a generation of community in the face of despair and alienation," Doane recalled. "I saw them build respect for each other. I had a clear sense of their responsibility toward each other." Doane said he felt uncomfortable with the macho attitude they had toward women, but at First Pres he learned not to write people off or get weighed down by public perceptions. One of his earliest memories at the church was a Sunday morning service with about fifty congregants. In the middle of the service, about fifty Stones walked in two by two down the center aisle. They stayed for part of the service.

One of Doane's responsibilities at the church was to be a liaison with TWO. Doane would also visit Fort at the Joliet prison to keep communication open between the church and the Stones. Doane always made sure to wear his collar. Like most people who came in contact with Fort, Doane immediately sensed his charisma. He also learned that Fort entertained a lot of guests while in prison.

By 1974, First Presbyterian had run out of benevolence for the Stones, and church members wanted to take back the third floor to expand a less controversial youth ministry. The original plan stipulated that the Stones were to take turns sharing the space. Doane visited Fort to break the news to him. "He was upset but restrained and obviously restrained because guards were watching the exchange. He was not pleased that the church decided other needs needed to be met, too. We didn't leave things in particular great shape," Doane said. He added that no one from the Stone Nation ever hassled him or others about the decision.

The next week Fort got transferred to the federal prison in Leavenworth, Kansas. A grateful Doane appreciated the distance, but he did continue some correspondence. The church received money for a new program that would allow forty schoolchildren to have classes and daycare. "The session voted to write you this special letter telling you what we are doing about the third-floor space, and to ask your support and prayers for the success of this new program. We think you would be proud to be a part of it, and hope to see you again soon," Doane wrote to Fort.

By the time Fort got out of jail, he had moved on from First Presbyterian. He was ready for a new phase with the Stones. And that didn't include Presbyterians, government money, or running a gigantic organization with thousands of members.

# 6

# Ushering in Islam

**J**EFF **F**ORT **GOT** out of federal prison in March 1976. A condition
of his release was that he couldn't live in Chicago. Fort—no longer the skinny, red-beret-wearing youth of Woodlawn—moved to
Milwaukee.

His supporters gave him a homecoming that had the pomp of a
war hero's return. Yellow buses loaded with Stones drove up from
Chicago. Hundreds of Stones formed a straight line on the street.
They stood at attention in their uniforms of red berets, green khakis, and black boots. Local residents gaped from the street, and the
press captured the moment. Milwaukee police and FBI agents kept a
low profile but were present nonetheless. An entourage of black cars
and limousines drove up. Black men exited the vehicles wearing big
gangster hats like urban Secret Service agents. The adoring Stones
chanted "Long live Jeff Fort!" to an enthralled crowd.

Chuck LaPaglia, former aide to Reverend Fry at First Presbyterian
in Chicago, had now settled in Milwaukee and told authorities that
he would help Fort get back on his feet. LaPaglia and his wife were
present on the day of revelry, and they got out of one of the cars in the
caravan. The guest of honor was now ready for his entrance. When
Fort exited his limo, those who knew him immediately noticed his
physical transformation: he had bulging biceps and a wide chest, and

he weighed more than two hundred pounds. The crowd cheered, and Fort spoke about a new religious movement for his devotees. The language might've been too deep for his followers, who were more preoccupied with their leader's discharge from prison.

But the bulked-up twenty-nine-year-old prepared to forge a new direction for his organization. A month after getting out of prison, Fort declared that the Blackstone Nation would now center around religion, Black Nationalism, and education. He enrolled in a community education program at the University of Wisconsin–Milwaukee, and LaPaglia helped the Stones with their community education program.

Some individual Stones lived in Milwaukee as early as the 1960s, but they did not represent the organization in any capacity. Many of them had relocated there with family and moved freely back and forth between the two cities. When Fort initially relocated to Milwaukee he brought with him a small group of Stones who served as personal bodyguards for him and his family. Some of his brothers and sisters and their families relocated to Milwaukee, too, and some are still there. Other Stones subsequently followed, their presence specifically connected to being with Fort.

Fort spoke about his new connection to Allah and told of having an epiphany about the Blackstone organization. "We now understand the symbolic meaning of the Stones as the cornerstone of the holy Kaaba in the city of Mecca. It is the Black Stone that will be the headstone of the future," Fort said in April 1976. The Kaaba is a mosque in Saudi Arabia that Muslims visit, and there is literally a black stone. Fort continued, "The divine mission of Muhammad was teaching the supreme truth through the universal perceptions of Islam. . . . It is only necessary to view the great Islamic brotherhood and I—the chief—stand witness today to the Blackstones' symbolic relationship to that truth."

Fort's epiphany led to a change in the organization that he had co-ruled since the 1960s. Fort incorporated his new knowledge into a structured, selective organization called the El Rukns, an Arabic term that refers to the cornerstone of the Kaaba. The word also means "foundation." They were tight-knit and fiercely loyal, cutting an imposing figure with their religious garb and spouting rhetoric that jolted law enforcement. The first Stones who converted to El Rukn were ones who had grown up in Woodlawn and Kenwood-Oakland, communities where the Stones had been strongest. Most of the original El Rukn converts were younger Stones (in their teens or early twenties) with extended family ties to the organization. They had greater loyalty than Stones from other parts of the city. Therefore, when Fort established this new direction, they followed him with no problem. Fort handpicked his new leadership, the generals, out of this group. The generals replaced the body of the Main 21. Leonard Sengali, Chester Evans, and Reico Cranshaw were the only Main 21s who were held over as El Rukn generals.

During this transition, Fort ran into resistance against the new direction from many of the older Stones, who challenged this new course by claiming to be Christians, not Muslims. The older brethren from the Stone days were neither ready to call their God Allah nor to adhere to devout rules. Fort wove in traditions from the Moorish Science Temple of America too, a religious organization with Islamic leanings mixed with biblical lessons and a pro-black outlook. Thus few Stones made the transition into what they viewed as a foreign El Rukn world. The weeding out was fine with Fort; there was no Main 21 governing body to consult with on decisions, no one with whom he was obliged to share power. In a short time, Stone stalwarts and leaders Eugene "Bull" Hairston and Mickey Cogwell would be phased out. Fort also adopted the new name Malik, which means "king" in Arabic, to match his new religious persona.

Chief Malik was now king of the El Rukns.

## Noble Drew Ali and the Moorish Temple of Science

As it is for many black men imprisoned in the United States, Fort's exposure to religion broadened while he served his federal sentence. In late 1974, Hairston and Fort were locked up together at a prison in Joliet, Illinois. They received visits from Christina Price-Bey, the national secretary of the Moorish Science Temple of America (MSTA). Moorish Science Temple teachings were thick in prison (especially from the 1930s to the 1950s). Their draw is similar to the influence the Nation of Islam has over groups of black men in the penitentiary today. National MSTA leaders employed a targeted prison recruitment campaign to bolster their membership, and Hairston and Fort were no doubt a part of those efforts. During those prison visits, Bey-Price extolled the teachings of MSTA founder Noble Drew Ali. She even continued to visit Fort when officials transferred him to federal prison in Kansas to serve his sentence for defrauding the U.S. government.

Price-Bey taught Jeff and the other Stones that black people in America are "Asiatics" and Moors. MSTA teachings claim that the ancestors of black people were the Canaanites who descended from Noah's son Ham; they are also descendants of the biblical Moabites. Their more recent ancestors inhabited West Africa, where they established the Moorish empire that ruled most of Europe and Asia. According to Ali, the blacks of America are therefore actually Moors and their natural religion is Islam, not Christianity. Ali taught that although Jesus was also a Canaanite, he was merely a prophet. The Romans killed him and then founded Christianity. Ali also preached to his followers that only by means of a deliberate distortion of the racial background of Jesus was it possible for white Europeans to claim him as one of their own and establish him as the head of their church. These ideals must have percolated in Fort's head as he served out his sentence.

The founder of MSTA had an intriguing life journey. Noble Drew Ali was born Timothy Drew in 1886 in North Carolina to ex-slaves living among the Cherokee. Legend has it that his mother foretold his greatness, predicting that he would do extraordinary things. However, when he was a boy his mother died, and young Timothy went to live with an abusive aunt. He would tell a story of how after

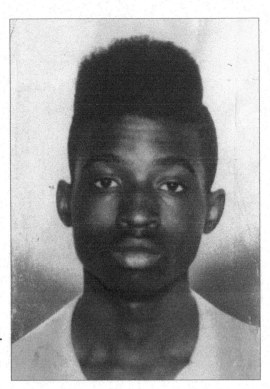

Jeff Fort mug shot, circa 1968.

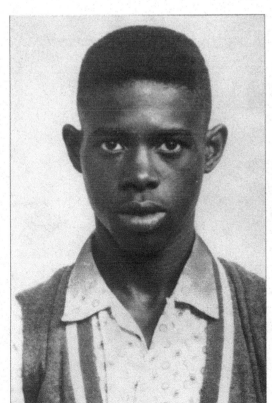

Eugene "Bull" Hairston
mug shot, circa 1961.

First Presbyterian Church, used as Stones' headquarters for several years in the 1960s.

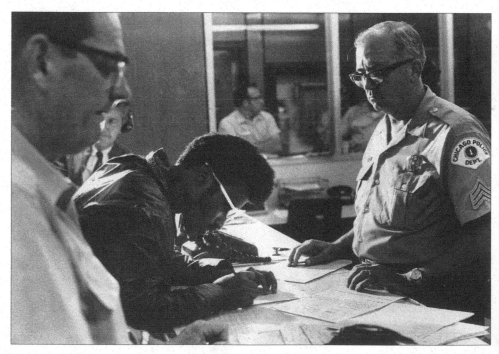

Jeff Fort posting bond, 1970.

Black P Stones press conference on police harassment, 1970.

Jesse Jackson (left), Jeff Fort, and Mickey Cogwell, 1971.

The Fort, El Rukn headquarters on South Drexel Street, 1980.

Jeff Fort at a criminal court appearance, 1981.

running away he joined a group of wandering gypsies. While with the gypsies he heard a voice say to him, "If you go, I will follow."

There are multiple versions of the stories of Drew's travails. One account said when he was a teenager he became a merchant seaman and traveled to Egypt, where he was supposedly initiated into a secret society that required him to go through a rite of passage. As part of the initiation he spent some time inside the great pyramid of Cheops. Upon successful completion of the ritual, he received the name Noble Drew Ali. At some point, the Circle Seven Koran was revealed to Ali, and he said he became a prophet. In the early 1900s, Ali had a vision that instructed him to start a religion that would uplift people of African ancestry, or black Americans, out of their desolate conditions. He subscribed to the Black Nationalist teachings of Marcus Garvey. In response to his vision, Ali founded the Canaanite Temple in Newark, New Jersey.

In 1925, the red-fez-wearing Ali moved to Chicago, declaring that black Americans weren't Negroes, coloreds, Ethiopians, or even black people. Members of the Moorish Science Temple of America always talk about the 1682 "Black Laws of Virginia" that exempted Moors (Moroccan nationals) from slavery. However, they say, in 1774 the founding fathers declared only "Negroes" were subject to slavery. Ali believed that Moors couldn't legally be slaves. His followers say that slave owner and U.S. president George Washington knew this, and he cut down the red banner of the Moors to hide the fact. This event, they say, is the origin of the legend of the young Washington not telling a lie about cutting down a cherry tree. This confusion over legalities led the Moors to forget their true identity and accept the label of "Negro." As a result they were made slaves. According to MSTA doctrine, if black people had honored their African ancestors and not converted to Christianity, they would not have been made slaves.

Ali founded the Moorish Temple of Science from the Canaanite Temple and legally incorporated it as a civic organization under Illinois law. In 1928, Ali changed the name to the Moorish Science

Temple of America and registered the organization as a religious institution. Simultaneously, Ali's movement—which he proclaimed a Mohammedan religion—gained footing in Detroit, New York, and Philadelphia. Ali once said:

> The problems of life are largely social and economic. In a profound sense, they are moral and spiritual. Have lofty conceptions of your duties to your country and fellowman in general and especially those with whom you deal. This includes honesty and righteousness as will cause you to put yourself in the other fellow's place. Look for the best in others and give them the best that is in you. Have a deeper appreciation for womanhood. Brighten the hopes of our youth in order that their courage be increased to dare and do wondrous things. Adhere at all times to the principles of love, truth, peace, freedom, and justice.

The primary objective of the teachings of the Moorish Science Temple of America was and is to connect African Americans with a proud heritage, thereby circumventing the stereotypical picture of Africa, its inhabitants, and their black American descendants as savage and uncivilized.

Fort's intellectual and spiritual thirst attracted him to MSTA teachings, and he wanted to spread that knowledge within his built-in flock. But there was a marked difference in how the followers of MSTA proselytized the teachings of the organization and how the new El Rukns embraced them. The El Rukns lacked the same fervor. Although they embraced some of the symbolism of MSTA, most didn't demonstrate the passion for the teachings that devoted MSTA followers did.

## Transition

**HENRY "TOOMBA" HARRIS,** a former El Rukn general, described his life in the organization in his book, *Epitome of Courage*. Born and raised in Milwaukee, Harris joined the Blackstone Rangers just as the group was transitioning to the El Rukn/MSTA era. Harris writes that he was invited into the house where the Fort family stayed in Milwaukee. There was a brief meet and greet before Jeff gave a speech titled "Chief Malik's Lesson." The eloquent lecture touched upon the new religious movement, but most of the Milwaukee membership didn't understand what angle Malik was coming from.

Harris describes the first day that he spent at Stones headquarters in Milwaukee in 1976. As he approached the structure, it looked like an old, abandoned building. Once inside, however, Harris realized that looks were deceiving, and his thoughts quickly changed. "The place was huge and freshly painted. A dance hall and kitchen were in the rear, a small book-lined study lined the north corridor." Books by black authors he'd never read lined the shelves: Richard Wright, Marcus Garvey, Timothy Drew, Malcolm X, Maurice Bishop, J. A. Rogers, Ishmael Reed. Chief Malik's portrait hung on a wall. Fifty men milled about wearing uniforms of green khakis and red berets.

When he first joined the Stones, Harris was given a uniform along with a list of bylaws that explained the dos and don'ts of membership. Among them were: no drinking in public, no drugs, no fighting each other, respect the black woman. He also received background about the meaning of his uniform. The new teachings of the MSTA explained the older Blackstone uniforms. The red beret stood for the blood of black people, who were supposed to be descended from the Berber tribe in West Africa that the white man later named Moors, who invaded Spain. Harris was told that the Romans threw one of the leaders—who donned a white fez that represented purity and godliness—from the Berber tribe into a lion's pit. The leader clung to the secret of his faith even facing death. When the rest of the tribe members pulled his body from the lion's pit, they discovered that the white fez was now red with blood. The green represented the motherland of Africa, and the black jump boots symbolized the black man's foot upon the white man's neck.

Harris entered a vast dance hall where the men faced east for prayer. They stood with their heads lowered, right hand balled into a fist, which was then placed across the left side of the chest. One of the Stones moved to the center of the floor and sang the Christian gospel song "Father Open Our Eyes."

A day after he arrived in Milwaukee, Jeff Fort enrolled in the Community Education Program at the University of Wisconsin–Milwaukee, a nontraditional academic program providing disenfranchised minorities access to the university. He later withdrew his application after the police chief raised a ruckus about him being paroled to Milwaukee.

Harris and other Milwaukee Stones later traveled to Chicago for another celebration honoring Fort at the Camp, located on 43rd and Indiana, which was the headquarters of the Black Hebrew Israelites. Several black men wearing colorful turbans and long robes were present along with the Stones. Other garish gear dazzled the place. Harris described a man in his fifties with dark eyes and thinning gray hair. Gold earrings dangled in both ears and nose, and a gold tooth glittered in his mouth. He wore diamonds on every finger, thumbs included. In the dance hall, Bull Hairston and Jeff Fort lingered. Fort urged the men to quiet down. He stepped to the center of the room, his pistol-flanked bodyguards moving with him.

Fort greeted everyone with a smile as he relayed to the membership his vision for a stronger, better-defined movement. It would start with scrapping the red, black, and green uniforms—as well as the leather jackets that bore the Stone logo of a pyramid enclosed in a circle. Fort explained there would be new garments for "the El Rukn Moorish Science Temple of America." This new organization would have an official look similar to monastic garb, but it would function with the unyielding structure of a corporate entity. Some of the Stones weren't ready for that heavy change. They didn't even really understand what a monastic order was without an actual description of the clothing. But mostly they acted like dutiful rank and file by responding "yes, sir" to Fort's speech.

Harris said that after the speech Fort and Bull Hairston gathered in a back lounge area to discuss the pros and cons of the new movement. Harris recalled an amicable conversation until Hairston raised his voice by disagreeing with his comrade's vision. Fort went on the defense, shouting that his plan would work.

But the ideological split between the two men was irreconcilable. Fort had spent considerable time in prison thinking of a master plan that centered around righteousness and this foreign Moorish direction. Hairston, who had been released from prison a year earlier than Fort, didn't think forcing a Stones about-face was feasible. In the 1960s, the Stones had obviously had religious influences all around them—First Pres, Reverend Brazier, African spirituality, a flirtation with Islam via the NOI and MSTA. But Hairston interpreted Fort's overhaul as incompatible with their lifestyle. He also told Fort that it wasn't right to use religion as a shield to do immoral things. Hairston snapped sarcastically that he was against them wearing turbans during the day and gangster hats at night.

After a heated exchange, Fort told Hairston unequivocally that he would not let him or anyone else interfere. The two faced off, and Hairston challenged Fort as to whether Jeff would kill Bull. Hairston wanted to know if the organization comprised gangsters or religious fanatics. Fort was ready to fight, but Hairston turned away in disgust, Harris remembered. He said Fort ordered his four bodyguards to kill Hairston. The men drew their weapons and placed the guns at his head. The old man adorned with diamonds and gold stepped in and pleaded with Fort not to kill Hairston. But Hairston turned to his elder and mocked that Fort wouldn't do it. According to Harris's account, Fort laughed and circled around Hairston. Fort told him that he was out of the organization. Hairston responded that Fort was wrong. As he stormed toward the door, he told Fort to never say he didn't warn him and then exited the room.

As Hairston left, Fort hollered, "Hey, Bull! If I ever see you again, it will be the day you die. Word to the Fatha!"

Harris said Hairston paused, turned back around to Fort, and shouted, "Fuck you!"

## El Rukn

HAIRSTON RECOGNIZED HE no longer had the power to stop Fort. He would need to gather together a posse of soldiers who were willing to engage in an all-out war with Fort and his new zealots. Most of the Stones who had been loyal to Hairston over the years were locked up, dead, strung out on dope, had quit the Stones, or had been co-opted by Fort. Without muscle, Hairston didn't stand a chance of challenging his former comrade. In his youth, Hairston would have been bold enough to try it. But now he knew he had lost. He wisely faded from the Blackstone scene quietly. With Hairston out of the way, Fort could show off his new passion. He now formally presented himself as Chief Malik. Gone were the Black Nationalist colors. In their place were red fezzes with long black tassels worn on special occasions such as funerals and group public appearances. It was not an everyday, ready-to-wear look. Some men kept the Circle 7 medallion.

The El Rukns made their first public appearance at the trial of Mickey Cogwell, William Stratton, and David McGowen in 1976. The men were on trial for buying and selling firearms without a license and possession of a sawed-off shotgun. The trio probably still identified themselves as Stones despite Chief Malik's El Rukn banner. There was no indication that Cogwell especially had accepted this new direction.

The public's introduction to the El Rukns was just the presentation Chief Malik probably imagined and likely the reaction he craved. He and seventeen El Rukns filed into the courtroom wearing red fezzes. Their appearance totally disrupted the trial. A paid police informer, Maurice Childress, was testifying when the El Rukns made their grand entrance. He was so unnerved that he spun around in the witness chair, faced the wall, and refused to testify. The judge immediately discharged the jury and declared a mistrial because five of the jurors told him they had been prejudiced by the incident.

Since the inception of the Blackstone Rangers, Henry "Mickey" Cogwell was always within the top five most influential Main 21s.

Not only did Cogwell have control over the Cobra Stones, he was brilliant and well connected outside of the organization. Cogwell had been tried and convicted with Fort for fraud, but his four-year sentence was reduced to probation. While Hairston and Fort served prison time, Cogwell's stature in the organization rose. He ran the day-to-day operations of the organization until Hairston got out of prison in 1975.

It was always believed that Mickey Cogwell had strong connections with the Chicago Mafia. As early as 1970, the *Chicago Tribune* reported about a financial alliance between Mafia chiefs and the Blackstone Rangers. The Gang Intelligence Unit of the Chicago Police Department claimed to have evidence accumulated from months of undercover work and surveillance, which produced the first-ever photographs of a rendezvous between mob emissaries and Blackstone Rangers leaders. According to the police, beginning in 1969, Cogwell and Charles "Reico" Cranshaw met with outfit representatives Joseph "Little Caesar" DiVarco, Joseph "Big Joe" Arnold, who also controlled the North Side lending racket, and Morris Lasky, a gambler who once worked for mob chieftains Jackie "the Lackey" Cerone and James "Monk" Allegretti. The police thought that the Mafia and the Blackstone Rangers were collaborating to control the policy racket, clubs, taverns, lounges, and liquor stores in the black community.

While running the organization, Cogwell engaged in union organizing. In 1974, he got the Hotel and Restaurant Employee and Bartenders Union to grant him an exclusive charter to organize workers on Chicago's South and West Sides. Using his organizing skills, Cogwell began to unionize restaurant, tavern, liquor store, hotel, and motel workers.

He obtained a charter for Local 304 of the Catering Industry Employees Union on May 20, 1973, at the international union headquarters in Cincinnati, Ohio. He made his buddy William Stratton the president, and Cogwell assumed the position of secretary of Local 304. Many people in the black community saw Cogwell's efforts as

an attempt to protect black folk, who had menial jobs in the emerging fast-food industry, from being exploited by their employers. The
police, of course, saw his work differently. Officers said he used his
street muscle to unionize an estimated two thousand saloons, restaurants, liquor stores, and prepared-food outlets doing business in the
black areas of Chicago for the purposes of financially shaking down
the owners of these businesses.

Having a foot in each world was dangerous. On February 25, 1977,
Cogwell was hanging out at a joint on 87th Street gambling into the
early morning. A former Black Disciple said that he was with Cogwell that night. The Disciple said it was not unusual for guys from
different gangs to frequent the same gambling spots and clubs. He
said the game ended at about 3:00 A.M., at which time Cogwell asked
his friend for a ride home. The man agreed, and he and the Disciple
dropped Cogwell off at his house on 78th and Seeley Avenue. The former Black Disciple said when they got two or three blocks away from
Cogwell's house, they heard shots but didn't pay them any attention.

Shortly afterward, police found Cogwell's dead body on the lawn
at 7820 South Seeley Avenue. Three bullet wounds pierced the thirty-
one-year-old's back. The city homicide police commander called the
shooting an assassination. Witnesses said a tall man wearing a dark
ski jacket and red pullover cap stood over Cogwell's body. Police
struggled with determining a motive because there were so many
possibilities. Investigators thought there might've been a falling-out
among gang members. Some of the Mains speculated that Cogwell
could have been slain because he was not in line with the new transition from the Black P Stone Nation to the El Rukns. Others believe
that his death had nothing to do with the Stones/El Rukns at all; they
say the Mafia put a hit out on Cogwell because of his involvement
with union organizing. They think that the mob felt that Cogwell
was becoming too powerful and had the potential to use his new
union to shut down hotels, fast-food joints, liquor stores, taverns,
and other businesses they were extorting. Just hours before Cogwell was killed, Al Bramlet, the head of the same union in Las Vegas,
went missing. Bramlet's body was later found in a shallow grave in

the desert. This points to the highly possible theory that Cogwell's and Bramlet's deaths were Mafia hits. The men had control of unions whose members worked for mob-controlled businesses.

Eventually the Cobra Stones became suspicious about their leader's death. Feeling that his hit may have come from the El Rukn leadership, the group dropped "Stones" from its name, dissociated themselves from the former Black P Stone Nation, and refused to fall in line with the El Rukns. They renamed the organization in honor of their fallen leader and became the Mickey Cobras, known on the streets today as the MCs or the Snakes. The El Rukns vehemently denied any involvement in Cogwell's death.

With Bull out of the organization and Cogwell dead, Chief Malik was for the first time the uncontested leader of the Blackstone Rangers turned Almighty Black P Stone Nation turned El Rukn Moorish Science Temple of America. With three exceptions—Sengali, Evans, and Cranshaw—all the Main 21s were either locked up, dead, or marginalized in the organization. Membership dwindled rapidly; a lot of Stones simply refused to adopt the tenets of Islam that were fundamental to the El Rukn Moorish Science Temple of America.

One Blackstone said that he was one of the leaders in an Illinois state prison when the mandate came down that all Stones were now to follow the new direction. This former Stone said that he had no intention of becoming El Rukn. He said his "mama didn't raise no Muslims." He considered himself a Christian. When it got back to the leadership that he refused to accept the El Rukn transition, he got a prison visit from a group of former Stones turned El Rukns—including his biological brother. They gave him an ultimatum, but the threat did not faze him, and he still did not accept the El Rukns. That bold decision put him on life support. He was shanked nine times, once in the neck, for disobeying a direct order. Upon his recovery he still didn't make the conversion.

The El Rukn Moorish Science Temple of America replaced the old Blackstone creed with the Royal Renaissance Allegiance. It was crafted to align the old Black P Stone Nation with the new direction of the MSTA and establish Malik as the organization's undisputed leader. There was a difference between the Blackstone creed of the prior decade and this language. The latter was taken directly from the MSTA. It went as follows:

This Unity that we the sons of Ancient Moabite blood have established upon these shores of North America in this alien civilization shall be preserved at all cost with the bonds of Ali's Holy laws. If we violate our principles may the flaming sword of our forefathers turn on us the wrath of Allah and strike us down seven times.

We pledge allegiance of Chief Malik under Love, Truth, Peace, Freedom and Justice.

The El Rukn Moorish Science Temple of America was governed by the seven acts of its "Divine Constitution" and bylaws:

Act 1
The Grand Sheik and the chairman of the Moorish Science Temple of America is in power to make laws and enforce laws with the assistance of the Prophet and the Grand Body of the Moorish Science Temple of America. The assistant Grand Sheik is to assist the Grand Sheik in all affairs if he lives according to Love, Truth, Peace, Freedom, and Justice and it is known before the members of the Moorish Science Temple of America.

Act 2
All meetings are to be opened and closed promptly according to the circle seven and Love, Truth, Peace, Freedom, and Justice. Friday is our Holy Day of rest, because on a Friday the first man was formed in flesh and on a Friday the first man departed out of flesh and ascended unto his father God Allah; for that cause Friday is the Holy Day of all Moslems all over the world.

## Act 3

Love, Truth, Peace, Freedom, and Justice must be proclaimed and practiced by all members of the Moorish Science Temple of America. No member is to put in danger or accuse falsely his brother or sister on any occasion at all that may harm his brother or sister, because Allah is Love.

## Act 4

All members must preserve these Holy and Divine laws, and all members must obey the laws of the government, because by being a Moorish American, you are a part and partial of the government, and must live the life accordingly.

## Act 5

This organization of the Moorish Science Temple of America is not to cause any confusion or to overthrow the laws and constitution of the said government but to obey hereby.

## Act 6

With us all members must proclaim their nationality and we are teaching our people their nationality and their divine creed that they may know that they are a part and a partial of this said government, and know that they are not Negroes, Colored Folks, Black People, or Ethiopians, because these names were given to slaves by slave holders in 1779 and lasted until 1865 during the time of slavery, but this is a new era of time now, and all men now must proclaim their free national name to be recognized by the government in which they live and the nations of the earth, this is the reason why Allah the great God of the universe ordained Noble Drew Ali, the Prophet to redeem his people from their sinful ways. The Moorish Americans are the descendants of the ancient Moabites who inhabited the North Western and South Western shores of Africa.

Act 7

All members must promptly attend their meetings and become a part and a partial of all uplifting acts of the Moorish Science Temple of America. Members must pay their dues and keep in line with all necessities of the Moorish Science Temple of America, then you are entitled to the name of "Faithful." Husband, you must support your wife and children; wife, you must obey your husband and take care of your children and look after the duties of your household. Sons and daughters must obey fathers and mothers and be industrious and become a part of the uplifting of fallen humanity. All Moorish Americans must keep their hearts and minds pure with love, and their bodies clean with water. This Divine Covenant is from your Holy Prophet Noble Drew Ali, through the guidance of his Father God Allah.

Another prominent symbol in the early development of the Almighty Black P Stone Nation was the Circle 7, a concept borrowed from the teachings of the Moorish Science Temple of America (MSTA) and the Nation of Islam (NOI). These organizations taught that the concept of 360 degrees represented the totality of universal knowledge.

They also taught that most of the founding fathers of America had been Freemasons. However, they claimed that the European form of Freemasonry was stolen from the original Freemasons, who were Africans. Europeans, they claimed, had traveled to Africa in ancient times to learn from the Egyptians. They taught that because the Egyptians believed the Europeans to be novices in the knowledge of the universe, they only shared with them a small portion of the totality of universal knowledge. Hence, the Europeans were only given thirty-three degrees of the truth, which is all they had to build their civilization with. According to the teachings of MSTA and NOI, it is the Europeans' underdeveloped knowledge of the universe that causes them to feel inadequate. These feelings of inferiority are projected on black people in the form of racism and oppression. Like the

MSTA and NOI, the El Rukns would often criticize those who were affiliated with Masonic orders for only having thirty-three degrees as their highest degree of attainment. In the late 1960s, Lance once heard Jeff expound, "Having thirty-three degrees of knowledge out of the whole 360 degrees ain't nothin' to be struttin' around like a peacock about." Jeff added, "The [El Rukns] be about the whole thang." This is the reason that they used a circle as one of their symbols, another emblem of 360 degrees of knowledge.

The circle would often have a seven written in the middle. The seven represented perfection. The El Rukns' text instructed that every number from one to nine had a spiritual meaning. The number one represented the oneness of the universe, in which everything is connected to universal order. The El Rukns were reminded to use this principle to stay unified among themselves. The number two represented the duality of all things. They represented two as a yin and yang symbol to mean the good and evil of all things. Sometimes this principle explained the importance of doing things that were not necessarily good. The number three represented the trinity of man. Jeff often talked about the importance of understanding that everybody had a spiritual, physical, and mental self. He taught that to be divine was to have balance among the three. According to Jeff, white people were ruled by their physical selves, and the world they built placed emphasis on the physical. For the El Rukns to be successful they had to do the same. He said getting money, cars, jewelry, clothes, and other material things were of the white man's world. He said that although the El Rukns should have these things too, they shouldn't let the pursuit of material things get in the way of their spiritual and mental development.

The number four represented stability. The El Rukns would often say "I put four on it" to emphasize that whatever they had done was solid, stable, or well done. The number five represented the five human senses: taste, touch, smell, sight, and hearing. It also represented the five fundamental principles of the Blackstone Nation: love, truth, peace, freedom, and justice. The number six signified evil and wickedness. They assigned this number to the government, which they saw as the enemy of all black people. The number seven represented perfection. Chippewa, one of the original Stones, says that when Stones were locked up together in jail in the early years they would comb the Bible for nuggets of wisdom they could use to establish a spiritual foundation for the organization. One of these nuggets included the Genesis story of how God created all things within the universe in six days, and on the seventh day he rested. The Stones interpreted that to mean seven was a number of perfection. In the El Rukn era, many of the members wore medallions and rings made of a gold circle with a seven in the center.

The number eight represented incompletion. Its opposite was the number nine, another prominent symbol in the El Rukn literature. Nine symbolized myriad things to the El Rukns, chiefly the representation of completion or finality. The El Rukns explained that it takes nine months for a mother to give birth to a child, there are nine planets that completed the solar system, and there are nine systems in the human body. They also used nine to symbolize death. The literature spoke to all things meeting their number nine, or end. It even referred to the eventual death of the Blackstone Nation; however, the teachings reminded the El Rukn organization and its members that if they strive for perfection in this life, they will be resurrected to rule again in the next life.

The El Rukns used a crescent moon with a five-pointed star to embody their orientation toward Islam. Similar to the six-pointed star representing Jewish nationality, or the cross symbolizing Christendom, the crescent moon and five-pointed star are commonly associated with Islamic power. For many black men incarcerated in America's penal systems, Islam has often been an attractive religion. Because white society proudly proclaims Christian morality and righteousness, it is natural for some black men who have been victims of white supremacy to reject Christianity. As the population of black men in American prisons began to rise after World War I, so did their adoption of Islam. The religion provided black men with an alternative to that of their white oppressors. Islam taught, and even promoted, going to war with one's enemies and oppressors. The El Rukns also accepted Islam as an orientation that they used to guide their worldview as an organization. Whether the tenets of Islam were practiced by the El Rukns at the individual level can be argued; nevertheless, Islam was without a doubt fundamental to the spirit of the organization.


## A New Era

THE BPSN HAD been instrumental in the creation of the system of "People" (five-pointed star) and "Folks" (six-pointed star) established within the Illinois Department of Corrections in the 1970s. This system allowed for extended alliances among the various street organizations and their members while incarcerated. The BPSN aligned with other "People" street organizations such as the Latin Kings and the Vice Lords. The "Folks" consisted of Disciple affiliates such as the Gangster Disciple Nation, the Black Disciple Nation, the Black Gangster Nation, and others. These alliances were later maintained on the streets of Chicago and elsewhere.

For the Stones, the five-pointed star represented the principles of love, truth, peace, freedom, and justice. Sometimes the El Rukns would stand in a five-point stance to represent the five principles. They would stand with their legs slightly spread, the right hand gripping the left wrist as their arms were folded across their stomachs. The head represented love, the top point of the star. The right elbow represented truth and the left elbow represented peace. The right foot represented freedom and the left foot represented justice.

From the mid-1970s to the early 1980s, gangbanging in Chicago died down, and the black community finally got a chance to take a collective deep breath after the marathon of gang violence it had been running from since the late 1960s. The leaders of most of the major street organizations—the Stones, Disciples, and Lords—had been locked up since the early 1970s. Fort, Hairston, and most of the Main 21 had been off the streets for most of the 1970s. David Barksdale, leader of the Disciples, and Larry Hoover, his successor, spent the better part of the decade locked up. Barksdale died in prison, and Hoover remains behind bars today. The spokesman of the Vice Lords, Bobby Gore, was locked up from 1969 to 1979. With the leadership of Chicago's major black street organizations incarcerated, a lot of the old vendettas ended. Ultimately, the dynamics that bred gang involvement during the 1960s and early 1970s had significantly decreased by the mid- to late '70s.

By the late 1970s a new youth culture began to develop on the streets of Chicago. While the El Rukns were still partying to the Chi-Lites, the Dramatics, and the old R&B singing groups of the Motown and post-Motown era, the new generation celebrated disco, funk, and a new thing called rap music. The youth culture during this time replaced the loud colors, platform shoes, and Afros with the designer threads of Calvin Klein, Jordache, Pierre Cardin, and Yves Saint Laurent. This was a new era of a softer, kinder, and gentler young, urban black male with a *GQ* look.

As Chief Malik returned to the outside world, his El Rukn Moorish Science Temple of America for the first time no longer represented the bastion of youth culture. The El Rukns found themselves in uncharted territory. In the past, whether it was their white T-shirts, khakis, Chucks, and bush-top fades (early 1960s Stones), Ray-Ban shades, black leather jackets, red berets, combat boots, and Afros (late 1960s Stones), or their Super Fly, full-length fur coats with the matching hats and canes, loud colors, platform shoes, and naturals, the Stones had always been fashion trendsetters. But El Rukn fashion was another story. The El Rukns seemed to cross Super Fly with a touch of ancient Morocco. One routine traffic stop turned into a high-speed chase as police officers pursued a speeding black limousine. When they cornered the limo, Jeff Fort and six other men emerged wearing full-length fur coats. In the summer, an El Rukn would sport a pair of shorts, alligator shoes, and silk dress socks pulled up as high as the knees. He would probably be rocking the signature El Rukn braids. The El Rukns were famous for their fat cornrows and braids. Wearing braids was popular among young black males in the 1970s, but the style played out toward the end of the decade. But not for the El Rukns; they wore their braids well into the '80s. And of course, only a real El Rukn wore a Fulani hat. These hats were straw with a conical shape laced with red leather and a chin strap. To the new generation, the El Rukns were social and fashion misfits.

As part of their religious iconography, the El Rukns wore a medallion with a number seven or a pyramid with a flaming sun on top inside a circle. Sometimes there was a black five-pointed star in the center of the pyramid. Behind the pyramid was a sun on the horizon. On top of the sun was an Arabian-styled sword with the word *Justice* written on the blade. On top of the sword were the letters L.T.P.F., which stood for Love, Truth, Peace, and Freedom. The El Rukn generals passed off the fashion direction to the rank and file. They started wearing the red fezzes gradually, sometimes looking like thugged-out Shriners.

Many MSTA members add the word *Bey* to their surname, a title of respect used for Turkish dignitaries and native rulers of Tunis or Tunisia. *El* is another reverent word used, and many of the El Rukns added the title to their first names or nicknames. For instance, Leonard was called Len for short. His name changed to Len El. A guy named Dwayne became Dwayne-El.

After the El Rukn conversion, the organization's Chicago headquarters known as The Fort changed its signage to read El Rukn Grand Major Temple: A.C. of the M.S.T. of A. A mural of the Kaaba flanked by two pyramids and palm trees was painted on the front of the building.

In 1978, Chief Malik left Milwaukee and returned to Chicago and began to subtly do away with the Moorish Science Temple of America in the name of the organization. By the early 1980s, the Moorish Science Temple of America identification seemed to have disappeared completely from the group's identity. Some say he had been granted a charter to the organization, but others say he hadn't. Meanwhile, others say he was granted a charter but lost it because the El Rukns refused to conform to the laws and constitution of the Moorish Science Temple of America. And still others say Chief Malik didn't like relinquishing the chance to be head of an entire organization. The Grand Sheik of MSTA was a national leader. In the hierarchy, Malik was like the head pastor, but the national church had many layers of leaders above him.

The El Rukn transition was visible on the streets, but Chief Malik's law enforcement adversaries reckoned it was nothing more than twaddle.

"Jeff Fort is a punk," declared Winston Moore, the Cook County jail director who had known Fort and Disciples leader David Barksdale dating back to the 1960s. Moore didn't believe that Fort wanted to rebuild the Black P Stone Nation into a religious or community-based institution. "He's a punk and he's just trying to start the shooting all over again and I object to the press giving him credibility. . . . Fort isn't into religion. All he's into is drugs, prostitution, intimidation."

The contradiction of righteousness and impiety became the foundation of the El Rukns. They prayed in their mosque. They sold drugs. They practiced entrepreneurship. They kept a stockpile of weapons. They celebrated their women at an annual feast with cake and adulation. They got arrested for murder. They started a security firm. They held community meetings. Chief Malik ran the organization as if he were the head of a monarchy. He actually sat on a throne at the El Rukns' headquarters.

As the Stones had done in the 1960s, the El Rukns dabbled in politics. In 1982, some El Rukns trekked to the Chicago elections board and registered over two hundred members. This grassroots movement was organized in response to police brutality, unemployment, and slumlords. In the 1983 mayoral race, the El Rukns inserted themselves in the racially charged politics of Chicago. After the mayoral primary, a tidbit surfaced: the El Rukns had been paid ten thousand dollars through the coffers of a black state representative to put up flyers and do other campaign work for Mayor Jane Byrne in her race for reelection against black candidate Harold Washington. Byrne called the gang despicable and said she was unaware of El Rukn participation. The El Rukns admitted to getting money from Illinois state representative Larry Bullock but insisted they acted as individuals, not members of their nation. The exchange was devised by Democratic party boss and alderman Ed Vrdolyak, who said Bullock received the money to lead a South Side effort for Byrne. The alderman—who became a legislative nemesis to Washington once he was elected mayor—denied knowing Bullock's plans. And Bullock said he was unaware of El Rukn involvement, and he defended his friendship with Vrdolyak and said he refused to play racial politics. But Vrdolyak had handily boosted Bullock's war chest; the alderman's committee gave Bullock seventy thousand dollars. Out of that pot came the ten thousand given to the El Rukns. The previous balance in the two-term state rep's coffers was $6,616. (A judge later sentenced Bullock to six years in federal prison for filing false statements with government agencies to get minority business certification for his construction firm. The corruption doesn't stop there: in 2009, Vrdolyak was sentenced to five years' probation for his role in a $1.5 million kickback scheme.)

Harold Washington operatives said the El Rukns also engaged in a great deal of voter intimidation. El Rukns would gather in large numbers outside polling places, trying to discourage people from voting. The Washington campaign sent volunteer workers to counteract intimidation with a show of force. Volunteers also drove people to the polls and escorted them in.

Chicago journalist Nate Clay never believed Vrdolyak's claim of not knowing about the El Rukn involvement. Clay said the El Rukns were co-opted by money and used in old-fashioned plantation politics by Vrdolyak and Bullock. Clay said he and a group of black activists approached the El Rukns about their political behavior. According to Clay, the El Rukn attitude was that Washington wasn't going to win, so they might as well get the money from Vrdolyak. But then Washington won.

Chicago police still saw Jeff Fort as a gang leader. They viewed his federal prison time as an inconvenient retreat that only boosted his power. The organization name change and Malik title meant little. Police openly monitored him. But his mother, Annie, defended him and said he was a devoted child. "Whenever I get sick, he comes to town to take care of me. I don't believe all these things I read about him in the paper. All I can do is hope for the best and pray for him every night," she said.

# 7

# Angels of Death

THE GENERAL JONES ARMORY on 52nd and Cottage Grove is a huge monstrosity on the South Side of Chicago. From time to time the side doors unlock and the public can sneak a peek at the military vehicles. But deep blackness swallows the camouflaged trucks even during the day.

On February 24, 1985, the armory opened its bulky doors and shone dim lights on the Chicago-based Nation of Islam for Saviour's Day, the annual celebration marking the birth of NOI founder W. Fard Muhammad. Inside the armory was dark and dingy. A cold draft blew through the cavernous space.

A sea of Saviour's Day participants did their NOI duty—wearing stony faces that created an orchestrated militaristic atmosphere, patting everyone down in security lines. Muslim women wore all white. Men in dark blue Fruit of Islam uniforms took their military posture. Thousands of regular black folk walked in, too, tolerating a frisk to hear minister Louis Farrakhan deliver an impassioned speech titled "Power, at Last . . . Forever."

Another posturing group came to the armory that Sunday afternoon—the El Rukns. The armory is just ten blocks north of Woodlawn. Farrakhan and the Nation of Islam courted an alliance with the local El Rukns. This alliance was not for the purpose of recruiting the

El Rukns to become registered NOI members; the Nation wanted the support of the El Rukns as street warriors they could unleash on those who sought to do them harm.

Farrakhan invited the El Rukns to Saviour's Day. At least five hundred men showed up. They entered the armory two by two, standing in the five-point stance while waiting to be searched. With red fezzes on their heads, the men looked more like a contingency of Moroccan dignitaries than gangbangers. Some generals sat on the stage, part of the ostentatious presentation that Farrakhan used at his headliner events.

Before the minister took the lectern, a large screen rose in the corner of the armory. From the other side of the ocean via satellite, Algeria's Ahmed Ben Bella and Ghana's Jerry Rawlings sent greetings. Then Libya's Colonel Muammar el-Qaddafi spoke. He said black Americans should quit the armed services and create a separate black state. Qaddafi said he wanted to help black people throw off the chains of bondage and oppression, and he'd assist in providing the means for armed struggle if desired. Farrakhan refused the offer. But there was something the minister previously hadn't refused—money. Qaddafi, persona non grata to the United States and President Ronald Reagan, had publicly lent Farrakhan five million dollars.

During Qaddafi's speech, Farrakhan asked the El Rukns to stand. He proceeded to warn the United States that if it tried to harm him, they would have to deal with his "angels of death," pointing to all of the El Rukns present.

The audience burst into feverish applause.


## Farrakhan

FARRAKHAN'S RELATIONSHIP WITH the El Rukns didn't come immediately or naturally. The minister had ended up in Chicago as part of sweeping changes to the Nation of Islam. In 1975, the Honorable Elijah Muhammad died, and his son Wallace Deen Muhammad,

later known as Warith Deen Mohammed, became leader of the NOI.
Warith Mohammad immediately introduced many reforms to bring
the NOI closer to mainstream Islam. He did away with his father's
teachings that Master Fard Muhammad was God on Earth, the white
man was the devil, and the black man was God. He established closer
ties with Sunni Muslim communities and introduced the five pillars
of Islam into the NOI's theology. He also exposed the corruption of
many of the NOI's top ministers, whom he claimed paid themselves
high salaries. These top NOI ministers included Louis Farrakhan. As
punishment, Farrakhan was reassigned from his prominent post as
minister of New York's Temple Number Seven—Malcolm X's former
position—to a lowly temple on Chicago's West Side. Warith Mohammad wanted to keep an eye on Farrakhan and limit his power within
the NOI.

Farrakhan saw his West Side NOI temple placement as what it
was—a demotion. He had been stripped of his national prominence
within the NOI and practically ostracized. The West Side was a foreign place to him, and he really had no desire to establish himself
there. Those close to Farrakhan commented that he seemed confounded by street culture in Chicago. Being from the East Coast, he
knew nothing of Chicago's street gangs. That put him at a disadvan-
tage when he came to an area associated with the Vice Lords. And
just as foreign as the West Side was to Farrakhan, so was Farrakhan
and the NOI foreign to those black denizens. From its inception, the
NOI held more influence on the South Side.

The NOI and the Blackstone Rangers even had some history.
FBI files document a rift between the Blackstone Rangers and the
Nation of Islam as early as 1969. According to an internal memo, a
confidential informant had told the FBI that the Blackstone Rangers sent a threatening letter to the NOI because the newspaper
*Muhammad Speaks* published an article on June 27, 1969, criticiz-
ing the Blackstone Rangers' violence. In the article, the redacted
name of a person within the Gang Intelligence Unit answered various questions about gangs engaged in slaughter on the streets and

schoolyards of Chicago. Apparently, when leader Elijah Muhammad learned of the letter, he responded that Jeff Fort and the Stones had better not bother the NOI. He also said he had no intention of meeting with the Stones. Farrakhan knew about the letter incident and carried the knowledge of it with him during his early years in Chicago.

In 1977, after struggling with his new status at the West Side temple, Farrakhan quit the Nation. Looking for a new direction, Farrakhan tried his hand at writing a Hollywood screenplay based on the life of Malcolm X. He moved to Los Angeles and lived with former football pro Jim Brown while shopping the screenplay. Having no success, he returned to Chicago in 1978 to rebuild the original Nation of Islam upon the foundation established by Elijah Muhammad. Farrakhan argued that Warith Mohammad had destroyed the NOI with his new direction. Farrakhan ran a renegade operation outside Warith's NOI.

Farrakhan eventually learned the extent and power of Chicago's street organizations. He also realized he could use them to his advantage. And as Jeff Fort matured, he, too, learned how to use Farrakhan to his advantage. Expediency, not trust, describes the relationship between the two men.

The El Rukns' exposure to Qaddafi came via the NOI, and the El Rukns would later drastically feel the repercussions of that association. Word spread that Qaddafi had provided Farrakhan an interest-free five-million-dollar loan in 1985. Even the black American almanac *Jet Magazine* published an article about the money. Farrakhan had said that the loan was to be used for a "self-contained economic system" for blacks in America, the Caribbean, and Africa. The NOI leader said he planned to use the money to start a marketing organization called POWER—People Organized and Working for Economic Rebirth—for members to sell toothpaste, soap, mouthwash, and skin oil. The personal care products line would be called Clean N Fresh. When criticism started to pile on Farrakhan for taking money from an international leader whom the United States considered a pariah, he defended himself. "I appeal to our own government: Don't be angry at Brother Khadafy [*sic*] for helping us," Farrakhan said. "I am not a terrorist, and don't you say I've taken this money to make bombs. And I have never been a prostitute; I don't sell myself to any man. I am my own man or, better yet, I'm God's man, and I cannot be bought for $5 million or $10 million or $100 million." Qaddafi's largesse toward the NOI and black Americans left an impression on the El Rukns—and, later, federal authorities.

During the time Farrakhan busied himself resurrecting the new NOI, he used various venues around the city of Chicago to hold meetings with his followers, including the Black Lawyers' Community College of Law and International Diplomacy at 4545 South Drexel. Farrakhan's friend activist Charles Knox had established the school in 1979.

Knox taught at Northeastern Illinois University's Center for Inner City Studies. Not only did he have strong ties to Black Nationalists, Knox also had an equally strong connection with Chicago street gangs. The leadership of the Stones, Lords, and Disciples respected him. Knox allowed Farrakhan and the NOI to use the Black Lawyers' College as a meeting place, and he also let the El Rukns host activities there. It was through Knox that Farrakhan and Chief Malik became acquainted.

Although the feds had tapered down the intensity of their surveillance of Black Nationalist groups after the U.S. Senate Church Committee Report (a 1975 committee formed to investigate the government's illegal spying on organizations and American citizens involved in political protesting), they still kept an eye on potential internal threats to national security. Their concerns were elevated when Farrakhan's rhetoric against the United States and Jews amplified. Farrakhan wanted to attract attention to his efforts to rebuild the NOI. Meanwhile, the anti-American and anti-Jewish sentiments that Farrakhan unleashed in the United States were being echoed in parts of the Islamic global community. In 1979, Osama bin Laden hooked up with his teacher and mentor Abdullah Azzam, a leading

Palestinian Sunni Islamic scholar and theologian, and began to fun-nel big money into Azzam's international jihadist movement. Bin Laden's money trained Muslim fighters to attack Western nations they perceived to be the enemies of Islam. And the icing on top, as far as the feds were concerned, was Farrakhan. The fiery leader began to encourage black Americans in his public speeches to forge stronger relations with their Muslim brothers abroad. He said that while America preoccupied itself with the Cold War, black people (including the Arab world community) should prepare to fight against America while the country was vulnerable.

The feds had had enough. Something had to be done about the growing anti-Americanism at home and abroad. The Joint Terror-ism Task Force (JTTF) was implemented in 1980 to investigate the emerging threat of terrorism against the United States. Lewis Myers Jr., a prominent civil and human rights attorney and activist, former national counsel to the NOI, and close confidant of Farra-khan, believes the JTTF used components of federal racketeering laws to circumvent the criticism that came out of the Church com-mittee. Myers said the feds used the JTTF and racketeering laws to justify spying on the political activities of black organizations as organized crime. The JTTF consisted of fifteen squads, each made up of local law enforcement officers deputized to work with a range of federal law enforcement agencies, including the FBI, the CIA, the Drug Enforcement Agency (DEA), and the Bureau of Alcohol, Tobacco, and Firearms (ATF), among others. They were strategi-cally located throughout the United States. Squad 13 was assigned to Chicago. Its targets were Farrakhan and the Nation of Islam, and Jeff "Malik" Fort and the El Rukns. While the FBI kept tabs on Farrakhan and the Nation of Islam, the DEA and ATF worked with deputized local law enforcement personnel to monitor the El Rukns.

This was merely a precursor. The feds would pull another rabbit out of their hat in the form of another task force to dismantle the El Rukns.

## Farrakhan and Fort

FARRAKHAN BELIEVED IN his "angel" Jeff Fort. During a 1982 Saviour's Day celebration at a downtown Chicago hotel, Farrakhan exalted Fort for his organizational skills and how they must have ostensibly scared the white man, saying, "When a man can organize men and discipline men and have men respond to his commands—that's called a dangerous nigger in this country." Farrakhan preached that perhaps Fort would eschew the negativity in his life and find another, more positive, way to organize. "See, a man that can organize men like this on one level can organize them like that on another level. . . . This brother is not just a Chicago man. This brother has the potential for national and international work." Farrakhan then compared Chief Malik to another leader, albeit one of a different ilk; it sounded like a backhanded compliment.

"Most of you who praise Malcolm, you're really hypocrites because you praise Malcolm as Malcolm X but that was the same man that was hustling women. That was the same man—you listen to me good—that was pimping black women. That's the same man that was selling drugs and bringing white folks up to Harlem to sell black women's butts to them white devils. But when he met a man that made a difference in his life, the same man that was one thing on one level became a monster on another level and that's Chief Malik's destiny." The audience, on cue, exploded with applause. What Elijah Muhammad was to Malcolm X, Farrakhan hoped to be to Jeff Fort.

Farrakhan and the Nation of Islam enjoyed street credibility among young, urban black men. The NOI brand of masculinity appealed to their manhood and encouraged their warrior spirits. NOI members called them the vanguards and protectors of the black community. This approach made young, urban black men somewhat tolerant of the NOI's posturing. The El Rukns knew that attending a NOI event would afford them the rare positive praise they craved. They would get to stand as a legitimate organization before thousands as Farrakhan heaped accolades on them as if they had done nothing but good in the 'hood. Their egos were stroked, and the NOI appeared as if it had some real credibility with the street warriors. In reality these superficial acts were the extent of the relationship between the NOI and the streets; the NOI rarely demonstrated the capacity to engage any other major street organizations in Chicago besides the El Rukns. When the El Rukns took on their Arabic name and Fort's flirtation with Islam became more prominent, Farrakhan used their conversion as an opportunity to feather his cap. In a 1982 speech, Farrakhan said, "The name El Rukn is a powerful name. It means the corner. And it's after the cornerstone that was laid in Mecca. A stone that is a sign of the last messenger of God. So the truth of the matter is, every black man, woman, and child in America that joins arms to the messenger who is the cornerstone of a new world government is El Rukn."

Michael Muhammad served as a youth minister for the Nation of Islam in the early 1980s. He first came into contact with Farrakhan as a student organizing against youth violence at his high school on Chicago's South Side. After graduation, Muhammad left for Tuskegee University but continued developing his relationship with the elder minister. When Muhammad returned to his hometown, he began working with gangs on behalf of the NOI. In the early 1980s, there was a bubbling resurgence of Black Nationalism and pan-Africanism and a revitalization of Elijah Muhammad's teachings.

Although the NOI cannot be categorized in a true sense as falling within any of these movements, Farrakhan capitalized on their revitalization by espousing elements of each. For instance, Farrakhan would talk about Malcolm X but only as a disciple of the Honorable Elijah Muhammad, not in his capacity as a Black Nationalist or pan-Africanist. He would praise the scholarship of John Henrik Clarke but neglect to mention Clarke's critique of Islam's historic and continued attack on Africa and its people. Farrakhan exalted the emergence of Afrocentrism but only to the extent that it didn't challenge the teachings of the Nation of Islam or Arabism.

Meanwhile, the Reagan era emerged at this time, and its ravishing effects soon began to hit America's cities. Street gangs made a brutal splash on these same urban milieus. Chief Malik no doubt saw all of this as he continued studying Islam and its iconography. These contradictions complicated the meaning of the El Rukns. The value system of the El Rukns—community and culture—coexisted with capitalism. So he convened the heads of the major street organizations, mostly from the South Side, to The Fort. Many of these gangs had been influenced by the earlier incarnation of the Blackstones. "There was a time if Chief Malik asked any group to come to the table—it wasn't an option to say no. I mean it's like being at the lowest level, like being in the mob, and Al Capone saying I need you to have dinner with me," Minister Michael Muhammad said.

About one hundred soldiers came, including the first and second in command in each organization. Those dozens of leaders met at the table. Most of them were not formally educated, but they were spiritual and not motivated by money, according to Muhammad. He said he was the only non-street gang representative. The concept was to solidify the organizations for one agenda along the lines of community and culture.

Nothing came out of that meeting, even though a press conference followed where claims of a truce between gang factions had been called and fiery talk about protecting the community was delivered. There are a couple of reasons why no follow-through happened: egos and beefs got in the way. "It's impossible to talk about these results," Muhammad says of the meeting outcome, "without talking about the federal government. The effort never got a chance to lay a good foundation or get set because that's when the feds started moving harder against the El Rukns."

## The Temple

THE SUNDAY AFTER Qaddafi's NOI Saviour's Day performance at the Armory, Father George Clements told his South Side Catholic church that he supported the efforts of the Nation of Islam, but he rejected Qaddafi's call for black America to form a separate state. Clements's sermon to the worshippers at Holy Angels Church directly responded to the Libyan dictator's message. "Our problems will never be solved by our sons and nephews facing court-martial for deserting the army and navy. Our problems are never going to be solved by taking up machine guns and grenades and trying to blow this land up. Our problems are never going to be solved by waiting around for Khadafy [sic] to supply us with military hardware to strike out against this increasingly racist nation," Clements told his flock, according to the *Chicago Tribune*.

The black priest was part of a politically active group of Chicago clergymen, and Clements had to mind what the El Rukns got up to because of proximity. Clements led a parish on Oakwood Boulevard, two blocks west of the El Rukn headquarters.

Located at 3947 South Drexel, The Fort became the El Rukns' headquarters around 1977. Police officers and news media often camped out at the organization's epicenter, the former waiting for the next bust, and the latter waiting to film it. The Fort bustled with incongruent activity: disco, an arsenal for weapons, mosque services on Fridays. There were pay phones and private phone lines. The Bamboo Room offered solitude. Phase II was a room for generals, ambassadors, or souls. The Cabar Room was a meeting space on Friday holy days. Chief Malik sat on a throne made of wood. Women were referred to as Moabites, and they had a midnight oasis room. The front of The Fort had a steel door with three bolted locks on the inside. A steel shutter covered a window. To gain entrance, one would ring a bell—if no police were around and the guest was legitimate, that person was let in. On Fridays and Saturdays, parties lasted until sunrise.

Formerly the Oakland Square Theater, The Fort was in the North Kenwood-Oakland community. The neighborhood had transformed from white to black after white flight. In the late 1960s, the building became the Affro-Arts Theatre, a space that showcased the talents of Chicago's black cultural nationalist community. Musicians Oscar Brown Jr. and Kelan Phil Cohran had worked with the Blackstones artistically at the theater in the late 1960s. In a way, the El Rukns returned to their roots when they bought and transformed the building into their temple headquarters. The surrounding community had lapsed into blight and poverty, which naturally made it an ignored community.

The Fort stressed an already distressed neighborhood. Drugs and crime riddled the nearby Ida B. Wells–Darrow–Madden Park Homes public housing complex. Residents had mixed feelings about the foreboding El Rukn presence and its headquarters. Emma McDaniel recalls how the perceptions of The Fort didn't always match reality in Mary Pattillo's *Black on the Block: The Politics of Race and Class in the City*. "All of our kids would go down there [The Fort] and nobody would get hurt. . . . And, honey, I was leery at first, you know. Because, doggone, my kids are like, 'Can we go down to the El Rukn party?' . . . And after they went one time, oh well, we knew every weekend that's where they was going. And they would go down there and dance and get together and come back and everything was OK." Some mothers thought the El Rukns protected their sons from gangs. On the other hand, resident Jerome Green had a less auspicious view of the organization. "They would actually break into people's apartments and beat up on them and things of that nature," he told Pattillo.

At the Wells development, some children were thrown down elevator chutes, fires destroyed units, and drug paraphernalia littered the area. Drug overdoses and violence shook the whole neighborhood. About 30 percent of the student body of Holy Angels came from public housing. Students sometimes faced harassment on their way to school. A group of teens who called themselves the Pebbles (a Stone affiliation) routinely bullied the Holy Angels students for lunch money or would chase them down the street. Fights broke out. Rampant drug use and drug selling left a stain, though it cannot all be traced back to The Fort or the El Rukns. Nonetheless, Father Clements saw the El Rukns as a powerful force in the community that could assuage the fears of children and their parents. And perhaps shield them from El Rukn activity. He came up with a plan in 1978.

"I decided to get a detente, a peaceful situation," Clements says. "So I confronted Jeff and some of his top people—told him I would offer to not go public about what they're doing if they would guarantee me that our kids would not be harassed. And they agreed. I stopped saying anything public about them and our kids were safe." Clements remembers being a little surprised that the El Rukns kept their word. "Every time I saw him [Jeff] I was amazed they would follow this nerdy-looking guy. He was short, he wasn't fierce-looking at all. It was amazing he could commandeer their attention. I always felt like he was kind of impressed that I would come and deal with him."

Clements said Fort showed respect in the meeting. Over the years Clements stood up to drug dealers in the community. When one of his valedictorians died of a heroin overdose, Clements turned his sadness and outrage into political mobility. In the 1980s, he went after nearby stores that sold syringes and freebase kits. He got legislation passed that shut those stores down. Clements's work garnered him national attention—and a made-for-television movie in 1987. Lou Gossett Jr. starred as the plucky priest in *The Father Clements Story*.

## The Rangerettes

**BACK IN THE 1960s** the girlfriends and female associates of the Blackstone Rangers christened themselves the Rangerettes. Although they could be considered a girl gang in their own right, they weren't as organized as the boys. They were more like fraternity sweethearts than a sorority. The Rangerettes hung out with the Stones in the neighborhood, at First Presbyterian, at the pool hall, and in various other locations. They went to the neighborhood parties. Some of them wore Rangers jackets to the parties. While they weren't involved in any of the Rangers' crime or fights with other gangs, they did fight a lot with other non-Rangerette girls. Most of these fights consisted of Rangerettes fighting other girls who dated the Rangers.

Tall, beautiful Penny Brown was president of the Rangerettes and considered the toughest girl in the group. Her sister, Diane, married Jeff Fort and became the mother of most of his children. The Stones didn't believe that the Rangerettes had a role in their affairs above and beyond companionship. Fort felt that the role of his woman was to take care of his home and children. His role was to be the provider for the family. He felt women had no role in the affairs of the organization.

Brown and the Rangerettes once got word that Pam Valenzuela, a neighborhood girl, claimed to be pregnant by Fort. The Rangerettes took it upon themselves to confront Valenzuela to take back her claim. It didn't work. She did have Fort's baby, Watketa "Keeta" Valenzuela, who rose to be the Prince of the Black P Stone Nation.

Valerie Mays made the shift from Rangerette to El Rukn princess; her title came via marriage to an El Rukn general. Born a Baptist, she read the Qur'an in the late 1970s. "But the Moorish religion didn't make any sense to me, so I just played the role. I could kick any lesson." She decided just to go along with the program, fueled by childhood loyalties from her days growing up in Woodlawn. Her brothers were Stones and El Rukns.

She wore the Muslim-style garments and head wraps. "I would go to service and stand in that circle. As soon as service was over, I was almost like Wonder Woman, running to the bathroom to change clothes." Sometimes her telephone booth transformation took place in a McDonald's bathroom where she put on T-shirts and gym shoes. She often carried a nine-millimeter in her purse, and sold and used drugs. (Mays caught a case with Fort's now-deceased son Antonio. She did two years beginning in 1992 for possessing a kilo of coke.)

While playing the role, Mays started to get a bad taste. One time during a service at The Fort, she and her sister noticed Jeff and his wife sporting minks. Members were supposed to give money to the "uplifting funds" on Sunday. That was it for Princess Valerie and her sister Princess Brenda. "We ain't finna buy them no more minks," they declared. No one paid attention anyway, she says.

In the El Rukn hierarchy, women were supposed to be seen, not heard. Hee-hawing with other women was discouraged. "Only decisions women would make was what was gonna be damned cooked on feast day. I wasn't cooking," Mays says. Women were supposed to leave the room when men entered. Mays says she ignored those edicts. One time it got her suspended for ninety days when word got back to Fort that Mays had smacked her aunt during a family row. Mays says she talked on the phone with Fort the next day. He was ready to amend her censure. "You know what?" Mays recalls telling the leader. "I don't think I'm coming back. You did me a favor. I was living two lives anyway." She still stopped by The Fort and remained loyal, but she shunned the formalities. Once she made the decision, Mays instructed her sister "to come to my house and get that shit out of my closet." She was done with the El Rukn attire.

## The Chase

IN EARLY FEBRUARY 1982, police arrested Fort—for the third time in four months—in an overnight raid at his Woodlawn residence. Police said they found twenty-six high-powered weapons, over a pound of marijuana, a quarter ounce of cocaine, and about four thousand dollars in cash. The previous arrests had been for concealing a fugitive and obstruction of justice. Fort was released on a sixty-five-thousand-dollar bond.

Several months later, thirty-nine police officers with police dogs raided The Fort. One can only imagine an onlooker's view of the dramatic scene. A helicopter circled and a fire department hook and ladder unit pulled up. The police first rang the doorbell. Someone peered through the peephole but walked away. When no one answered, officers tried to burn the steel door with a torch. When that didn't work, officers used the hook and ladder unit to hoist themselves to the second-floor window. They entered, came downstairs, and unlocked the front door. Police arrested two people; they seized two Thompson submachine guns, a twelve-gauge shotgun, marijuana, and cocaine. The police commander said that the raid was conducted based on information gathered from people who claimed there were machine guns in the temple.

These two incidents—and there were many others—demonstrated the long-running serial between the police and El Rukns. Raids, arrests, charges, and bonds. Repeat. A number of forces convened to shut down the El Rukns—from Washington, D.C., to South Side informants—reminiscent of the campaign of the 1960s. The Cook County state's attorney's office filed lawsuits to recover back taxes on property owned by the El Rukns. The office also challenged the sale of the organization's headquarters because it said a shady deal allowed for no property taxes to be paid. The state's attorney wrote a letter to a judge that said the following: "Jeff Fort and his entourage, known as the El Rukns, have developed into the single most dangerous street gang in Cook County. Their activities include murder, robbery, prostitution, the sale of narcotics, the intimidation of witnesses and fraudulent and coercive real estate transactions." (Richard M. Daley, future mayor and son of Richard J. Daley, became state's attorney in the 1980s.) Chicago police got some help in their El Rukn chase, which was too much for local authorities to handle. The timing couldn't have been better for Chicago law enforcement when the political climate in Washington, D.C., shifted. In 1982, the Organized Crime Drug Enforcement Task Force (OCDETF) started as a broad interagency attack on drug trafficking and money laundering. Housed in the DEA, the task force comprised the FBI, Immigration, the ATF, the U.S. Marshals Service, and the IRS. Agents were looking for possible violations of the Racketeering Influenced and Corrupt Organizations Act. Congress had enacted RICO in 1970 to fight organized crime and the mob. Officials realized that they could use the law beyond that scope, and in the 1980s street gangs increasingly saw RICO charges leveled against members. The government justified using RICO by arguing each of those events was committed to attain power, control, and wealth for a criminal street gang.

Prosecutors connected the El Rukns to a sweeping plan to distribute hundreds of pounds of various illicit drugs. The defendants unsuccessfully challenged the RICO conspiracy.

The federal task force initiative launched between two major drug signposts in this country: First Lady Nancy Reagan's vapid "Just Say No" antidrug campaign targeting schoolchildren and the declaration of the War on Drugs. President Richard Nixon had declared the "war" in 1971 and established the DEA two years later. The rise of international drug cartels brought on widened accessibility to drugs and accompanying shoot-outs among major traffickers, which spilled into U.S. foreign policy. In 1981, Ronald Reagan, fresh in office, declared the drug war a priority. Public awareness had risen when large, multimillion-dollar cocaine seizures took place at U.S. airports and Miami residents began feeling the onslaught of drug violence in their port city.

Yet again, Fort found his organization smack in the middle of new federal policy. In the 1960s, it was the War on Poverty; now it was the War on Drugs.

Chicago police detective Richard Kolovitz and his high school best friend, Dan Brannigan, got assigned to the federal task force that went after the El Rukns. "It became very en vogue among police departments to do gang, to do the El Rukns—because we were getting headlines," Kolovitz recalls. What the Chicago Police Department couldn't give, they got from the task force. In this unit they received financing, cars, and overtime. At one point Kolovitz and Brannigan were sworn in as deputy U.S. marshals to give them greater authority. They even had money to relocate informants who testified and gave consequential tips against the El Rukns. Informants also bought drugs, but not in large enough quantities to cause suspicion. Kolovitz, who's rare on niceties about the other federal agents, said the DEA didn't want to be involved with the El Rukns because there wasn't enough drug weight.

"There aren't going to be no monster weight in the gang, because you cannot send an informant in to buy dope and say, 'Listen, I've got some street thug and he's going to walk in [and] buy three, four, five, ten kilos.' They'll shoot him and rob him, which they are notorious [for] doing." And officers couldn't conduct buys because the dealers wouldn't do business with strangers. Kolovitz said the unit would send in the informants for dope buys a few times before cracking down with an arrest. That kept the Cook County state's attorney's office happy.

There were some foils in this operation. Kolovitz said authorities set up a dummy jewelry show at a convention center so they could hire the El Rukn–owned security firm. The guards came, showed their guns, and filled out faux paperwork. Law enforcement used the caper to get information from members. No felony arrests came out of it, and Kolovitz admitted that most of the guards weren't even El Rukns.

Kolovitz and company kept tabs on the El Rukns as they built cases for prosecution. Officers worked twenty-four-hour shifts to watch El Rukn buildings. Authorities said that Fort formed a group within the organization called the Key Soldiers or the Thirty Soldiers to provide security for various El Rukn–controlled buildings, sell narcotics, and protect lower-level street workers from rival drug dealers. This cat-and-mouse cycle was all part of the game. "The thing is, is that we had an understanding with Jeff," Kolovitz says. "Jeff had us followed, Danny [Brannigan] and I followed. They followed us several times. We had discussions with Jeff over the situation, and he understood it. Business is business and don't make it personal. It was an understanding we had; we had several conversations with him over it." He acquiesced that he had a formidable enemy in Fort. Then Kolovitz adds, as if he were being too generous in his assessment, "His intelligence lies in the good used-car salesman, for lack of a better way of putting it. [He'll] sell you a pile of crap."

Fort turned himself in to begin a ninety-day sentence at Cook County jail in June 1983. The charges were obstruction of justice and concealing a fugitive. Six police detectives watched Fort surrender. "I came to wave good-bye," said Edward Paleinef, a gang crimes unit commander at the time. He said Fort had previously told him, "You'll never put me in jail."

But Fort had a bigger quandary coming up, a Mississippi mess.

Prosecutors indicted Fort, Henry Timothy, and William Doyle on federal narcotics and racketeering charges while the men were already in the county jail. Mississippi authorities had arrested Timothy and Doyle that spring on charges of conspiracy to possess marijuana and distribute cocaine. The duo were allegedly carrying two hundred grams of coke. They got caught from a wiretap run by narcotics agents. They allegedly had phone conversations with a man in Chicago named Angel—Fort's nickname. Prosecutors said El Rukns made several trips to Mississippi to buy marijuana to sell in Chicago. Kolovitz says Fort, a Mississippi native, once traveled there to attend his grandfather's funeral and took care of drug business as a bonus. The drug connection he made happened to be with an undercover informant. The conspiracy said that Fort, in Chicago, arranged with Bill Marshall, in Tupelo, Mississippi, to exchange eight ounces of coke and $18,750 from Fort for one hundred pounds of marijuana from Marshall. Marshall, a Mississippi Bureau of Narcotics agent, posed as a drug dealer nicknamed Tank. After this conversation, Doyle and Timothy traveled to Mississippi. They met Marshall in a Ramada Inn for the exchange.

This arrest was not a planned drug task force operation. Kolovitz said a friend of his in the Mississippi narcotics department called bragging about the two Chicago fellows he had arrested—Doyle and Henry. The detective recognized the names. "Well, my little half-Irish dick got hard," Kolovitz says. He said Fort's weed connection had caught a case and turned to work for the narcotics agent. The connection hooked Fort up with Marshall, and Marshall called the provided phone number and asked for Angel. Marshall could be heard on the phone saying, "I hope you don't mind, I'm white." Kolovitz listened to the tape. "Holy fuck! That's Jeff," he said after recognizing the voice. The next morning Kolovitz and one of the task force members grabbed their badges and hit the road in ATF cars for Tupelo.

When Fort finished his ninety-day stint in Cook County, the feds greeted him. Kolovitz took him to Mississippi to face the drug charges. It was their last interaction. The feds rented a prop jet out of Meigs Field, a small airport on Lake Michigan. Kolovitz says that during the flight he leaned over to Fort. "I said, 'Jeff, look out the window,' because we flew over 39th Street. 'Look out, Jeff, you are never going to see the South Side again.' And Jeff doesn't swear as a rule." But Kolovitz says Fort broke his tenet and lobbed back, "Fuck you, Kolovitz." The detective resumed antagonizing Fort by saying, "I'll take care of Mama." Fort retorted, "Fuck you," again.

In late August, Fort and the other two defendants pled not guilty to the federal drug charges in an Oxford, Mississippi, courtroom. Later the underlings took a plea. The trial got under way that fall. Fort stunned the courtroom one morning by pleading guilty to the conspiracy charge to deliver drugs. Kolovitz said the change of heart came when several people came in and identified Fort's voice. "The judge, like an idiot, gave him time to spread out." A few weeks later, in November, Fort failed to appear for his sentencing and a warrant was issued for his arrest.

Fort's lawyer said an anonymous caller had phoned him with the news that Fort would not be appearing for the sentencing. His fifty-thousand-dollar cash bond was forfeited along with the balance on the five-hundred-thousand-dollar bond. The rumor is that Fort fled to Pakistan during this period. In the middle of December, Fort turned himself in and a U.S. District Court judge sentenced him to thirteen years.

## Crack Comes to Chicago

CRACK DEVELOPED IN the early 1980s as a cheaper, stronger form of cocaine. It hit California first as a way to freebase safely. By 1985 the drug had gained national attention and began its cruel, addictive, violent choke hold on American inner cities.

Not in Chicago. Not yet.

Rudy Nimocks, a Woodlawn resident who ranked high in the Chicago Police Department, said he and other officers initially worried when stories about crack surfaced. "We had info that some gangs in Chicago were resisting the importation of crack cocaine because of competition of heroin and marijuana," Nimocks says. Crack was also unfamiliar at the time, and dealers may simply not have known how to handle it. But just like fashion and music sometimes come late to the Midwest, so do drugs. Crack came to Chicago amid the hysteria but didn't really hit hard until the early 1990s.

Residents took note, too. Michelle Campbell lived in north Kenwood-Oakland. She told Mary Pattillo in *Black on the Block*: "The El Rukns kept it more safer so far as keeping drugs out of the neighborhood. You know, they sold, I think they allowed for them to sell marijuana, but it wasn't cocaine. It wasn't crack cocaine in the neighborhood."

Kelan Phil Cohran, the musician who had worked with the Stones back in the 1960s, said the El Rukns had a vision to improve black people. "Everyone knows the El Rukns was about family. I always supported them. I think they ran drugs out of town. They ran the crack people out."

Lance's research years ago led him to a guy from Los Angeles nicknamed Freeway, who said he first brought crack cocaine to Chicago. He got his name from being a member of Ricky Ross's Los Angeles street gang called the Freeway Boys. Originally from Chicago, Freeway went to live with relatives in L.A. after being kicked out of Kenwood High School for getting caught smoking weed in the washroom. He was a tennis player. When he got to California and started playing tennis for his high school team, he met a young man named Ricky Ross, one of the top high school tennis players in L.A. Ross played tennis by day and stole cars by night. Ross was so good at tennis that several colleges offered him scholarships to play. However, the colleges later found out that Ross could barely read so they withdrew their scholarship offers. With no future in tennis,

Ross resorted to his next best strength—hustling. His high school tennis coach had a cocaine habit that he fed by selling cocaine. He turned Ross on to the hustle, and before too long the legendary Ross was the champion of selling cocaine just like he was once the man in tennis. Ross found a connection to purchase cheap Nicaraguan cocaine from two Nicaraguans, Oscar Danilo Blandon and Norwin Meneses Cantarero. This cheap cocaine became known as "crack" cocaine. Ross made plenty of cash selling the new drug to L.A. gangs. Ross got so big that he built a drug-distribution network across the country including Texas, Seattle, New Orleans, Oklahoma, Kansas City, St. Louis, Indiana, Minneapolis, Cincinnati, Cleveland, South Carolina, and Baltimore. This is the same Rick Ross from whom the popular rapper took his moniker.

Freeway joined the ranks of thousands who worked for his high school tennis buddy selling crack across the country. Freeway said that since he came from Chicago, he talked Ross into allowing him to be the first to set up distribution in his hometown in the mid-1980s. Having gone to Kenwood High School, he knew a lot of El Rukns because they were strong in the communities not far from the school. He also knew the El Rukns had the syrup (codeine) and weed markets on lock, so he approached them about distributing this new drug. He said they had no interest at all. Undeterred, Freeway set up shop on his own. In less than a day, he said, he got a visit from some of his El Rukn buddies, who told him that not only was he to stop serving, he shouldn't be seen again in Chicago unless he wanted to be killed. He knew what time it was and immediately headed back to L.A. When asked if the El Rukns refused to distribute crack because they were protecting the black community, he laughed. He said the El Rukns only wanted to protect their control of their drug market. He said they wanted complete control of the distribution and selling of the product and since they didn't have the direct connection to the source, they wouldn't let it happen at all. Their decision not to sell crack was strictly business, not moral, according to Freeway.

The El Rukns inhabited the drug world, but their narcotic trade of choice was a drug known on the streets as Ts or Blues, a mixture of the prescription painkiller Talwin and a blue antihistamine tablet called Tripelennamine. When crushed together and injected, the drug provides a heroin-like rush, but it was much cheaper.

Several reputed El Rukns landed in the court system over the drug trade and the accompanying violence. Fort's brother Andrew was convicted of killing the brother of a suspected El Rukn drug competitor. El Rukn Alvin Toney received consecutive sentences of forty years for murder and attempted murder after he opened fire in a Harold's Chicken Shack. El Rukn James Walker missed the death penalty that prosecutors had sought, but a jury convicted him of triple murder. Walker insisted he belonged to a religious group, but the judge gave him life in prison. The judge said he spared his life because of Walker's background as a former Northeastern Illinois University student and youth center worker.

The drug task force got a break in its RICO strategy in 1985. A high-ranking El Rukn flipped as an informant and gave information on the organization—eliciting glee from the Cook County state's attorney. The thirty-two-year-old high school dropout was the first El Rukn who could give testimony about murders to ever cooperate with authorities. "This is the most significant break [against Fort] since Fort went to the federal penitentiary in the 1960s," said assistant state's attorney Larry Wharrie. Before this break, the authorities had hit brick walls. The informant gave testimony on several unsolved murder cases. Among them was the 1981 killing of a rival drug dealer who had shown disrespect to the El Rukns by mimicking them. The informant said El Rukns killed two men in spring 1985 who'd had a drug operation directly across the street from The Fort.

Buoyed by their penetration into the El Rukn organization, prosecutors used the opening to destabilize Fort's muscle from his prison cell. If they could nab him on murder and/or drug charges, he'd face additional years on top of the thirteen he was already serving. When Fort was transferred from Mississippi to Bastrop, Texas, authorities succeeded in getting a wiretap put on Fort's phone at the federal prison. Agents listening in on those calls soon claimed that they heard new code words that had nothing to do with drugs.

As Fort was biding his time in federal prison, he remained at the helm of the powerful El Rukn enterprise. Like any other inmate, he had telephone privileges that allowed him to make collect calls. Using a combination of black dialect, street slang, and some coded terms, Fort communicated his orders to the El Rukn leadership. Prison officials, who were mostly white, couldn't understand Fort's communication. Law enforcement listening to those calls concluded that Fort directed narcotics, murders, and the organization. One newspaper article called him the "crafty El Rukns" chief for whom prison had never been much more than a minor inconvenience. That was the same attitude law enforcement had held about Fort when he was in prison.

Also, Fort had learned about the five-million-dollar loan Qaddafi had bestowed upon Farrakhan and the Nation of Islam, and he started to make his own plans. Federal authorities scurried to prepare another wave of indictments in a case that had much bigger implications than drug trafficking. It would lay the foundation for linking American street gangs to homegrown terrorism.

# 8

# Qaddafi and the Domestic Terrorism Trial

IN JUNE 1986, ex-con/police informant/coke 'n' dope dealer Sam Buford, also known as Black Magic and Magic Man, made an introduction. He hooked up El Rukn Alan Knox with an undercover FBI special agent named Willie T. Hulon. The trio sipped drinks at the Southern Girl Lounge on East 39th Street and negotiated a cocaine deal; Hulon bought half an ounce from Knox. Later Hulon told Knox about a friend who worked at an army base down South who stole bulletproof vests. That intrigued Knox, who asked whether this friend could also get a grenade launcher. Knox had seen this weapon used by Clint Eastwood in the movie *The Enforcer* to shoot a man off a tower. Hulon promised he would check on it.

A month later Hulon had the goods.

Hulon, Buford, and undercover FBI special agent James Cross waited in a room on the second floor of a Holiday Inn in Lansing, Illinois, a suburb south of Chicago. That night Knox arrived with El Rukn general Melvin Mays. There was a lot of back-and-forth about money, a viewing of Polaroids of the rockets, and talk of possibly purchasing additional weapons. Knox mentioned he had an enemy who owned a building, and he wanted to blow it up. Cross and Hulon exchanged looks. Knox assured them, "But you don't have to worry. I'm going to wait about a year before I can blow anything up." Meanwhile, Mays left to get money and returned ninety minutes later. They paid nineteen hundred dollars for the M-72 Series Light Anti-Tank Weapon. Knox took the rocket launcher downstairs to a car in the hotel parking lot. What the El Rukns did not know was that the rocket was inert.

Another El Rukn associate put the weapon in the trunk of a car and drove it to an apartment building in Woodlawn known as the Hut or the African Hut. Several days later, police raided the building. And thus the penultimate episode of the El Rukns began.

**THE LAW** ROCKET became the linchpin for the feds in their long-running pursuit of Jeff Fort. It built the case for the 1987 *United States v. Jeff Fort et al.* trial. Alan Knox ("General Gangster," "General Gangs," "G.G."), Melvin Mays ("Maumee," "Mau"), Reico Cranshaw ("General Rico," "Amir Rico"), Leon McAnderson ("Officer Mufti Exec"), and Tramell Davis ("Tacu," "General Tacu," "Amir Tacu," "Ta") joined Fort as defendants in this domestic terrorism trial. They collectively faced fifty counts in the September 1986 indictment. Federal prosecutors argued that Fort masterminded a deal—while serving time in Bastrop, Texas, on a drug conviction—to commit acts of terrorism in the United States on behalf of the government of Libya for $2.5 million. The charges detailed phone calls and meetings in Libya and Panama regarding getting the money. Law enforcement posited that Fort had broken ties with Louis Farrakhan because the Nation of Islam minister wouldn't share any of the money he'd received from Qaddafi with the El Rukns. Police culled all this information and interpreted it from wiretaps.

"Wiretaps were initially obtained based on an ongoing drug business being operated by the El Rukns with Jeff Fort at the helm," Fort prosecutor Susan Bogart says. Those wiretaps produced hours upon grueling hours of tape recordings in a code that would have confounded the sharpest CIA operative. "There was a code relating to drug activity and law enforcement was deciphering this code when coded words that were unfamiliar arose and, which, when deciphered, revealed the [terrorism] conspiracy," the former assistant U.S. attorney says. And it wasn't a wunderkind government code breaker but an El Rukn turncoat, Tramell Davis, who helped the government with its playbook.

The trial began in October 1987. Mays was, at the time, on the lam. Davis cut a deal. Roosevelt Hawkins joined the defendants for his alleged role in transporting the LAW rocket. The government was convinced that Libya, an enemy of the state, had lured this street gang into the arms of terrorism. But there was no proof that money ever changed hands between the El Rukns and Libya. No explosives were launched. No buildings or airplanes were blown up, either. None of the men who visited Libya, according to the prosecution's time line, were the same El Rukns who met at Southern Girl Lounge or the Holiday Inn. The defense's riposte was that Fort sought money as a mosque leader trying to build a bigger temple and grow his religious flock. The defendants also unsuccessfully argued that they were victims of entrapment.

The trial—taking place before the age of the twenty-four-hour news cycle, cable talking-head analysts, witty bloggers, and camera flashes from the paparazzi—proved to be sensational for its time. The trial also pulled the curtain back on some of the inner workings, language, and culture of the El Rukns, which had turned into a menacing household name in the Chicago area.

And it wasn't cheap. The trial cost an estimated half a million dollars; over half went toward security.

**THE JURY DID** not relate to Jeff Fort.

El Rukns crammed the courtroom in a powerful show of support for their Chief Malik. They wore white prayer caps and sunglasses. Metal detectors greeted entrants at the door, and King, an Illinois state police dog, sniffed spectators for explosives. Federal security guards stood inside. All of this pageantry was arguably not hyperbolic. Some jurors said they had received threatening phone calls during the trial, and several alternates were forced to step in as replacements. The jury was sequestered during the trial due to threats. The judge ordered jury members to have no more than two drinks per night. They couldn't use the telephone without permission, and a U.S. marshal read all of their mail.

During the trial, Fort and the defendants wore religious garb and beards. Reporters noted Fort's legendary intimidating stare, which he imposed upon the press and visitors. "Fort drills holes through everyone in the courtroom. His head never moves, but the eyes dart about until they lock in on a victim. Like a pit bull, they don't let go," observed two *Chicago Sun-Times* reporters. At one point the judge granted the government's motion to ban someone from the courtroom and the federal building. A marshal testified that the man sat on a bench close to the aisle and got Fort's attention. The marshal said that Fort made a gesture with his fingers on either side of his nose. The man nodded his head, and Fort gestured some more. Upon witnessing the exchange, the marshal had the man removed from the courtroom. Fort denied, through his attorney, any gesturing or signaling. The judge and prosecution kept a cautious watch over the defendants throughout the court case.

Terry Gillespie represented Fort at the trial. "It would've been very difficult twenty-five years ago for a jury not to be threatened by that scenario," says Gillespie, reflecting on his former client. "It was primarily black men in a Muslim-type organization. Very secretive, supposedly very militant." Gillespie surely suggested that Fort don a suit and tie during the trial as a humble nod to the jury and a signal to the judge that he understood the gravity of the circumstances. Naturally, any such suggestion fell on deaf ears; his client marched to his own drummer as he had throughout his life. Fort wore a white prayer cap and flowing, colorful robes. Chief Malik dressed the part as revered leader to his El Rukn congregation, an image that dovetailed with his defense. It didn't matter if the jury interpreted his

aesthetic as that of a solemn man. If Islam seems foreign to mainstream America today, it was quite the exotic religion in 1987. The
prosecution curiously asked questions such as What does *salaam alai-
kum* mean? What is Ramadan? What is an imam?

Gillespie pegged the trial as problematic from jump, and Fort
never considered taking a plea. It just wasn't an option, Gillespie says.
Prosecutors displayed weapons and machine guns as evidence. They
played clips from the Clint Eastwood movie. "The content of the
case and allegations of the case were so sensational. The allegations
and physical evidence they brought in [were] so sensationalist," says
Gillespie. Each of the defense attorneys routinely objected whenever drugs and guns dominated direct examination testimony. They
kept reminding the judge, and later the jury, that the case was about
conspiracy to commit terrorism, not drugs and guns. That frustration gnawed at the entire defense team. In one exasperated moment,
Reico Cranshaw's attorney objected when a witness went into detail
about where cocaine was stored at The Fort.

"At the risk of saying, those who trudge up the long, weary road
to Calgary with me shall share in its glory, we have been through this,
Judge," attorney Rick Halprin complained to federal judge Charles
Norgle. "I thought you had ruled, and I thought the government
understood and we had understood, that this was not going to be
permitted into evidence any more, these blanket assertions as to narcotics." The defense then collectively, as they did many times during
the trial, asked for a mistrial. And, as usual, the request was denied.
And one wonders if Halprin, or the court reporter, meant the long
Biblical road to Calvary.

But the government had found a star witness with whom they cut
a deal: Tramell Davis. After his arrest on August 5, 1986, Davis did
not initially cooperate with law enforcement. After the FBI told him
that his wife could be charged, he changed his tune. Then he said he
hadn't told the FBI the whole truth. He had omitted the explosives
and the relationship with Libya. The terms of Davis's plea agreement
required full cooperation, and in turn the feds gave ten thousand

dollars to Davis's family. Davis pled to three counts: racketeering, conspiracy, and receipt of the LAW rocket. He said he spent five hundred dollars on himself and the rest went to his wife and seven children for bills and relocation. Davis became the passport to the land of El Rukn. He had a glass eye and wore dark brown–tinted sunglasses in court. It was rough being a government witness. During the trial two of his sisters-in-law were shot and wounded by a masked assailant in front of a public housing development. A U.S. attorney said the shootings weren't connected to the trial, but the *Sun-Times* reported that one police investigator felt it could've been an attempt at intimidation by El Rukn supporters. And, citing alleged threats, inmates at a suburban jail asked authorities to separate them from Davis; they even presented the jail with 227 signatures.

In court, Davis refuted that the code words were masked religious principles.

Prosecutor Bogart asked him, "Mr. Davis, is the principal purpose of the El Rukn organization a religious purpose?"

"No, ma'am," Davis replied.

"What, from your viewpoint, is the principal purpose of the El Rukn organization?" Bogart asked.

"They are most like—they be practicing Islam. But then in another way, they do other things. It's just like a cover-up . . . doing things illegal and stuff," Davis explained. He described distributing cocaine and being number three in command for the organization. And Davis sold himself as the Rosetta stone for interpreting the El Rukn language.


## Grape Manifestations

FORT'S TIGHT-KNIT organization had its own tongue.

It was English but not really. It was a carefully constructed argot. Synonyms didn't have obvious meanings. *Oatmeal* meant cocaine or one million dollars. *Star* meant money. *Palm justice* meant a handgun.

A favorite phrase was *demonstration*, which could be a noun, adjective, or verb. As in "need more demonstrations [pistols with silencers] like the current one as it does not make much noise." "Na, based on the fact that he demonstrated with our young friend there. Nam. That's, we drawin' that's the demonstration, but he was drawin' that we should, ah, he's preparing now and some demonstrations in the science of how they going to reachin' for one in, in the name of like that twelve man type demonstration there." This example also points toward other favorite language staples—*drawing* and *the science of*. Put all together, there were sentences like "In the science of star where you know, where all where . . . where you brothers could . . . get in full manifest." Some meanings triggered a chuckle. *That actor* or *Cleemonkey* was Ronald Reagan. Police officers were the *gentile chumps*. They also sprinkled the five El Rukn principles in their speech: love, truth, peace, freedom, and justice. Sometimes it sounded like bad poetry: "Love, time never was, a love, circle peace." The translation? The terms were numbers: 1-(7+1)-0, a phone code. *Grape* was often the number ten. The El Rukns liked other pieces of fruit—*tangerines, oranges*—to express dollar amounts. *Manifestation* was another crutch word that often popped up. The jury listened to excerpts of the tapes and were given handy translation sheets. They were often reminded that the translation CliffsNotes were not evidence, only the tapes.

The wiretaps came from collect calls and pay phones at The Fort. Fort's code name sometimes was *Mr. Wood* or *the N*, and the feds contended that he communicated often with his faithful followers, never relinquishing control of the El Rukn organization while incarcerated. It appeared that Fort had a carte blanche deal to use the phone while in prison. In a bit of irony, at the federal facility, a plaque above the phone reminded inmates that phone calls could be recorded.

Bogart alluded to flagged code words beyond the scope of drugs in the vast El Rukn investigation. Those key words were *peanut* or *pecan* and *young friend* or *our friend*. The former referred to Farrakhan and the latter meant Qaddafi, according to government analysis.

Fort dissed Farrakhan as someone with a lot of bark but no bite that would translate into real assistance. It was a mistake on the part of the Libyans to think Farrakhan was a real warrior! Fort threw salt on the minister receiving that unrestricted five million without having to do anything in exchange. "But we know Pecan can't wasn't [*sic*] a live soldier from jump," Fort told McAnderson via phone. "He's a good mouthpiece, but he's not a live soldier." McAnderson chimed in, "That's right, yes, sir."

The El Rukns could certainly do better, Fort believed; if they had received that kind of money, the organization would have already mobilized black Americans. In recorded phone conversations, the government picked up on Fort's adulation of Qaddafi: "We admire our friend a whole lot because you know, you know, he remind us of ourself and our tribe." Fort instructed that the El Rukns needed to support Qaddafi by making a video as an overture. They needed to show Libyans that they would help in any way they could in the international clash the country had with the United States.

However, Fort said something else about needing *star* (money) in the wiretap, which the prosecution did not mention. The string of sentences intimated black economic self-sufficiency. Fort said: "You know, but the bottom line, brothers, is that us we need to, we need support, we need star support that we could be able to set up a, a economic base, uh, to where we could a ourself [*sic*] support, get our people off into a self suppostin [*sic*] type demonstration, that's what we need."

Whatever kind of relationship that Qaddafi actually had with the El Rukns, these tapes played directly into the hands of U.S. foreign policy.

## The United States and Qaddafi

PRESIDENT GEORGE W. BUSH took Libya off the United States' list of state sponsors of terrorism in 2006, partly because the Libyan government took some responsibility in the 1988 Pan Am airline crash over Scotland. But in 1980s Reagan-era parlance, Libya equaled terrorism, and that image dominated the decade and the American mind-set. It's easy to see how the feds and the police felt they had stumbled upon a wiretap windfall when they connected Fort to Libya.

But the two countries hadn't always shared a hostile relationship. In 1949, the United States and Libya signed promissory notes to establish a military base in Tripolitania. "From 1954 until 1971, the USA enjoyed a profitable presence in Libya through the Wheelus Air Force Base, 'a little America . . . on the sparkling shores of the Mediterranean.'" The United States paid an average of two million dollars a year to cash-strapped Libya for the largest U.S. base outside the continental United States. It was a training center for American and NATO pilots. Next, oil was discovered in Libya in 1959, and American companies benefited. The discovery dramatically changed Libya politically and economically. A social movement began among Libyans against the perceived occupation of foreign governments with military bases and the contradictions of the moneyed oil industry. That led to protests from students and intellectuals alike. Muammar el-Qaddafi's group staged a successful coup against the monarchy in 1969, and he assumed power.

Relations between the United States and Libya didn't immediately turn sour. The air force base was more about bombers, and the advent of nuclear missiles made Wheelus less important. The rickety relations surfaced when Qaddafi decided in the 1970s to partially nationalize the country's oil resources.

It didn't help that Libya supported the cause of Palestinian liberation and denounced Israel, a staunch U.S. ally. As detente diminished in the Cold War, Washington fumingly saw Libya align with the Soviet Union. Qaddafi sent troops to Uganda to support the tyrant Idi Amin. The United States gave aid to Tunisia when the North Africa country crossed swords with Libya. In 1979 the United States declared Libya a state sponsor of terrorism. In August 1981, two Libyan jets fired on a U.S. aircraft flying over Mediterranean seas claimed by Libya. The

U.S. planes returned fire and shot down the attacking aircraft. That same year, under newly elected president Ronald Reagan, the state department invalidated U.S. passports for travel to Libya and closed its embassy. Washington tried unsuccessfully to overthrow Qaddafi's government. That same year the U.S. Air Force shot down two Soviet-made Libyan fighters over the Gulf of Sidra; in 1982 Reagan imposed an embargo on oil imports from Libya and banned technology transfers to the country. The United States blamed Libya for the bombing of a German disco that Americans frequented. In response, in 1986, the United States bombed Libya, and Qaddafi's daughter was among the casualties in the carnage. The Libyan leader had a decidedly anti-American, pro-Arab, anti-Western stance. Previous U.S. presidents had ignored him. Not Reagan. He thought that Qaddafi epitomized third world leaders who had no respect for American power in the post-Vietnam era.

The El Rukns found themselves in the midst of a pissing match between two world leaders who harbored an intense disdain for each other. This is the cloud under which the El Rukns traveled to Libya. It wasn't a secret that some of them went. The prosecution had passport evidence. Nate Clay, a *Final Call* journalist, saw them in the capital city of Tripoli.

In the late 1970s Clay wrote a column for the Nation of Islam newspaper, and he was close to Farrakhan. He helped start another newspaper, the *Metro News*, on Chicago's South Side. Around 1985 he got to know some of the image-conscious El Rukns when they used to stop by the newspaper's office. Fort might've felt indebted to Clay—he tipped the mainstream media that Chicago police were busting into Fort's mother's house every day looking for Fort's brother. Clay said Fort called him from Texas to thank him. That's when the El Rukns started dropping in at Clay's office to show off a new and improved image and to demonstrate some gratitude toward him.

"They had tried to change from Blackstones to El Rukns and they were trying to project this notion that they were concerned about uplifting the community. But at the same time, as it turned out, that was nothing but a cover. This whole doctrine of Islam served as a shield. So they continued dealing drugs, and a lot of black folks fell for it." Clay admits he at first didn't buy the police's reasoning that the El Rukns' form of Islam was a front.

Clay had traveled for a conference of radicals—white Northeast liberals, members of the American Indian Movement, Black Nationalists—in Libya. He was there when the United States started dropping bombs on the Gulf of Sidra. Americans started rushing to get on the first available flights out. He said he didn't recall which El Rukns he saw in that Tripoli hotel lobby. "As I'm running out of the hotel, the El Rukns were sitting there in the lobby, casually just uninterested in the fact that place was being bombed. I said, 'Hey, aren't you guys leaving?' 'No [they said], we got business,'" Clay said. "Well, I didn't bother asking. I just wanted to get the hell out of there. So I didn't bother seeing what kind of business but I had come to find out later they were staying behind to meet Qaddafi."

## Key Witness

TRAMELL DAVIS JOINED the Blackstone Rangers in 1965 and stayed with the organization as it morphed into the El Rukns. Davis testified that from 1982 to 1986 he was in charge of security at The Fort. Either a .38 or a .45 stayed by his side. In the indictment, he was charged with participating in phone calls with Fort about explosives and obtaining money from Libya. Over several days of direct examination, the prosecution often asked for minutiae about the El Rukns to prove to the jury that he was entrenched in the organization. Davis recalled listening to Mays, Cranshaw, and McAnderson at The Fort talking about how they were going to get money from Qaddafi. Davis went into detail about various meanings from the wiretap: Qaddafi waiting to see the El Rukns, the El Rukns not backing down off their word to him. However, during many of the conversations Davis was not present.

He did recount being in a room with generals and ambassadors on April 10, 1986. Cranshaw and McAnderson handed them all cards to read aloud while being videotaped by Mays. Davis said the gist of the recital went along these lines, according to the trial transcripts: "'I'm brother Amin. I'm from New York City, and I have three hundred men behind me, and we pledge our support to our brother Moammar Khadafy [sic] of Libya. And we disapprove of what happened—what the United States had did.' And it was a little bit more to it, but I can't recall all of it." Davis testified that different men from different cities did the recitations.

He said he viewed the videotape that same night, and it had fifty-five testimonials with a picture of Fort on a throne and a poster of Qaddafi next to it. Davis also testified that Mays discussed with McAnderson knowing a person who could make explosives. This demonstration was meant to prove El Rukn muscle to Qaddafi so they could get a share of some money. The Libyans made arrangements for the El Rukns to visit.

Attorney Charles Knox ran a law school on the South Side of Chicago. The National College of Black Lawyers, an old converted mansion just a few blocks away from The Fort, was controversial because it had no accreditation and investigations alleged El Rukn business took place in the facility. Although Charles Knox—unrelated to defendant Alan Knox—wasn't charged in this federal case and didn't testify, he acted as a conduit. He apparently had conversations with Qaddafi and facilitated introductions. Davis said Charles Knox didn't know El Rukn code. (While he didn't get charged with terrorism, he was sentenced to three years in federal prison for impersonating a lawyer while trying to visit Fort in prison in 1987.)

When it was time for another El Rukn visit to Libya, the diplomatic strain between the country and the United States made it too tough to go. Davis said some El Rukns exchanged their tickets for Panama (code name *straw hat*) because it had the closest Libyan embassy.

Prosecutor Bogart asked Davis what kind of promises Cranshaw made to the Libyans after Cranshaw, McAnderson, and Charles Knox returned from Libya.

> Davis: "The Libyans was under the impression that Reico [Cranshaw] was going to do like the Libyans do."
> Bogart: "What was he saying he was going to do?"
> Davis: "Exactly what the Libyans do. The Libyans would be blowing up planes and stuff."
> Bogart: "Was there anything else said in connection with what Reico Cranshaw promised to the Libyans that the El Rukns would do?"
> Davis: "Just planting things around—no, planting explosives and stuff around different buildings and stuff like that there and on the airplane."

Davis said Fort gave instructions over the phone in June 1986 to send fifty El Rukns to Libya. Davis said he and others went to fill out passport applications. Fort wanted them to be able to travel back and forth effortlessly to Libya.

One day at The Fort, Davis claimed, Mays handed him a picture of a rocket with some explosives around it while talking on the phone with Jeff. Mays then talked in money code that added up to about the amount the El Rukns had paid for the LAW rocket at that Holiday Inn. Finally, there were instructions from Fort about what to pay, the hookup with Sam "Black Magic" Buford, and who would handle the rocket. When the El Rukns returned to the Hut, Davis saw them because he and his family lived there. Davis said that Mays then "just zipped up the bag and showed me—said he got that there, what he showed me on the pictures."

Bogart clarified Davis's testimony by asking, "When you say that, that there, what you saw in the picture, what are you referring to?" Davis answered, "The rocket."

The defense strategy sought to strip Davis of credibility and mention some of the positive activities the El Rukns did—delivering turkeys and food baskets during the holiday season, adhering to a pious Islamic way of life. Fort's lawyer Gillespie poked holes in Davis's story. In those early conversations with the FBI, Davis had told agents that the purpose of getting two million dollars from Libya was to build or renovate the mosque. He also told a U.S. attorney that he didn't know what the El Rukns were required to do for the Libyans in return for the two million. During cross-examination, Gillespie and Davis danced around this for a bit.

> Gillespie: "So, you lied then to the United States Attorney, is that right?"
> Davis: "I didn't tell the whole truth."
> Gillespie: "What do you say now you knew the two million dollars was to be for?"
> Davis: "I knew all along."

Gillespie also tried to raise doubt among jury members about Davis's knowledge of the El Rukn code. Davis admitted that he learned some words as late as 1987 while listening to tapes with government agents. And there were words that he either didn't know or became familiar with only by looking at the prosecution's book of terms. He also acknowledged that he read prosecutor notes in the margin of the wire transcripts while the tapes were playing. Gillespie pounced on that revelation during questioning.

> Gillespie: "And sometimes you were able to look at books for the testimony that's coming up, isn't that right, sir?"
> Davis: "Yes, sir."
> Gillespie: "And go over the testimony that's coming up and the words in the margin with the prosecutors, isn't that right, sir?"
> Davis: "Correct."

DAVIS NEVER HEARD Fort talk to Qaddafi or heard the Libyan leader's voice on tape or the phone. He did not see any money come into the organization from Libya. Gillespie characterized Davis as an opportunistic witness who had spent the last few months listening to the tapes as if he were cramming for a final exam. Gillespie pointed out how much time Davis spent talking to FBI agents, Chicago police, federal prosecutors, and ATF officials in the lead-up to the trial. The implication was that Davis became a government parrot who helped bring in a case against Fort—a case that government officials had been itching to bring home.

## An Opposing Witness

ONE DEFENDANT TOOK the stand to paint a different portrait of what it meant to be an El Rukn: family, respect, even protesting against apartheid in South Africa. It was as if there were two El Rukn organizations running around on the South Side of Chicago. College-educated Leon McAnderson's testimony provided what was hoped to be a foil to Davis's. McAnderson said he knew nothing of a LAW rocket, drug dealing, a cache of weapons, or plots to blow up even a balloon on behalf of Qaddafi.

Leon Clarington Cortez McAnderson, thirty-seven, was born into a large Baptist family in Kansas City, Kansas. He received his GED, attended junior college, and became a GED instructor. McAnderson met attorney Charles Knox in Missouri while doing community work. McAnderson moved to Chicago—his wife and their five children in tow—in summer 1975 to study criminal justice administration at Northeastern Illinois University. Knox was on faculty at the university, and the professor recommended a scholarship for him. In Chicago, McAnderson said, he worked with the National Conference of Black Lawyers, the Urban League, Operation PUSH, and other neighborhood groups. In 1978, McAnderson earned a bachelor's degree.

While at Northeastern, he met some El Rukns. The conversations were not about the organization per se, he said. Instead they revolved around "the work that they were doing." McAnderson testified during direct examination by his attorney Sheldon Nagelberg. "They were involved in some educational programs at the University of Illinois. They worked with the commission dealing with racial problems in the Englewood and Woodlawn area," he said.

He attended his first El Rukn function at The Fort in summer 1979. McAnderson and his family joined the group's annual family feast at the 39th Street headquarters. He met Jeff Fort, members, leadership, and their families. "At the time, I was under the impression that they were just a community organization," McAnderson said. "You might say a real cultural-type foundation. They believed that black people here in America who were descendents of slaves came from the northern part of Africa, namely Morocco, and that their religion was Islam, as opposed to Christianity."

A couple of El Rukns invited him to a service in January 1980. Flattered, McAnderson accepted the invitation. That same year he joined the organization, lured in by their progression toward Sunni Islam tradition and strong family values.

McAnderson: "I wanted to get involved with some of the projects that the organization was doing. One of the things is that they worked closely with prisoners. They also had programs designed for young people. . . . They were involved in different programs in the community, and that was my forte then, you know, working in the community."

Nagelberg: "At the time that you joined the El Rukns formally in 1980, had you ever used drugs?"

McAnderson: "No."

Nagelberg: "Had you ever been arrested and charged with any crimes?"

McAnderson: "No."

Nagelberg: "When you joined the El Rukns in 1980, were you

aware of anybody within the El Rukn organization who was using
and abusing drugs?"

McAnderson: "I would say abusing drugs; but this was not allowed."

McAnderson listed the rules and regulations for the El Rukns: no pill
popping, no profanity, no drug selling, and no possession of narcotics. Members paid ten dollars a month for dues, and the fabric of
family was a key tenet. McAnderson was drawn to Fort and looked
up to the revered leader. They talked about politics and family life.
Fort acted as a counselor, or minister, for many of the El Rukns.

McAnderson said he and Cranshaw prepared to travel to Libya in
March 1986. Professor Charles Knox had told them about a nation-
wide delegation of Americans going to a peace conference. He said
the Islamic Cause Society, a group that acted as a missionary agency
for Islamic activities, sponsored the gathering. McAnderson said he
told Fort about his plans and how visiting Africa would be one of the
greatest opportunities in his life.

Nagelberg: "What did Mr. Fort say?"

McAnderson: "He was real happy for us, you know."

Nagelberg: "Did Mr. Fort command or tell you to do anything
while you were over in Libya?"

McAnderson: "Nothing, other than—that if we could go, go."

Nagelberg: "Did he tell you that you should talk about commit-
ting any violent acts in the United States?"

McAnderson: "None whatsoever."

Nagelberg: "Did he in any way give you any direction as to people
to contact when you got over there?"

McAnderson: "No, he did not."

Cranshaw and McAnderson flew to Libya via Morocco due to the
U.S. travel ban. They landed in Tripoli on March 13, 1986. The duo
soon saw Charles Knox at the hotel with a large American delegation. Thousands of delegates from around the world were at the con-

ference, McAnderson said. It was a week-and-a-half transformative experience.

"It was a very emotional experience for me, personally. I enjoyed every minute of it," McAnderson testified, reflecting on his first trip to Africa. "We were—there were people from all around the world, people from different countries, different Muslim countries, being represented. It was just a time to socialize and get to know everything that was going on as far as Libya went . . . it was just an educational experience that I'll cherish for the rest of my life." He said he didn't speak to Qaddafi, nor did Cranshaw or Charles Knox.

McAnderson said he and Cranshaw left the country after the U.S. bombing. They traveled with an American delegation of about twenty-five—Morocco to Amsterdam to New York. While in New York, McAnderson said, he and Cranshaw talked about submitting a proposal to the Islamic Cause Society for money. McAnderson believed this agency gave Farrakhan his five million dollars. The El Rukn thought it would be a good idea to use the money to renovate the mosque. Another idea bubbled, too.

"We also hoped to establish a legal defense fund, because we had a number of people who were going to trial and who needed attorneys. This was always a constant thing with the El Rukn organization. We always had some legal battles to fight," McAnderson recounted.

When they finally returned to Chicago, Tramell Davis was one of the men who picked them up. On the way back to The Fort from Midway Airport, two Chicago policemen, including El Rukn nemesis Richard Kolovitz, stopped them on 55th Street. The officers ordered them out of the car and frisked them. Police opened the trunk, McAnderson said, and removed the luggage. A dog sniffed the contents. The officers arrested Davis for using false identification.

The remaining trio returned to The Fort. McAnderson had brought back posters of Qaddafi and pamphlets on politics in African countries. A month later there were still ongoing discussions about how to get money from the Islamic Cause Society. McAnderson said only he, Cranshaw, Charles Knox, and some of his students worked on the proposal. Because they couldn't get back to Libya, McAnderson and Cranshaw went to Panama, where the Islamic Cause Society had an outpost. (The prosecution never elaborated on what exactly the Islamic Cause Society did—a point Cranshaw's attorney pointed out in his closing argument. Why didn't they establish whether there was a sinister aspect to it?) McAnderson testified that Charles Knox had given him the name of two imams to look up in Panama City. In McAnderson's words, it was a pretty uneventful trip. They ate, went to services, and brought the pro-Libya videotape that Tramell Davis mentioned in his testimony. McAnderson gave it to some Muslims for their viewing pleasure. Then the traveling duo returned to Chicago with not much but lint in their pockets, still determined to formulate a proposal to present to the Islamic Cause Society but no closer to that $2.5 million. "We didn't bring back absolutely anything. In fact, we had trouble paying our hotel bill," McAnderson recalled.

Their return flight stopped in Miami, and customs officials pulled them out of line. They didn't know that customs had searched their luggage and found a document in Cranshaw's handwriting discussing plans to destroy government property in retaliation against U.S. antagonism toward Libya.

McAnderson had testified earlier that he wasn't aware of any illegal activity that the El Rukns carried out. He conceded that they developed their own language—a language he quickly pointed out lacked profanity as proof of their pure hearts. McAnderson explained that the El Rukns invented the communication because they knew there was a possibility that the feds would be monitoring Fort's conversations from prison. The organization didn't want law enforcement all up in their financial affairs, McAnderson said.

McAnderson revealed the subject of the clandestine El Rukn code: ginseng.

"Well, ginseng is an oriental drink that basically we have been acclaimed to have a root that—a ginseng root that is over three hundred years old. In fact, we've been acclaimed to have one of the oldest roots in the United States of America. And we sell the extraction of this juice, which is in liquid form. Our membership, we buy it," McAnderson testified.

He said the symbolic words the El Rukns used referred to the sale, income, and development of ginseng. The five principles—love, truth, peace, justice, freedom—meant money. This wasn't drug talk, McAnderson implied. The phrase *young friend* didn't necessarily mean Qaddafi; it could mean national leaders or Louis Farrakhan. And McAnderson concluded by saying Fort never instructed him to participate in any violent or illegal acts.

The prosecution tried to get McAnderson to recall phone conversations with Fort in which he told the leader that the Libyans had given them recognition. The cross-examination was a tedious back-and-forth. McAnderson didn't remember conversations or wanted to hear an entire conversation from the wiretap played back, not just portions of it. Through it all, McAnderson recited the party line—the El Rukns were a humble religious organization.

DURING A SIDEBAR CONVERSATION, the other prosecutor, John Podliska, made a surprising statement. "We did break the code before Tramell Davis had anything to do with it," Podliska told the judge. FBI special agent Edward Hamara took the stand as the prosecution's witness. Podliska made the case for him. "This witness would be testifying to how that [code breaking] was done during the course of the investigation." This was a curious piece of testimony because Davis had sat on the stand for several days interpreting El Rukn code. Hamara said he began compiling lists of words in the El Rukn language and formulating his beliefs around them in April 1986. During cross-examination, the defense attorneys seized on this. It seemed hard to believe those several hundred words were defined in a short period by a man who was not an official code breaker. Hamara said he and Davis sat down together and did a compilation.

[Alan Knox's attorney] Kent Brody: "And the special assignment that you were on at the FBI Academy had nothing to do in training you with code breaking, is that correct?"

Hamara: "That's correct."
Brody: "You are not familiar with the proven techniques for—or the established techniques in the science of cryptanalysis, would that be fair?"
Hamara: "Or some of the methods now, you know, but I do not have extensive knowledge as an expert would."

Hamara's lack of expertise didn't outmaneuver the defense.

## Final Arguments

ON NOVEMBER 18, 1987, closing arguments began. They took two days. The six-man, six-woman jury had already labored through six weeks of testimony and fifty witnesses. The prosecution walked through much of it again, a tactic to drill down their assertion that the El Rukns reeked of guilt.

Bogart's contention served as a summary: "This case concerns organized crime, with a twist of terrorism." She portrayed the El Rukns as a separatist organization that concocted its own rules, ethics, and language. Bogart tried to invalidate the religious purpose of the organization, insisting it centered on criminal activity. She listed the missiles and weapons authorities had found on El Rukn property, including The Fort.

"Now there was testimony that over the last year, 1986, there was some changes taking place. They were trying to refer to it as a mosque, a Sunni Muslim mosque, but the fact of the matter is that the reference to The Fort still appeared over the entrance to that building, and the way in which that building was maintained, was, in fact, in the manner in which a fort would be maintained," Bogart proclaimed.

She reminded the jury of the power Jeff Fort wielded behind bars, the way he gave instructions and orders from a prison phone in Texas. Bogart told the jury to remember listening to a telephone call from a man describing himself as Brother Raul from Libya. He looked for "the people who had met with the Libyans in Libya to negotiate on behalf of the El Rukns." Bogart played several pieces of tape again. She circled back to a conversation that Mays and Fort had had about putting a bomb on an airplane.

"These conversations concerning the discussions of money, ladies and gentlemen, to obtain money from the Libyans are conversations occurring in the course of the conspiracy, and as you listen to them and as you see with whom it is the defendants are talking or about what they are talking, you can make the determination that those telephone calls are occurring in the course of those negotiations, which is charged in the conspiracy count . . . the object of which is to have damage to buildings, to kill or injure people, or intimidate them, to have damage done by means of fire or explosives," Bogart said. She referred to the trips to Libya, the painstakingly recorded conversations cloaked in code, and the LAW rocket sale.

Bogart's closing arguments took so long that the judge offered a welcomed break.

When Gillespie took the floor on behalf of defendant Fort, he acquiesced that some of the El Rukns went to Libya and Panama, but insisted they didn't go as members of organized crime. Gillespie didn't doubt that the El Rukns tried to get money from various sources—banks, Sammy Davis Jr., anybody willing to open up a checkbook. But he underscored that no buildings, airplanes, or property had been earmarked for destruction on behalf of Libya. Gillespie even conceded that weapons were located at the African Hut and that the El Rukns had purchased an inert LAW rocket. He reminded the jury to weigh whether that weapon was purchased to commit acts of terrorism. He trashed Tramell Davis. "He didn't know anything the El Rukns were supposed to do on behalf of Libya, and he told you in this courtroom, under oath, that that was the truth at the time he said it. . . . He told you, ladies and gentlemen, that he told the agents when he began cooperating with them that he did not know what the guns were to be used for."

As the case wrapped up, Gillespie sensed that the jury found the El Rukns as foreign as Libya. The El Rukns were not part of the mainstream. He directly addressed that unfamiliarity. "Even if you don't like Jeff Fort. Even if you don't like his organization. Even if you think he's guilty of other crimes that aren't in the indictment. If you think, if you believe after deliberation, that this prosecution has not proven him guilty beyond a reasonable doubt as to any particular count, it is your duty to find him not guilty as to that count," Gillespie argued.

The next day the other defense attorneys echoed strains of Gillespie's theme.

THE JURY DELIBERATED several days. All of the defendants were found guilty. Fort got eighty years and was fined $255,000. Cranshaw received sixty-three years. McAnderson received fifty-one years. Both were fined $241,000. Alan Knox got fifty-four years and was also fined $241,000. Hawkins received nine years and no fine.

According to the *Sun-Times*, Fort, forty, sat stone-faced at the sentencing. But he did find time to bring a bit of levity. After sentencing, Judge Norgle said he was free to leave the courtroom. "Out this door?" Fort joked as he gestured to the public exit. Everyone, including the judge, laughed.

Cranshaw is dead. Hawkins and Davis are out of prison. Mays became a fugitive who spent years in Morocco, Holland, Switzerland, and Saudi Arabia. He came back to Chicago and got caught on the South Side in 1995.

Fort is in a supermax facility in Florence, Colorado. He's scheduled for release in 2038. Chicago Gangster Disciples kingpin Larry Hoover is also in Florence. Mays is currently serving a life sentence. Mays has tried to seek political prisoner status under the Geneva Convention, claiming he is a citizen of the Republic of New Afrika. A court denied the motion. Alan Knox is scheduled to get out in 2018. McAnderson is scheduled for 2016. Fort has tried to get the El Rukn Nation established as a religious organization.

TERRY GILLESPIE WAS a young, naive lawyer fresh out of the state's attorney's office when he took this case. Gillespie is now a sought-after defense attorney in Chicago. He represented Rod Blagojevich shortly after the Illinois governor dominated national news stories for his corruption scandals; Gillespie's partner Ed Genson was part of the team that successfully defended R&B singer R. Kelly on child pornography charges in 2008.

"This was the most difficult case I ever had and one of the more unique individuals I represented," Gillespie says of Fort. "Such a waste to have someone who was such a strong leader of young men all these years locked up in the penitentiary." Gillespie never viewed Fort as a terrorist. "I don't think he wanted to bring or would bring that kind of attention to his organization. He saw himself as a very serious leader. Jeff was too smart for that." Like many, Gillespie believed Fort simply wanted to con Qaddafi out of some money.

# 9

# $\mathfrak{Prosecutorial}$
# $\mathfrak{Misconduct}$

**F**EDERAL AGENTS DIDN'T rest after Fort's terrorism conviction. In October 1988, he and four other El Rukns were convicted of a 1981 drug murder. "We made a real dent in the organization," said special prosecutor Randy Rueckert after the criminal court's verdict. "This should go a long way to ensure that he [Fort] will spend the rest of his life in jail." Fort was serving a thirteen-year drug term when the terrorism trial began. He received eighty years from that conviction. This latest murder conviction piled on an additional seventy-five years.

Law enforcement had received a big break in 1985 with the help of an inner circle El Rukn officer who told police about the drug murder and provided details on other wrongdoings. The mother of that informant was shot, which prosecutors portrayed as retaliation. Three El Rukns were convicted in a Rockford, Illinois, courtroom because of fears that a Chicago jury couldn't be impartial. Meanwhile, Fort's brother Bennie was stabbed to death in June 1988.

Prosecutors finally felt satisfied with Fort's prison sentences, and now they wanted to finish demolishing the El Rukns. But accomplishing that came at a steep price.

ON OCTOBER 27, 1989, a Friday afternoon, rank-and-file El Rukns hustled into The Fort to be on time for *Jum'ah*, the Friday congregational prayer that is obligatory for all Muslims. The Qur'an says: "O ye who believe, when the call is proclaimed to prayer on Friday [the day of assembly], hasten earnestly to the remembrance of Allah (*subhanahuwa ta'la*) and leave off business [and traffic]. That is best for you if ye but knew" (Qur'an 62:9). Federal authorities knew many of the high-ranking El Rukns they had been investigating would be there. Agents camped out around the clock, and at approximately 1:30 P.M., while almost half of the El Rukn membership was making *salat* (prayer), over fifty federal agents, including the FBI, DEA, and ATF, with the assistance of thirty-plus Chicago police officers, stormed The Fort. They used sledgehammers and blowtorches to break down the doors.

Darryl Lamb ("Ambassador Khan") was one of the El Rukns worshipping on the day of the raid. The El Rukns were already prostrate in prayer when federal agents swarmed them. Agents screamed for the El Rukns to remain facedown on the floor while aiming M-16s at their heads. Ambassador Khan said agents loaded up the El Rukns in police trucks and transported them to the Chicago Police Academy on the West Side. They were escorted to the gymnasium and shackled to bleachers draped with chains. Agents separated out the lower-ranking El Rukns; they were transported to Cook County jail and charged with disorderly conduct and mob action. Most of them were later released. The leaders, including Khan, were processed at various tables set up around the gym. Mug shots and fingerprints were taken before shipping them over to the Metropolitan Correction Center (MCC), the federal jail in downtown Chicago.

Subsequently, sixty-five El Rukn leaders were indicted on racketeering, conspiracy, murder, kidnapping, witness retaliation, drug, and firearm charges. "My hope is that ultimately, if our prosecution is successful, we will take out the entire organization," said U.S. attorney Anton R. Valukas after the indictments. He said the indictments should be a "deathblow" to the organization. The government filed a single indictment against thirty-eight El Rukns. It included 175 crimes over a twenty-year period. The indictment was 305 pages long and weighed almost four pounds, and it detailed a labyrinth of illegal acts.

The indictment included RICO conspiracy and narcotics conspiracy. The government explained that it had included so many otherwise unconnected criminal activities in one indictment because each crime was allegedly committed to attain power, control, and wealth for a criminal street gang. Despite protestations from the defendants, the court allowed the unifying RICO conspiracy. Some defendants pled guilty, others fled and became fugitives, and twenty actually went to trial. Jeff Fort was an unindicted coconspirator whom the government said masterminded the activities of the El Rukns, assisted by his generals and officers. Among the charges: twenty murders, twelve attempted murders, eleven conspiracies to murder, one kidnapping, wide-scale drug trafficking, numerous acts of obstruction of justice, an attempt to bribe a judge, and witness intimidation/retaliation/tampering. Fort was not charged because he was already in prison.

Khan and the El Rukns knew the feds were coming. Agents let them know in 1986 during a raid of The Fort. But they didn't expect the feds to take so long. Khan never worried about the feds coming after him. He said he knew he hadn't been caught doing anything illegal. Besides, although Khan sold drugs, he didn't sell at the level he thought the feds would be interested in. Like many other drug dealers, Khan mistakenly thought if you weren't caught in the act of selling drugs, you didn't have a problem. Khan didn't realize that the RICO act allowed the feds to indict individual members of organizations considered to be involved in racketeering and corruption.

Attorney Standish Willis represented Lawrence Crowder. Willis was part of a group of private lawyers appointed to represent people charged with federal crimes. Defendants like Crowder couldn't afford lawyers, so judges appointed attorneys like Willis to those cases. Willis remembered that indictment as the first kind of massive prosecution. Prosecutors wanted a mega-trial. "It was so large we filed motions to try to break [it] up. If we went to trial no one could get a fair trial," Willis said. There was just too much evidence to comprehend. The judge did break the trial up into five separate trials. The prosecution even reduced the volume of evidence against each defendant unrelated to his active participation in El Rukn affairs and his alleged crimes.

A sampling of the charges:

The El Rukns committed a slew of other murders and attempted murders related to narcotics activity. On March 12, 1980, Fort ordered two defendants to kill Douglas Ellison because of a dispute involving a narcotics debt. Three months later, eight defendants conspired to murder Lemont Timberlake because he failed to accede to demands to stop dealing narcotics in El Rukn–controlled territory. This plan was carried out on June 17, 1980, when Timberlake was shot and killed in a vacant lot on the south side of Chicago.

From about April 1981 to January 1983, as a result of a drug territorial dispute, 23 defendants conspired to kill the top leaders and members of the Titanic Stones, a rival gang, including Eugene Hairston, George Thomas, Barnett Hall, Ray East, Robert East and Willie Bibbs. During that same time period, Bibbs and Hall were killed and Thomas was the target of an attempted murder. In the course of the Thomas attempt, on January 23, 1983, five defendants and other gang members killed Charmaine Nathan and shot and attempted to kill Sheila Jackson.

In April 1985, as a result of another drug territorial dispute with a rival gang, 23 defendants conspired to kill various members of the King Cobra street gang. Rukns cruised the streets of Chicago in efforts to locate and murder King Cobra members. During this time, several defendants and other El Rukn members murdered Robert Jackson, Rico Chalmers, Glendon McKinley and

Vicki Nolden and attempted to murder Theotis Clark and Andre Chalmers. McKinley and Nolden were innocent bystanders swept up in the wave of violence.

Conspiracy to possess with intent to distribute, and to distribute, multi-kilogram quantities of heroin and cocaine, hundreds of pounds of marijuana, thousands of amphetamine pills, thousands of Talwin and Tripelennamine pills, multi-liter quantities of codeine syrup, and large quantities of Phencyclidine (PCP). From 1966 to 1989, various defendants purchased narcotics from sources in at least seven states, including Florida, South Carolina, Mississippi, New York, Wisconsin, Illinois and Michigan. The government further contended that the defendants sold narcotics from numerous El Rukn–controlled buildings and territories throughout the Illinois cities of Chicago, Evanston, Skokie, and Harvey, and also from Milwaukee, Wis.

The indictment also included Noah Robinson, Reverend Jesse Jackson's half-brother. Robinson was one of the first people arrested. He had an MBA from the Wharton School of Business, and he held patents on a traffic device and floor wax. But people who knew him said the brilliant Robinson also had a gangster mentality. Chicago journalist Nate Clay said he picked up on a sibling rivalry going on between Robinson and Jackson. While Jackson had established himself as a civil rights leader, Robinson desired to be the leader of the gangster movement. Reverend Al Sampson said Robinson really wanted to be at the helm of the El Rukns. He was indicted on a number of charges including skimming $650,000 from Wendy's restaurants he owned in Chicago. The Wendy's corporation conducted an investigation of his stores and found that he ordered the cash registers turned off during part of business hours to keep the company from knowing the true total sales.

Robinson was also indicted for paying the El Rukns twenty thousand dollars to commit two murders for hire. One of the murders he

was accused of soliciting involved the individual who was investigating Robinson's attempt to defraud Wendy's. The murder never took
place. The other murder Robinson was accused of soliciting involved
an El Rukn whom Robinson had hired to provide security for his
fast-food restaurants. He and the El Rukn eventually fell out when
Robinson accused him of stealing from the restaurants and fired
him. Later Robinson traveled back to his hometown of Greenville,
South Carolina, for a Christmas holiday. The El Rukn followed him
to Greenville for a confrontation. The El Rukn caught up with Robinson at a pool hall that Robinson owned. According to federal prosecutors, Robinson paid Chief Malik with cash and a drug connection
to kill the El Rukn. Chief Malik supposedly sent two El Rukns to
Greenville in a raggedy car to murder the El Rukn who was harassing
Robinson. They did the hit, but on their way back to Chicago their
car broke down in the mountains of Tennessee. When cops raided
The Fort, they found Robinson's private number in an El Rukn general's phone book, along with a newspaper article about the murder
of the El Rukn who had been harassing Robinson. Putting two and
two together, the feds were able to solve the case. The feds said he
had heroin and cocaine connections, too. Robinson went to prison
for life with no parole.

TWO YEARS AFTER the extensive indictments, the El Rukns remained
locked up without a trial. Instead of staying in the MCC, they were
transported to the federal penitentiary in Terre Haute, Indiana. The
feds said they were a threat to the safety and security of the inmates
and staff at the MCC. They were placed in segregation in the Indiana
penitentiary for the two years they awaited trial. There were hearings held during this period concerning the cases of the indicted El
Rukns, but the defendants were not permitted to attend.

It wasn't until the spring of 1991 that the feds finally began to try
the El Rukns. The system broke them up into groups that reflected
their organizational ranks. There were twenty generals or amirs. The
next ranking group was the officer muftis, followed by the ambas-

sadors. The last ranking members were the key soldiers. Most of the key soldiers who had been swept up in the raid had been released immediately and were never indicted. The first to go on trial was a group of 13 ambassadors. Khan was in that group. The ambassador trial ended with three being acquitted of all counts, but ten were convicted on charges from racketeering to conspiracy to commit murder. Khan was convicted. The trial, which lasted for months, was the first in which the government hoped to strike a deathblow to the gang by imprisoning its leadership. More El Rukn turncoats came forward, detailing the drug operations, intimidation, and murders. Many convictions ensued. Fugitives were caught.

The feds were forced to throw out many of the charges against the El Rukns because too much time had lapsed since the indict-ments. Nevertheless, officials seemed pleased with the convictions because they believed the ten ambassadors who were found guilty were being groomed to be the future leaders of the gang. The ver-dicts were returned from jurors whose identities had to be shielded to protect them from retaliation. The jury convicted the first two El Rukn members, one on charges of racketeering, narcotics conspiracy, and conspiracy to commit murder and the other on a charge of dis-tributing drugs. Eight others were convicted on charges including racketeering, conspiracy, and drug distribution. The jury also changed its verdict on an El Rukn who had been previously convicted. That defendant, Paul Downie, was cleared of racketeering, racketeering conspiracy, and drug distribution, although the jury let stand his con-viction for narcotics conspiracy and other drug distribution charges.

## Prosecutorial Misconduct

A YEAR AND A HALF after the convictions and pleas, a major glitch surfaced. Rumors and innuendos that had been spreading through-out the MCC by jailhouse snitches raised questions about whether prosecutors had provided special favors to El Rukn government witnesses. At the core of this scandal was the question of whether prosecutors knew that two El Rukn generals, Henry Leon "Toomba" Harris and Harry Evans, tested positive for morphine in 1989 while in custody.

Khan said that the federal prosecutors didn't realize that snitches don't just tattle to the feds; they give up everyone they come in contact with. These special witnesses bragged to the other MCC inmates that they were getting drugs from the outside, having sex with their wives and girlfriends, and making outside phone calls that were supposed to be prohibited. Eventually word got back to the defendants and their lawyers. The defense lawyers subsequently filed motions to the federal court to have hearings on prosecutorial misconduct. Their requests were granted.

Hearings before federal judges Suzanne B. Conlon and James F. Holderman were held to determine if the accusations were serious enough to warrant new trials or dismissal of the indictments. William Hogan, the chief prosecutor, denied wrongdoing; the federal court nevertheless proceeded with hearings to determine if the U.S. attorney's office was involved with prosecutorial misconduct by concealing evidence in its prosecution of the El Rukns.

During the hearings, a former prosecutor testified that he had learned that government witnesses Harris (Fort's brother-in-law) and Evans had tested positive for drugs. He relayed his concerns to Hogan, whom he said brushed him off. Hogan denied having any such conversation. The defense argued that the drug evidence might have swayed jurors. "It's one thing to be charged with all these crimes while they're on the street," said Peter Schmiedel, a defense lawyer, "but it's quite another to be indulging in narcotics when in government custody." Testimony included other assertions: a prosecution paralegal admitted she gave a sip of beer to a witness in a government office and smuggled "Ex-Lax" to an El Rukn in prison. The defense and Judge Holderman suspected that the laxative brand name could have been a code for drugs. Unaware that she was being taped, the paralegal also had sexually explicit conversations with an El Rukn, saying she would like "ten minutes in a locked room" with another El Rukn.

Judge Holderman, expressing shock that the paralegal was not dismissed, ordered that the prosecutors involved be reported to a state disciplinary group because they did not report the accusations against her. One El Rukn said another El Rukn had stolen a memorandum from Hogan's desk that outlined the government's case. Another gang member said Harris told him that part of his testimony was "a pack of lies." Other testimony showed that some El Rukns were allowed special family visits. Holderman said prosecutors had failed to disclose certain benefits given to the witnesses, which might have been relevant in determining their motivation for testifying—and their credibility. For example, the witnesses were allowed contact visits with their wives or girlfriends while in the MCC, a violation of jail policy. Complaining about lax security at the jail, the judge said the women were rarely searched before seeing the prisoners and may have used the visits to smuggle cocaine, marijuana, and heroin into the jail.

Evans was caught having sex with his wife while in the MCC. Although his visiting privileges at the jail were revoked, he later was allowed to have contact visits with her at the U.S. attorney's office. Holderman said the authorities had also granted the witnesses unheard of and "especially troubling" telephone privileges. In light of the evidence indicating that the witnesses received drugs from outside sources, the judge wrote, "The court can only infer that the El Rukn cooperating witnesses utilized their telephone privileges to contact their illegal drug suppliers." The inmate witnesses even answered the telephones in the office of a special government task force, in some cases pretending to be federal agents.

In light of all this, new trials were ordered in the summer of 1993. The federal court ruled that prosecutors had tainted the trial by misconduct and withholding information. A federal judge dismissed the racketeering convictions against six top leaders of the El Rukns. Judge Marvin Aspen cited misconduct by the prosecution. A total of

thirteen convictions were overturned. Defense lawyers were successful at getting new trials for twenty-four. And sixteen El Rukns who
had pled guilty were allowed to back out of their plea deals. William
Doyle was tried and convicted again of murder in 1995.

THE DAY AFTER the October 1989 raid on The Fort, federal agents
and workers used bricks and cement to seal off the El Rukn headquarters, entombing it until such time when it would be forfeited to
the government. Floyd Davis, an original El Rukn general who was
one of the sixty-five El Rukns caught in the raid and indicted, said
that he believes the criminalization of the El Rukns was really about
the city's desire to grab valuable land that the Stones owned. The
Stones owned a lot of properties on the South Side in neighborhoods
like Oakland and Woodlawn that the city wanted to gentrify. Davis
said he believes that the city's plan was to trump up charges against
the El Rukns, lock them up, and take their properties by claiming
they seized them due to the commission of crimes. When the El
Rukns got out of prison, they had no properties to come back to.
Davis claimed there was no one in their communities to protect the
incarcerated El Rukns from internal and external predators.

One of the most symbolic antigang gestures was the razing of The
Fort in summer 1990. The word *symbolic* was used many times by dignitaries. A six-thousand-pound wrecking ball tore into the temple as
Mayor Daley, police superintendent LeRoy Martin, and other political and prosecutorial VIPs watched. Martin said the demolition was a
symbolic victory in the War on Drugs. Daley said the building symbolized drugs and destruction to young people. "Today we are here to rid
the community of the El Rukn blight once and for all." Three hundred
people watched the ball smash into the building, and some collected
chunks of the rubble for souvenirs. Police drug task force member
Dan Brannigan said, "It would have been nice if they used dynamite."

Father George Clements, of nearby Holy Angels Church, wasn't
so quick to break out the party favors. He tempered the celebratory
mood by reminding people that gangs still thrived in many Chicago

neighborhoods. The El Rukns may have been past tense but homi-
cides were peaking overall in the city in 1990.

After federal agents seized The Fort, Mayor Daley said the property would be transformed into a park, housing, or a health center.
The neighborhood has been completely converted. The public housing that surrounded The Fort is now gone. Its proximity to the lake
makes the neighborhood attractive, so in the 2000s the Oakland
community has seen an increase in property values and middle-class
families. Today a single-family home sits on the former Fort site. By
2010 some nearby houses cost five hundred thousand dollars.

RETIRED CHICAGO POLICE detective Richard Kolovitz has RUKN86
on his license plate. The number represents an old restaurant term
from the 1950s, used when a diner ran out of the blue plate special.
The cook would yell out, "That's 86," meaning it's done, gone, over.
That's what Kolovitz felt about the El Rukns in 1986.

While working on the organized drug task force that nailed the
El Rukns, Kolovitz lost his leg and now walks with an artificial one.
He won't say how it happened except that it wasn't related to his
work. The brawny and balding Kolovitz spent his career chasing Jeff
Fort. We're not sure if Kolovitz imagined himself in a superhero-
archenemy relationship, but the cop pursuing the villain for decades
has a comic-book aspect. The hunt revealed the frailties of law
enforcement.

"It cost me two marriages and it cost [partner Dan] Brannigan
one. A couple houses, and all this other crap," Kolovitz said. "For lack
of a better phrase, we sold ourselves to the devil to get the devil."

# 10

# The Legacy of Terrorism on Street Gangs

**N**ARSEAL **B**ATISTE **WAS** so excited about his meeting that he couldn't sleep the night before. But he overslept the morning of December 16, 2005, and arrived three hours late for his appointment at the airport. Batiste, a black American originally from the South Side of Chicago, wore a long white robe and a red-and-white checkered turban, and carried a large wooden staff to greet his friend's uncle, Brother Mohammed, a rich funder of al-Qaeda from Yemen. Batiste wanted to impress the potential benefactor. Ten minutes into the conversation, Batiste told Brother Mohammed about a Chicago man toward whom he felt kinship.

> Batiste: "There's a man that you probably don't know and he was probably in the same situation that I was in like right now. And that's kinda hard to tell you so many things in such a short little time. What I want to explain . . ."
> Mohammed: "I have my whole time. Don't worry about my time. My time is for you now."
> Batiste: "His name is Jeff Fort. Jeff Fort."

Mohammed: "Jeff Fort."
Batiste: "Jeff Fort was a leader of one of the biggest gangs . . .
[inaudible] and it started off of Islamic philosophy."
Mohammed: "Do me a favor. Can higher your voice because I
have problem hearing."
Batiste: "He got arrested and he went to jail back in ah, nineteen
eighty something. He was the first black man to ever be indicted
in United States Court for terrorism. He was being, he was being
helped by Libya."
Mohammed: "By Libya?"
Batiste: "And, the reason why I tell you about him cause you can
go on the Internet, you can always, always look at it, it's called
the Black Stone Nation."

What Batiste didn't know was that his friend's "uncle," Brother
Mohammed Ali Hussein, was not a rich al-Qaeda operative from
Yemen but a paid FBI informant raking in ninety thousand dollars
a year and living in a safe house in Mexico. Batiste's friend Brother
Hamas had knowingly hooked up the introductions, and several
meetings took place in south Florida—in person and on a wiretapped
cell phone.

In his encounters with the Arabs, Batiste falsely bragged that he
was a leader of the Stones in Chicago and controlled five thousand
gangbangers who would help him revolt against America. The feds
listened in on every word.

THE FEDS CONTINUED chasing Blackstone phantoms twelve years
after the events of the early 1990s. In a twist, Batiste found his fate
inextricably linked to the legacy of Jeff Fort and the Blackstone
Rangers. The feds used the same tactics to punish Batiste they had
used in the 1980s to entrap Fort on domestic terrorism charges. In
both investigations, the federal government set up elaborate stings
with posing informants who purported to have incredible access and
means. The FBI accused Batiste and his ragtag followers of plot-

ting to work with al-Qaeda operatives to blow up the Sears Tower in Chicago and several FBI buildings. The 1987 conviction of Fort and the other El Rukns had paved the way for prosecutors to connect street gangs—and their affinity for Islam—with terrorism. Although Batiste wasn't actually involved in a street gang, his boasting and perceived promises fit a certain profile that the feds searched for. But there is one key difference in these terrorism scenarios: Batiste functioned in a post-9/11 bizarro world. The nerdy kid who grew up to be a community organizer found himself in the cross fire of zealous prosecutors determined to assuage the nation's fears of homegrown racial terrorism.

A post-9/11 world means living under a candy corn–colored system that rates the levels of terrorism threats against the United States. It means a new federal agency, Homeland Security, engages in counterterrorism. It means that the crumbling of the World Trade Center is an image that will stay burned in the American psyche for decades. It means dealing with the PATRIOT Act. It means any scathing critique of the United States can raise suspicious eyebrows about terrorism. Under George W. Bush, the phrase "War on Terror" seeped into the American lexicon and imagination. The former president planted fears about "evildoers." Two wars, in Iraq and Afghanistan, were built on this premise. Furthermore, federal authorities didn't want to be caught with their pants down again. Many people blamed the U.S. intelligence community for not taking threats from al-Qaeda seriously sooner. The bipartisan 9/11 Commission pointed out the failures of the Clinton and Bush administrations. Both administrations missed several opportunities to prevent al-Qaeda's plot, according to the commission report.

In between Fort's trial and Batiste's trial, another Chicagoan was labeled an enemy combatant. Jose Padilla, a former Chicago gang member who converted to Islam, was charged and convicted of conspiracy to provide material support to terrorists. Authorities said that Padilla had worked to support jihadist campaigns in Afghanistan and other Central Asia locations. In 2008, a federal judge in Miami sentenced Padilla to seventeen years in prison. Even though this was considered a victory in the Bush era, the conviction was weaker than what prosecutors had at first sought.

The dogged pursuit of Batiste presented federal prosecutors with a difficult course. There were two mistrials. But that hardly deterred the government. Living under the cloud of the War on Terror gave prosecutors the chance to use the old adage: third time's the charm.

ON JUNE 22, 2006, police arrested seven men in Miami and accused them of collaborating with al-Qaeda operatives to blow up the Sears Tower and FBI buildings in five cities, including North Miami Beach, Florida. Those seven men would later be referred to in the media as the Liberty City Seven because the area they organized and were arrested in was Liberty City, a poor Miami neighborhood. The names of the Blackstone Rangers and Jeff Fort surfaced prominently in the case because prosecutors argued that they set the precursor for Batiste's copycat terrorism ambitions. The four-count indictment included conspiracy to provide material support to a foreign terrorist organization, conspiracy to provide material support for the commission of an act of terrorism, conspiracy to destroy or damage a building by means of an explosive, and seditious conspiracy to levy war against the United States.

All seven defendants were denied bail at their arrest in 2006. The feds said they were a radical Islamic group known as the Moorland Organization whose ringleader, Batiste, wanted to wage a jihad from within the United States to overthrow the government and replace it with an Islamic government. Their first trial started in October 2007, with the threat of up to seventy years in prison if convicted of all charges. The first trial ended on December 13 with one defendant acquitted and the jury unable to return a verdict on the other six. A retrial was scheduled for January 2008. On April 16, 2008, the judge in the case declared a second mistrial for the six remaining defendants after the jury had been deadlocked for thirteen days. After the first two mistrials, there was hope that the government's case against the Miami men would be dropped. Many people saw the case as a Bush administration attempt to entrap the men in order to justify their War on Terror and the billions of dollars spent on homeland security. There was a great deal of hope that with the new Obama administration coming in, the Liberty City case would be dropped and the men would be released. However, the new head of the FBI, Robert Mueller, called up the prosecutors to urge them on and let them know they were doing a good job.

During the first two trials, the U.S. attorney's office's strategy was to link the Liberty City Seven as terrorists committed to a terrorist plot. When that approach failed, the lawyers decided to sensationalize the case by trying to connect the group's actions to the Blackstone Rangers and Jeff Fort. Batiste's lies about his relationship to the organization ultimately brought about his demise. During the third trial, Batiste's attorneys asked Lance Williams to be a witness. They wanted him to testify about the Moorish Science Temple of America and the Blackstone Rangers. According to the feds, Batiste was a member of the Moorish Science Temple of America who claimed to be a leader of the Blackstone Rangers. Williams was prepared to refute some of those details and the prosecution's inaccurate description of the Chicago organization. In actuality, Batiste ("Brother Naz," "Prince Manna") led a tiny religious group called the Seas of David in Liberty City.

Batiste's path to prison seemed an unlikely one. It had nothing to do with drugs, street gangs, or leading a throng of thousands of adulating followers. The government had suckered Batiste into trying to extort money from a rich, radical "al-Qaeda" operative who got Batiste to say stupid things on tape to cozy up to the man. "I don't know how he wound up in all this mess," says his father, Narcisse Batiste. "My son was brought up under strict supervision, and he's a good person. I taught him how to work hard and be honest. I sent him to Catholic school and high school."

## Narseal Batiste

**BATISTE WAS BORN** on Valentine's Day in 1974 into a religious family in Chicago's West Pullman community, a mix of working-class and middle-class African Americans. The family later moved to the south suburbs. Family members and former teachers alike described Batiste as a good kid, somewhat of a loner, not affiliated with any gang, and kind of nerdy growing up. He was also a Guardian Angel and enjoyed protecting people. After high school, Batiste enrolled in community college, but he quit to pursue a certified truck driver's license. Unsatisfied with driving around the country, he relocated to Louisiana to work in a family venture led by his father. In 1994, he announced his conversion to Islam. His estranged brother Craig Batiste, twenty-five years Narseal's senior, said Narseal left Louisiana after a big family dispute over money.

Narseal Batiste then moved to North Miami with his wife, Minerva, and their children. People described him as sociable, charismatic, a bit egocentric and loquacious. Batiste was a vegetarian, enjoyed martial arts, and had no regular source of income. In 2001, he filed for Chapter 7 bankruptcy. Batiste described his occupation as a FedEx delivery driver who netted forty-four dollars a month after paying bills, and who owed thousands of dollars to creditors and collection agencies.

While in North Miami, he frequented a drug-infested park with his family. The conditions appalled Batiste so he started to organize the surrounding community. He wanted to clean up the park, get rid of the drugs, spread the gospel of physical fitness, and advocate for jobs in the construction industry. Batiste had success in recruiting people to his movement. His most loyal followers were a group of six or seven Haitian men who were several years younger than Batiste. (These young Haitians ended up being his accused coconspirators.) Batiste led daily activities in the park that included martial arts training, outreach to reduce drug selling in the park, dissemination of cultural and religious teachings, and job training.

Batiste's trouble began when he started frequenting an Arab-owned convenience store in the neighborhood. The unidentified owner was notorious in the area for his alleged involvement in welfare fraud and polygamy and had a questionable immigration status. A second Arab man also regularly patronized the convenience store. He was known to Batiste as Brother Hamas. Hamas was also of dubious character, and he convinced the merchant to transfer the ownership of the business to him so as to avoid losing his license for illegal activities. Through his daily visits to the store, Batiste formed a friendship with both men. In 2005, they often discussed ideals and world affairs. Many of their conversations centered on Western imperialism and America's oppression of black people in America and Arabs in the East.

At some point the store owner and Hamas fell out over money. Batiste found himself stuck in the middle, and he tried to mediate the dispute. But Hamas had a reputation for reporting Arabs with whom he beefed to the feds. When he didn't receive the fifty thousand dollars he demanded from his merchant friend, Hamas went to the feds to blow the whistle on the store owner's illegal activities. Alas, Batiste didn't know that Hamas had gone to the feds. Later Hamas told Batiste he would give him fifteen thousand if he helped get the money. Broke Batiste saw this as a way to earn some cash, and he began to pressure the store owner to give Hamas the money, arguing that it was the Muslim thing to do. Meanwhile, the thirsty feds were putting pressure on Hamas for more substantial information that would result in an easier case. Hamas had nothing. But he did dangle a carrot. He told authorities that Batiste visited the store daily railing about how much he hated America and how he was training black people to rise up against America. The feds' ears perked up. They made Hamas a paid informant to go get more information from Batiste. They gave Hamas about fifteen hundred dollars to give the unsuspecting Batiste as a payment for his role in helping Hamas obtain his money from the store owner.

The feds continued to use Hamas to see how far Batiste might be willing to go with his anti-American sentiments. Hamas agreed to wear a wire and meet with Batiste more frequently, and he recorded some of Batiste's anti-American rhetoric. Following the feds' instructions, Hamas told Batiste that he had a rich uncle from Yemen who was connected with al-Qaeda. All Batiste had to do, Hamas said, was convince his uncle that he had a good plan to attack America. The uncle would happily give him all the money needed to carry out the violence on behalf of al-Qaeda. Desperate for money, Batiste agreed to the meeting.

During this period of subterfuge and wiretapping, Batiste continued doing community work while attempting to open up a branch of the Moorish Science Temple of America because he was inspired by their teachings. He found a complete dump of a building located across the street from the projects in Liberty City. An Arab man owned that structure, and Batiste agreed to pay two thousand dollars per month in rent for this place that he would call the Embassy. With the labor of his loyal Haitian followers, Batiste fixed up the place and turned it into a de facto headquarters. The feds would depict the Embassy as a place Batiste wanted to establish as headquarters for his new Muslim government. The men would meet there for religious lessons.

Finally the feds were ready for their plan. They instructed Hamas to coordinate with Batiste for a meeting with his rich Yemeni "uncle." Prior to the meeting, the feds installed video recorders in the airport and the Embassy to record the conversation between Batiste and Brother Mohammed Ali Hussein, the informant.

A FEW DAYS after the airport meet and greet with Brother Mohammed in which Batiste invoked Jeff Fort's name, Batiste visited Hamas's apartment. Hamas wore a wire. Batiste bragged that he led the Blackstone Rangers back in Chicago.

> Batiste: "This world war can be won if we win one city. You know when [unintelligible] in Chicago."

Hamas: "How many brothers we got down here?"

Batiste: "Shew. [unintelligible] Let me tell you something. Ooc [short for *aki*, Arabic word for "brother"], you know I'm not kidding you. I can get five thousand [unintelligible] soldiers in Chicago."

Hamas: "Why you didn't mention anything about that to me, brother?" [laughing]

Batiste: "'Cause I save the best things for [unintelligible]."

Hamas: "I heard that."

Batiste: [laughing] [unintelligible]

Hamas: "I heard that. But seriously, we can get five thousand soldiers going?"

Batiste: "Yep."

Hamas: "I'm serious, brother. Brother, this is real guerrillas or . . ."

Batiste: "Shew . . . Nothing like you ever seen before. Crazy."

Hamas: [unintelligible] "Four thousand. You have already five thousand, brother."

Batiste: "Come on, God. You [unintelligible] trying to record there or what?"

Hamas: "But you got me thinking about, about five thousand soldiers now, man. I haven't thought about that. That's a big army. Five thousand soldiers."

Batiste: "I used to be a leader of the Blackstone Rangers. I had fifty soldiers. They would had did any fuckin' thing I told them to do."

Hamas: "And that's in Chicago? Are they still there? So why we don't go [unintelligible] to Chicago for a while?"

Hamas: "OK, brother. Do you want go to Chicago?"

Batiste: "Got to go to Chicago."

Hamas: "When you want to go?"

Batiste: "As soon as we get the money. Soon as we get the money."

Hamas said he would try to get ten thousand dollars and get them to Chicago. Batiste promised to introduce him "to some of my soldiers that are Arab and black."

In various other meetings, the feds said, Batiste outlined his plans to destroy the Sears Tower and wage war against the U.S. government. He asked for weaponry and financial backing for his group's mission. Details of the mission included poisoning the public and/or water in public places, taking control of National Guard installations in Miami, and getting some of his Marine friends to train people. Batiste noted that his experience in the construction industry would help him blow up the Sears Tower. "If I can put up a building, I should definitely know how to take one down," Batiste said. He also said he owned land, or had access to land, in Louisiana and Alabama where soldiers could train and that he had approximately ten guerrillas across the United States. Records in Florida showed that he and his wife opened a masonry business in March 2004.

Batiste may have had his suspicions about the relationship between Hamas and Brother Mohammed. He cut off communication in January 2006. The feds worried, but Brother Mohammed ingratiated himself back into Batiste's life. He even claimed, in an attempt to bolster his credibility, that he had assisted in the planning of the attack on the USS *Cole*. By March, Batiste had fortified his alliance with al-Qaeda by swearing an oath of *bayat*, or loyalty, in front of Brother Mohammed, who said he was acting as an agent for Osama bin Laden. In a warehouse ceremony, the defendants individually did the same. Batiste said how grateful he was for the support he was receiving from bin Laden and how much he admired his work, characterizing him as an angel sent from Allah. The feds acquired this from a grainy video camera they had installed in the Embassy warehouse.

At the same ceremony, one of the FBI informants outlined a fictitious plan to conduct coordinated attacks against FBI buildings in five cities, including the one in North Miami Beach. This was drawn out in front of all of the defendants. Batiste said he would get good footage of the FBI building to assist in the bombing plot, but he expressed concern that such a plan would make it difficult for the other men to do the Chicago mission. Batiste stated that although he was seeking funding from al-Qaeda for the mission, the money could be received through other means. The FBI informant assured Batiste that the Chicago mission and al-Qaeda's plan would be coordinated.

Another part of this fiasco was the complicated involvement of two Chicago men named Sultan Khan Bey (James Stewart) and Master Althea. Master Althea was Batiste's martial arts teacher from suburban Oak Lawn and a former friend of the Batiste family. Master Althea claimed to be the leader of a group called the Universal Divine Brotherhood that ran out of Oak Lawn. He ended up in Miami and roped Batiste into his web. Khan Bey was a leader of the MSTA in Chicago.

Batiste paid for Khan Bey and his wife to come to Miami under the pretense of starting an MSTA chapter. Khan Bey thought the trip was about building up the religion, but Batiste wanted to use him as proof to the Arabs that he had credence and weight in the Chicago streets. He invited Khan Bey to some meetings. But Khan Bey recognized something amiss and went off on Batiste, kicking him out of his own Embassy. Master Althea confronted Khan Bey about his treatment of Batiste, and in response Khan Bey pulled out a gun and started shooting at him. Master Althea escaped and reported the incident to the police, who arrested Khan Bey and charged him as a convicted felon with possession and discharge of a firearm. He landed in jail. But he hollered that he was a sovereign citizen and that the United States had no authority over him.

MSTA leaders refuted that Batiste and his followers were members of the movement. They spoke out in 2006. "If anybody is involved in any terrorism, anything that is against our purpose, if they say they're with us, they're not," said Sister Susan Russell Dunbar-Bey, press secretary of MSTA. Back in Chicago another affiliated temple took a stand against Batiste. "America should know and understand that [alleged plotter] Narseal Batiste and his co-defendants are not members of the Moorish Science Temple of America and have never been considered as such," said Sheik Clifford Jackson-Bey, of the Subordinate Temple Number One in Chicago, in a written statement.

After this debacle with Khan Bey and Master Althea, Batiste went back to negotiating for money from the Arabs by himself. Hamas emphasized to Batiste that Osama bin Laden needed his help because he was planning to blow up federal buildings all over America. Hamas relayed that bin Laden needed Batiste to take pictures of all of the federal buildings in Miami. Batiste expressed opposition to taking the pictures; he said that he'd rather blow up the Sears Tower and kick off the jihad in Chicago. After hours of trying to convince Batiste to take the pictures, Hamas broke down and cried. Batiste then acquiesced, and Hamas took him out to buy a camera. After he took the pictures, Batiste and his wife hocked the camera for money to eat at McDonald's.

The feds raided the Embassy shortly afterward and arrested Batiste and the six Haitians. After two hung juries, one of the six Haitians was released. However, he was immediately rearrested and deported. The other five Haitians went to trial with Batiste, although the feds agreed to let them go with two and a half years of time served. During the third trial, four of the five Haitians were under house arrest and one was still locked up with Batiste. Lance Williams met and talked to all of the defendants who were under house arrest. They appeared to be humble men. In 2006, the mother of defendant Stanley Grant Phanor said her son was a God-fearing Christian who studied the Bible and was a man of Jesus Christ. Elizene Phanor said he was not a jihadist. "One thing I know. My son is no criminal. My son, no gun. My son don't have no bomb. My son never killed people. My son loves people."

IN THE THIRD and final trial in winter 2009, the Batiste defense wanted to use Williams's testimony to counter the prosecution's so-called expert witness. Williams had been referred to the defense team by professor John Hagedorn, a leading gang expert at the University of Illinois at Chicago and a defense consultant. As soon as the prosecution heard about Williams's background (professor who studies gangs, witnessed the Stones/gangs up close as a kid hanging out with his dad, youth advocate who worked with gangs), they objected to him testifying. The prosecution asked the judge to immediately dismiss the jury so that they would not be prejudiced by what was taking place in the courtroom. She agreed and dismissed the jury. Williams was also asked to leave the room. The defense attorney told him afterward that the prosecution argued he was an expert witness being carried as a lay witness. Since the defense didn't have time to process him as an expert witness, the prosecution argued that he couldn't give expert witness testimony. He was allowed to give preliminary testimony; however, the jury was dismissed while he was giving it. Williams was supposed to continue his testimony with the jury the following morning. When the court asked the defense to call him back to the stand, the defense said to the judge (in front of the jury) that since she restricted his testimony, they decided not to call him back. The defense hoped that planted a seed in the jurors' minds that he was going to say something that would hurt the prosecution's case.

While the first two trials were based on the defendants' being terrorists, the third trial focused on their being gang members who were plotting terrorist acts to overthrow the U.S. government. The prosecution's star witness was former ATF agent Dan Young, now Homeland Security's expert on Chicago gangs. However, his testimony only provided public information that could have been found by perusing documents published by the Chicago Police Department and the Chicago Crime Commission. In addition, there were strikingly inaccurate and biased statements within Young's testimony. Young's role was to depict the Stones as a street gang that only existed to further its criminal enterprise. The prosecution likely felt that since the previous two juries didn't believe that Batiste and his associates were terrorists, maybe the third could be convinced that the defendants were gang-bangers plotting with terrorists to attack America. Young proved to be the perfect expert witness for the prosecution.

He testified about "a little known fact" that Gangster Disciple leader Larry Hoover was a member of the Black P Stone Nation. However, it is common knowledge that Jeff Fort tried to get Larry Hoover, then leader of a gang called the High Supreme Gangsters, to incorporate his gang into the Black P Stone Nation. According to Rod Emery, author of *The Blueprint: From Gangster Disciple to Growth and Development*, a history of the Black Gangster Disciples, "In Hoover's mind, such a merger would swallow up the Gangster identity. Therefore Hoover declined."

Young testified that "the Blackstone Rangers' primary mission in life was to fight the Disciples over turf." While the Disciples and the Blackstone Rangers were indeed vicious rivals, they also collaborated in The Woodlawn Organization's job-training program from 1967 to 1968. They also united in 1969 in a coalition to push for jobs for African Americans in Chicago construction projects. The bitter 1960s turf war between the Stones and Disciples was just one facet of the Stone Nation's history.

Agent Young had a plethora of other claims in his testimony. He suggested that the P in Black P Stone Nation stood for "prince of darkness" among other extreme titles. However, Fort himself often openly said that the P stood for "people, peace, power, prosperity." Back in the 1960s, the Stones also promoted the idea that black men were "princes" who were proud of their heritage.

Young testified that Fort defrauded the federal government of eight hundred thousand dollars and had control of the TWO job-training program, which allowed the BPSN "to become one of the premier street gangs in Chicago." In truth, the administrators and fiscal agents of the TWO job-training program were reverends, Arthur Brazier and Leon Finney, not Jeff Fort. Plus, a modestly funded job-training program wasn't enough to propel the BPSN to become a "premier" gang.

Young also testified that the BPSN staged marches in the areas under their control to intimidate and recruit. He noted that Fort and Mickey Cogwell were invited to attend the Nixon inauguration. In fact the BPSN was involved in a number of political and social activities where marches and demonstrations were common. While it is indisputable that the gang was deeply involved in local drug sales, they also were strongly influenced by the civil rights movement and Black Nationalism.

Young told the jurors, "Fort goes to bed one night leader of one of the largest and most powerful street gangs in the city of Chicago—wakes up as the Imam of the El Rukn Tribe/Nation." Nevertheless, the evolution of the Blackstone Rangers into the El Rukns was a long and complicated process. Young also claimed the El Rukns would do anything for money. In the sense that money is a motivator for most people to act, including lawyers, prosecutors, judges, and witnesses, such a statement is merely self-evident. The El Rukns were not Boy Scouts, and they were involved in street-level and wholesale drug sales. But they also were involved in the life of the communities where they lived all their lives and were not seen by all residents as evil. Their persistence in several neighborhoods for over fifty years is evidence of at least a small amount of community support, whether misguided or not.

Young said that Fort claimed the BPSN had fifty thousand members across the nation. The Chicago Crime Commission most recently estimated BPSN membership at twenty thousand, with three thousand more in prisons. Fort's fifty thousand likely dates back to the early 1970s, but the recent estimates are so far apart as to be nearly meaningless. Young testified that Fort had already "downsized the gang to his most loyal members." Research and knowledgeable observers within the communities, universities, and law enforcement believe that the incarceration of almost the entire Stones leadership crippled their organization and reduced their influence.

Young's testimony did not mention one of the most salient features of gangs in Chicago today. All of the major gangs, the BPSN included, have fractured into "renegades," or outlaw factions. These are now more numerous than loyal membership. This renders estimates made by ATF, the Chicago Crime Commission, or the Chicago police lacking. In any regard, the influence of leaders like Fort has been vastly reduced over the past twenty years.

Despite Young's weak testimony, after a three-month trial a Miami jury convicted the defendants—Narseal Batiste, Patrick Abraham, Stanley Grant Phanor, Burson Augustin, and Rothschild Augustine—of multiple charges that included conspiring to provide material support to the al-Qaeda terrorist organization and conspiracy to levy war against the United States by discussing and planning attacks on targets in the United States, including the Sears Tower in Chicago. Naudimar Herrera was acquitted on all counts.

The case ran up a tab of millions of dollars. "This is not a terrorism case," Batiste's lawyer, Ana Jhones said. "This is a manufactured crime." The defense team said their clients were hapless fools who fell victim to a government snare. Knowing that Batiste's claim to be a leader of BPSN was as inert as the LAW rocket they convinced El Rukn Alan Knox to buy, they used his claim to justify his prosecution nonetheless.

TERRORISM IS DEFINED as the unlawful use or threatened use of force or violence by a person or an organized group against people or property with the intention of intimidating or coercing societies or governments, often for ideological reasons. In the United States, this definition is now elastic and *terrorism* is increasingly a loaded word.

After the 9/11 terrorist attacks, a flurry of states added terrorism-related laws to their criminal codes, according to the National Conference of State Legislatures. From 2002 to 2005, states from New Hampshire to Texas identified new laws. But some states took it to the next level. In New York, a gang member from the Bronx was one of the first people ever charged under state terrorism laws. The district attorney said members of the St. James Boys street gang were shooting with the intent to intimidate or coerce a civilian population. Edgar Morales was convicted, though critics argued that this case did not fit the scope of terrorism. In 1992, the Illinois General Assembly passed a street gang terrorism prevention act. Part of the language says: "The General Assembly finds, however, that urban, suburban, and rural communities, neighborhoods and schools throughout the State are being terrorized and plundered by street gangs." The act says the street gangs' activities present a "clear and present danger to public order and safety and are not constitutionally protected. No society is or should be required to endure such activities without redress."

Former Speaker of the House Newt Gingrich hosted a FOX News special in 2005 called "American Gangs—Ties to Terror?" in which he investigated how international gangs pose a risk to national security, not just personal security. "Fueled by the global nature of the drug trade, gangs are increasingly international operations. With the infra-structure in place to move and distribute drugs across the border, the danger exists that they will use their network to, for the right price, traffic terrorists and weapons into the country." He concluded that groups driven by greed and hatred would find a need to collaborate.

Prosecutors have in the past used new laws to creatively fit crimes. RICO laws were originally put on the books to nab mobsters, but a decade later they were employed to take down drug cases involving gangs like the El Rukns. In the frenzy after 9/11, and the initial arrest of Jose Padilla, experts and academics questioned whether al-Qaeda would have a natural campaign in recruiting foot soldiers from prison gangs. Some argue that the problems that beset inner cities create a natural breeding ground for attracting disaffected and disenfran-chised youth to the al-Qaeda cause. But that can also be seen as a myopic view of what al-Qaeda stands for. Do the upper-middle-class, educated Saudi Arabian men who were behind the 9/11 attacks have much in common with male black and Latino gang members who often come from poverty-stricken neighborhoods? Can bin Laden craft literature that would attract American gang members? Islam may not be enough. Anti-American sentiments don't necessarily equate to waging a holy war against the United States. Al-Qaeda members don't maneuver in the United States and are generally offended by the country's foreign policy and way of life. Gangbangers tend to enjoy a capitalistic society that is conducive to the drug trade and other illegal vices.

Terrorism cases involving gang members run the risk of being red herrings for the government and society. If the word *terrorism* is used simply in the urban context to prosecute lawless gang members, the definition's intent is watered down. Many residents in struggling urban neighborhoods might describe ongoing street violence as terrorism, but one must question whether that's really accurate terminology. For Jeff Fort and Narseal Batiste, the terrorism connections become more complicated. Hustling Qaddafi or al-Qaeda members out of money was likely the intent of both Chicago men. Of course, making contact with terrorists or U.S. enemies of state is going to do more than raise the ire of government officials. But these men and their flocks got caught up in U.S. foreign policy. Perhaps it won't be the last time for street organizations and their sympathizers.

# 11

# The 8-Tray Stones

IN 1991, an 8-Tray Stone named Quinn called a Friday night service and invited Lance Williams. Service was a weekly meeting Stones, or Moes—as they began to refer to themselves around that time— held to discuss Nation or organizational goings on. In 1976, when the Blackstones became El Rukns and claimed to have an affiliation with the Moorish Science Temple of America, the El Rukns began to refer to themselves as Moors, or Moroccans. Following the tradition of black vernacular, the El Rukns altered the pronunciation of *Moor* to "Moe." Like some of the other words, symbols, and rituals that existed during the El Rukn era, Moe is a Blackstone moniker that remained in the new era of the organization. Thirteen-year-old Quinn asked Lance to "come talk to the Moes about some of that black stuff you be telling us about at school."

The service took place in the basement of a three-flat building on the corner of 85th and Morgan. Teenaged boys on security detail set up elaborate checkpoints around the building. They looked out for police or enemies who might have found out about the meeting and could try to do a drive-by shooting. The teens were decked out in Starter jackets, baseball caps, hoodies, and gym shoes. Many of the Stones preferred Chicago Bulls Starter jackets because the team's colors were the same as the Stones'—red and black. Plus, the Stones used BULLS as an acronym for Brothers United Living and Loving Stones. The Stones cherished the new Nike Air Jordan gym shoes, also red and black.

Everyone got frisked at the entrance to the basement. The men and boys were politely asked to remove their hats. As each Stone entered the room, he greeted every other Stone with the standard Blackstone handshake and direct eye contact. He then joined the cipher, a circle that the body of Stones stood in to carry out their standard rituals of service.

As a visitor, Lance observed from the sidelines. Quinn started the meeting by having the forty middle school to early high school–aged Stones recite the Blackstone Creed in unison. All Stones had to be able to recite it verbatim:

From out of the darkness into the light, Blackstone gives us courage, Blackstone gives us sight. Blackstone gives me something no man can be deprived of and that is the undying love called Blackstone. All means everything. Mighty means great. Many have been called, but few have been chosen. I now know nine thousand miles due east in the holy city of Mecca, there lies the Kaaba. The Blackstone is kept there. Many have tried to move the Stone but couldn't. So it is written who ever tries to move the stone will be crushed. Whoever falls upon the Stone will be grinded to dust.

Behold the Almighty Blackstone!

After the group recited the Blackstone Creed, Quinn turned to face the east, slightly bowed his head, and extended his arms out, bent at the elbows with his hands cupped. The boys followed his lead. He then led them in a call-and-response prayer. The Stones repeated in unison and with reverence:

Allah, the Father of the Universe.
The Father of Love, Truth, Peace, Freedom, and Justice.

Allah is My Protector, My Guide and My Salvation, By Night and
By Day, Through His Holy Prophet Noble Drew Ali.
Amen.

The creed recitation and prayer brought a deep silence over the group
of boys. Quinn broke the intensity with a loud greeting: "All well,
Moes!" The group responded in unison: "Blackstone love!" Quinn
instructed the group to "spit some lit," gang vernacular for "spitting
literature," or reciting the laws of the organization by memory. The
activity required the Stones to form a circle, or cipher as they called
it, so that each Stone could enter the center to "spit lit." At this meeting the Moes recited from a portion of the Blackstone literature they
called the Preliminary Moorish Questions. The thirteen questions
originated from the El Rukn era's affiliation with the Moorish Science Temple of America. The first Stone stepped into the center;
Quinn asked him question number one: "Who are you?" The young
Stone answered, "a Asiatic Moslem." The group applauded enthusi-
astically and shouted "yes, sir, yes, sir!" The response let the Stone
know that his answer was correct. The second Stone proceeded to
the center of the cipher and waited for Quinn's question. "What
are you?" The second Stone had no idea what the answer was so he
bowed his head and quickly went back to his place. The third Stone
took his place and attempted to answer the question. He said, "I
am the spirit of, uh, huh . . . the neverending, uh, uh." The group
immediately chimed in, shouting "no, sir, no, sir" to let him know he
was wrong. The fourth Stone eagerly jumped into the middle of the
cipher and asked himself the question, "What are you?" And then he
answered his own question with confidence. "I am the spirit from
the everlasting past unto the neverending days to come." The group
exploded with applause. "Yes, sir, yes, sir, all well, Moe, all well, Moe."
Quinn used this method to lead the group through the remaining
eleven questions and answers.

Once they successfully answered the thirteen questions, they
started over again until each member had a turn to spit. Next they
had a general conversation about internal business, including ways

to raise money (all legal) to buy matching T-shirts for an upcoming neighborhood party, personal beefs, and the payment of dues. During that general conversation, the boys would always say "Pardon me, Moe" or "Pardon oneself, Moe" whenever they wanted to make a comment while someone else was talking. There was no arguing, cursing, loud talking, silliness, or rude jokes. To witness this reverence and politeness was amazing, because most of the boys in attendance at this so-called gang meeting were the same boys who caused the most disruption in school. They were the ones involved in most of the fighting and overall disorderly behavior. However, at this Friday night basement meeting the teens demonstrated complete and total respect from the beginning to the end of the service. Clearly they had reverence for this service that they didn't have for school.

At the end of the meeting, Quinn told the body that he had asked Lance to come to the meeting to talk to them about black history. He said all Blackstones were required to know about being black, and since the schools didn't really teach them anything about their history, he wanted Lance to teach them. Some of the Stones responded to Quinn's comments by saying "yes, sir!" He also told them that Lance would take a group of youth to Africa in the summertime, and he wanted to go on the next trip. Quinn asked Lance to tell them something. Lance obliged and talked to the Stones for about an hour. The meeting ended with a group prayer and an encore recitation of the Blackstone Creed. The Stones concluded with the Blackstone handshake and they left the building in an orderly way.

Quinn, a young Stone wise beyond his years, continued to provide guidance and maturity to the 8-Tray Stones until his untimely death of an asthma attack in his twenties.

IN THE MID-1980S, Lance started the Know Thyself program, a community-based organization that provided African-centered enrichment activities to school-aged youth. A key component was a rites of passage program for elementary school students. Know Thyself sponsored fifteen-day trips to Egypt and Greece for students in the program. Because the program launched during a time when there was a great deal of national concern around young black men being an "endangered species," Lance readily sold the services of this new program to many elementary schools in the Chicago Public School system. Principals identified their most at-risk boys to participate, many of whom were affiliated with gangs and engaged in risky behaviors. Like his father, Lance found himself working with gangbangers. Although his father drew from the popular Black Nationalist social and political consciousness movement of the 1960s and early '70s to try to encourage the boys he worked with to become more socially responsible, Lance was not so fortunate. By the time he started his work with inner-city black kids, the Black Nationalist social and cultural revolution had been replaced with a drug culture exacerbated by the rabid right-wing conservatism of the 1980s. Therefore, he had to create artificial cultural activities that served as interventions for the plethora of social problems experienced by inner-city black youth.

As a youth worker, Lance witnessed an escalation in antisocial behavior—particularly among young African American males. It appeared to him that a lot of this behavior took cues from a new "gangsta/thug culture" emerging from popular culture expressions like gangster rap music. Lance instinctively felt he could counter this new thug mentality by introducing the young people to cultural resources promoted by African-centered youth development programs. He hoped these programs might reduce the antisocial behaviors that lead to violence among these kids.

Lance implemented the Know Thyself program at Gresham Elementary School in the Auburn Gresham community. He conducted a classroom-based cultural awareness program for the fourth- through eighth-grade students, but his primary responsibility was working with a group of fourth- through eighth-grade boys the school had identified as being at risk. A couple days a week Lance conducted group sessions that used transitional initiation rites to instill the boys with an African cultural social ethos that promoted a sense of purpose and meaning. Lance also spent a significant amount of time with the boys in the community after school, on the weekends, and during the summer.

When Lance first arrived at Gresham he quickly found out that the overwhelming majority of the boys identified themselves as Blackstones. They called the community that they lived in 8-Tray. The South Side community was composed of black extended family households. Morgan Street divided 8-Tray. The west side of 8-Tray had many brick bungalows and large frame homes; although these were single-family homes, most of them were occupied by extended families where grandparents, usually the owners, housed their unemployed adult sons and daughters. Grandchildren and other adult children lived there, too. On the east side of the Tray, multi-unit apartment buildings mixed with two- and three-flat buildings. Single mothers and their children usually occupied the rental apartment buildings and flats. There was a great deal of turnover in the rental units, families always moving in and out and, of course, some evictions here and there.

Many families had lived in their homes long enough to pay off their mortgages and so owned their bungalows and frame homes. The homeowners were usually elders who had raised their children in the neighborhood as they worked and retired from government jobs like the post office or unskilled jobs in factories. Whereas the grandparents were able to secure living-wage jobs despite having no education beyond high school—many of them weren't high school graduates—their children weren't so lucky. Even though most of their children had graduated from high school, and some went to college, the ones who only had a high school diploma were unable to secure more than menial jobs. That forced them to continue to live with their parents, who were nearing retirement age.

Those children began to have children who also lived with the grandparents. Eventually many of the second generation, frustrated by feeling stuck and like failures, resorted to abusing alcohol and drugs and engaging in a range of other risky behaviors. Many of the young women self-medicated with multiple sex partners, resulting in children from different fathers. The men coped by drinking, using drugs, and doing petty crime to make money. Many of these young men ended up addicted to alcohol and drugs while simultaneously being incarcerated for their petty crimes and hustles. The grand-children ended up being raised by their dysfunctional mothers and their grandmothers, who by now have outlived the grandfathers. The mothers and grandmothers struggled to raise children amid a failing educational system, economic isolation, and the deterioration of the community's social fabric. The third generation is beginning to have children now and the vicious cycle continues.

The boundaries of 8-Tray ran from 83rd Street on the south between Halsted and Racine to 85th Street on the north. It was bordered by Stone Terrace, a Blackstone set, to the east. George Town, a Gangster Disciple (GD) set, fell south of 8-Tray, making it a conflict border. To the north of 8-Tray was a middle-class neighborhood occupied by single-family homeowners. There was no gang activity in this neigh-borhood, so it served as a buffer between the 8-Tray Stones and the GDs on 79th Street. To the west of the 8-Tray Stones was Foster Park, another Blackstone set. Although 8-Tray and Foster Park were both Stone sets, beefs arose between the two. Most of the conflict revolved around interpersonal disagreements. There were approximately 450 8-Tray Stones in the mid-1980s, with some as young as nine.

Calumet High School served as the neighborhood school for 8-Tray kids. Prior to Calumet being transformed into a charter school in 2007, approximately thirty 8-Tray Blackstones were enrolled at the school. Most of the Stones were freshmen and sophomores, because they began dropping out of school after their second year. The larg-est population of Stones on 8-Tray were men between the ages of sixteen and forty—most of whom were high school dropouts and unemployed. Their population ranged from 350 to 450 with another hundred locked up in prison. Although the number of Stones fluctu-ated from set to set, the demographic categories were essentially the same. Compared to other Blackstone sets, 8-Tray was essentially a medium-size set. Stone Terrace, the Blackstone set just east of 8-Tray, was half the size of 8-Tray, and Motown, one of the largest Blackstone sets, was twice as big.

## History of 8-Tray

LIKE MOST BLACKSTONE sets of the last twenty years, the history of the 8-Tray is a direct result of the fracturing of the Blackstone Nation itself. Although federal prosecution and incarceration of the Stone leadership mostly contributed to the fall of the Stones, internal strife, the crack cocaine era, Chicago public housing policy, and Chicago public school transformation policy were prominent forces in helping to fracture the Blackstone Nation into small renegade sets. The infrastructure and leadership hierarchy that has been in place within the Blackstone Nation for the last twenty years is a direct result of federal law enforcement's destruction of the El Rukn organization. From 1976 to the mid-1980s, the El Rukns were the dominant representation of the Blackstone organization on the streets. However, through massive downsizing and the adoption of Islam, most of the kids who lived on Blackstone sets didn't even realize that the El Rukns were Blackstones who had converted to Islam and taken on another name. They thought the El Rukns were some strange new cult. At the same time, because the El Rukns had downsized so much and its leadership came under attack by the feds, it didn't have the capacity to micromanage the day-to-day affairs of its sets. The older Stones on the streets who refused to convert to El Rukns remained underground because they didn't want problems with the organization or law enforcement officials who were in hot pursuit of the El Rukns. Thus, El Rukn's inability to manage the affairs of its sets left a leadership vacuum within the sets.

The Stones began to take it upon themselves to bring leadership and organization to their individual sets. However, because most of them did not have any type of guidance from the older Stones, they didn't really know what they were doing. They used the little that they had learned about what it meant to be Blackstone growing up as boys and made up the rest as they went along.

On 8-Tray, two Stones, Terry "T-Bose" Davis and Christopher "Loopy" Keys, emerged as leaders of a group of young Blackstones who lived on 83rd Street between Halsted and Racine. The Stones who lived in the general area between 83rd Street and 87th Street anywhere between Western Avenue and the Dan Ryan Expressway had no specific name. They were just considered members of the Black P Stone Nation. At the time, T-Bose and Loopy were attending Calumet High School, which the Gangster Disciples dominated. Known for being gladiators, the two single-handedly fought off the GDs and eventually mobilized Stones from the neighboring Foster Park and Stone Terrace communities to come together to drive the GDs out of Calumet High School and convert it to a school dominated by Blackstones.

With their success, T-Bose and Loopy developed a reputation for being leaders. The two took advantage of their victory by appointing themselves generals of a renegade set that they would call 8-Tray, street slang for 83rd Street. They used the title "general" because they had heard it was the highest rank under Chief Malik. Having the rank of general, they naively believed, would make them subordinate only to Chief Malik. They didn't know that general was a rank within the El Rukn organization, not the Blackstone Nation. There were only twenty generals in the whole El Rukn organization, and only Chief Malik appointed them.

This type of confusion and discontinuity has been common among Blackstone sets since the mid-1980s. T-Bose and Loopy also believed as leaders of a set they would have to pay a "Nation tax," a sort of franchise fee that sets had to pay to the governing body of the Blackstone Nation. Due to the collapse of the established organizational leadership, they really didn't know how much or to whom they would have to pay. They didn't like the idea of owing anybody anything; they also didn't like the idea of some ambiguous higher-ups coming in and telling them what to do. Loopy wanted the 8-Tray to establish itself as a renegade set with complete and total independence from the Black P Stone Nation. They would remain Blackstones but with autonomy from the main body. T-Bose was a little hesitant but he didn't see anybody who could stop them, and it didn't appear that anybody really cared what they did.

Hence, the 8-Tray Stones emerged, distinguishing themselves from other Stones in the area. The Stones who lived west of 8-Tray subsequently began to call themselves Foster Park Stones. The Stones east of 8-Tray began to call their set Stone Terrace because most of them resided in a housing development with that name. Simultaneously, but not necessarily influenced by the 8-Tray Stones, other Stones throughout the South Side of Chicago began to establish a new era of Blackstone sets. Some were the sets of Terror Town (Dominate Set), Duck Town, Moe-Town (Dominate Set), and a host of other fractured Blackstone sets too numerous to list. Each one of these sets had its own leadership that generally operated independent of any outside force. The leaders of these sets often change due mostly to simple attrition. The set names also frequently change.

## Rise of a New Set Leader

DUE TO THE LACK of an organized leadership hierarchy within the Blackstone Nation, individuals emerged as leaders in organic ways, often through specific events. One such event occurred on a hot summer morning on 8-Tray in 1991. Lance helped CK run a summer league basketball tournament on the grounds of Gresham Elementary School. CK had organized the tournament for elementary school boys, but he also had a division for guys sixteen and older. Born and raised on 8-Tray, when CK returned home from the army he took it upon himself to get involved with youth in the community. He became a baseball coach at Harlan High School while organizing sports events for the kids in the neighborhood. Although he did not actively gangbang, 8-Tray Moes and Moes from neighboring sets respected him. When he pulled together this particular summer tournament, all of the Moes from 8-Tray, Stone Terrace, and Foster Park entered teams. On game days, there would be over a thousand Moes at the court.

Before the game started, CK got into an argument with a young guy named Antoine. Although Antoine was not a Moe, he played on one of the 8-Tray teams. The argument stemmed from Antoine's team having to forfeit its game because neither team had enough players present at the scheduled start time. Antoine joked with CK about giving his team the win since he was the only one there from either team. Apparently CK, in a bad mood, pushed Antoine and told him to get his punk ass off the court. Antoine slowly backed off, retreating off the school grounds altogether to stand across the street from the courts. A large crowd gathered as CK continued to berate Antoine by calling out his name as he stood across the street. CK even threatened to send his thirteen-year-old nephew, Greedy, over to whip Antoine's ass. Antoine said nothing; he just stood there. Eventually everything died down and the next scheduled game went on. Under normal circumstances, CK would not have overreacted this way. He was an intelligent young man who sincerely wanted to help improve his community. He coached baseball at one of the local high schools, so he knew how to behave professionally. However, in this situation his behavior was out of character. He had pulled together a basketball tournament for hundreds of straight-up gang-bangers. CK wanted the gangbangers to know who was in charge. If he let Antoine challenge his authority, he would be perceived as weak by the rest of the guys. The streets don't respect or tolerate weakness, so CK felt that he had no other choice but to go off on Antoine. His overreaction sent a message. In the process of exerting his manhood, he also emasculated Antoine. It is this type of emasculation that leads to much of the violence that exists between young black males in the 'hood.

About twenty minutes into the game, CK's girlfriend, who had been standing along the sidelines, hollered to CK that Antoine was coming and he had a gun. The barrel of the gun was so long that its tip almost scraped the ground as Antoine's six-foot-four frame took long, quick strides. Everyone stood frozen with shock as Antoine took the barrel of the forty-five and jabbed it at CK's head and said, "Motherfucker, who's the punk now?" He continued to press the gun to CK's head, asking him repeatedly, "Bitch, who's the punk now?" Suddenly, amid a sea of Blackstones, one Stone slowly glided out from among the crowd. This Stone was as lean and tall as Antoine and he wore long, draping cornrows. He slowly approached Antoine, almost whispering, "Toine, Toine," trying to get his attention without startling him.

"Toine, Toine," he said, "slow up, Toine, it ain't worth it, Toine. It ain't worth it." Antoine didn't seem to hear a word; he stewed in a rage. By now, the approaching Stone stood next to Antoine, whispering in his ear. CK kept his head raised high but didn't say a word. The Stone continued to whisper in Antoine's ear and soon Antoine's heaving chest slowly contracted. His breaths became deeper and slower and then he gradually lowered the gun from CK's head. He backed off, facing the thousand-plus Moes. He turned and walked away.

Once Antoine was out of sight, CK ordered the game to continue without him. He told his girlfriend to go home. He gathered up a few of the Moes, jumped in a car, and quickly left. The game resumed. Half an hour later, automatic gunfire rang out in the distance, but nobody stopped to inquire what was going on. Nothing needed to be said. What had just happened on 8-Tray typified the most common type of violence that takes place within the Blackstone Nation and other gang sets. To outsiders who don't know, it's called gang violence; to those on the inside, it's simply beefin'.

On that day, the future 8-Tray leader emerged. The Stone who came out of the crowd to save CK's life was Skip-O. He earned the respect of many on the Tray that day for the way he handled Antoine. Likewise, CK established himself as a capable leader, too, by not cowering in the face of death. Many would have understood if CK had apologetically begged Antoine for his life. But in the eyes of the streets, CK kept his head up, looked death in the face, and held his ground. He also immediately struck back with force, another trait admired by the streets.

## The Alakhbar

WITHOUT ANY FORMAL PROCESS, the Stones of 8-Tray began to claim Skip-O as their alakhbar, or set leader. While no continuity remained among the various sets within the Nation, all Blackstone sets usually had at least one person who served as a figurehead and carried some sort of title. When the fragmented Blackstone sets began to emerge during the decline of the El Rukn era in the mid-1980s, many sets used the title of general for their leader. On 8-Tray, T-Bose and Loopy were the original two generals, but later five other guys simultaneously held the rank. By the early 1990s, however, 8-Tray began to recognize the title of alakhbar as the person who served as the leader of the whole set.

The alakhbar held rank over the generals. *Alakhbar* was an Arabic word the Stones used to mean "a great leader." The job of the alakhbar was to oversee the whole set. The alakhbars called and officiated over regularly scheduled Friday service meetings. Even though they were supposed to appoint and supervise lower-ranking positions to help them manage the day-to-day affairs of the set, that rarely happened. The alakhbar also supposedly functioned as the ultimate decision maker of the set. However, Stones in all sets pretty much did what they wanted to do with little accountability to anyone. The alakhbar was the chief mediator/judge of conflict within the set. If he felt that one of the Moes of his set needed to be punished, he could order lower-ranking lawmen called muftis, another title borrowed from the El Rukn era, to give the Moe being disciplined a violation. A violation, or V, usually meant that a Moe would have to stand in a circle of other Moes and take a beating for a prescribed period of time. Sometimes he would have to take a punch to the mouth from a lawman. Usually only a weaker Moe would be given a violation. More aggressive Moes wouldn't tolerate being violated by anybody for any reason.

The alakhbar serves as the official representative of the set to the Nation and other Nation sets. No sets may involve themselves in the affairs of another set without permission from the alakhbar. Depending on the set, the alakhbar has varying degrees of influence on the Stones within it. Only in rare cases, however, does the alakhbar rule over his set with an iron fist; he simply doesn't have the power. In the cases where an alakhbar has complete power and dominion over his set he usually acquired the power on his own and not through his association with the hierarchy of the Blackstone Nation. In the 1960s and early '70s, the leader of a set would be empowered by the authority of the organization because he had received an appointment. Today, alakhbars are self-appointed or assumed through some form of default. For instance, in the late 1980s to the early '90s, the 8-Tray set went several years without anyone holding the position of alakhbar.

## Skip-O

SKIP-O COULD HAVE been the leader of any organization. He was charismatic, sociable, and smart. Those attributes combined with his imposing six-foot-four, slender but muscular frame and his fearlessness made him the perfect leader of gangbangers. Skip-O's first approach to leadership was to appeal to his members' hearts and minds. If that didn't work, he didn't order a subordinate to exact punishment on the rebellious person or individuals—he did it himself. In the event he had to regulate someone, it was never personal; once he checked you, it was over. His intelligence and brilliance was beyond reproach. He had the Blackstone literature, which consisted of thousands of laws, principles, iconography, rules, and regulations, committed to memory. This isn't surprising, though; he graduated from Whitney Young High School, one of Chicago's top college preparatory schools. He also had a couple of years of college under his belt. He had received a scholarship to play basketball before he ended up back in the 'hood as the leader of the 8-Tray Stones.

As the alakhbar, Skip-O could have used his status to line his own pockets. In keeping with tradition, a set leader could impose a nation tax on anyone making money, legally or illegally, in the territories they controlled. During Skip's reign as alakhbar, the selling of crack cocaine on the 8-Tray generated a lot of money. Skip could have taxed the guys selling drugs on 8-Tray, but that wasn't his style or part of his personal value system. Most other guys in his position got rich from taxing drug dealers. They had the cars, clothes, and money to show for it. Skip, on the other hand, didn't even have a car. He walked around the Tray like Jesus tending his flock.

In some cases, the drug dealers paid the set leader an agreed-upon percentage or weekly fee for the right to sell drugs on his set. In return, the gang leader would use his soldiers to sell drugs for the drug dealers and/or provide them with protection from people trying to rob them or gangster their drug spots. If drug dealers didn't follow his protocol, the set leader would prohibit his members from selling for the drug dealers and/or send his subordinates at the noncompliant drug operation to shut it down. More sophisticated set leaders had their own drug connections and therefore could supply their own members with drugs to sell while the leader controlled the proceeds.

Like Bull Hairston, the cofounder and leader of the Blackstones from the 1960s, Skip-O saw drugs as a plague among black people in and out of 8-Tray. He really wanted to shut down selling drugs altogether on 8-Tray, but he knew that most of his Stones were victims of social and economic marginalization and had no other real opportunities to make money. Since he couldn't provide them with a better alternative he didn't try to stop them from selling. At the same time, he would preach to them about the detrimental effects that selling drugs had on them and their communities. He encouraged some to use selling drugs only as a stepping-stone to opening legal businesses. Those who were capable he encouraged to go back to school to acquire some skills that would allow them to get a decent job. Skip also had a pragmatic streak; he knew that he really didn't have the soldiers necessary to shut down the drug dealers on the Tray anyway. He understood that his most loyal followers were even more loyal to the drug dealers because they put money in their pockets. So he left it alone and didn't get involved in their affairs. When they got robbed or needed protection from competitors, he let them fend for themselves and ordered his men to stay out of the battles.

After serving as alakhbar of 8-Tray for close to seven years, Skip-O stepped down from his position. Today, Skip-O has a job. He comes through the Tray every once in a while to briefly holler at the Moes, but he keeps moving. For a period of time after Skip-O stepped down, the alakhbar position on 8-Tray remained vacant. No one seemed interested in the job. They saw it as a hassle with no real benefits. The drug dealers were too strong to extort. Lording over a set was too risky. There were too many hotheads on the set willing to shoot even the alakhbar over minor conflicts. The members were more loyal to the drug dealers than to the Nation. Trying to govern a renegade set was a problem that nobody wanted.

## The Crack Cocaine Era

ILLICIT DRUGS HAVE always been available on 8-Tray. In the early 1980s, freebasing cocaine became more affordable and popular in some black communities. Prior to the 1980s, black folks viewed cocaine as a "rich man's drug," and heroin was for dope fiends. During this period one could easily buy "bud"—marijuana—on the Tray, of course, and one could get syrup too, but not too many gang-bangers were even into selling drugs then. By the mid-'80s, cocaine in the form of ready rock made cocaine much cheaper. The demand increased the market, and the opportunity to make money on a large scale attracted the gangs. The Tray delved into selling ready rocks, and by 1990 the crack era had come into its full effect on the Tray and other Blackstone sets.

The Stones' relationship with crack cocaine in the 1990s looked curiously similar to their relationship with heroin during their early history. From their inception, the Stones were adamantly against the selling of heroin in Woodlawn. Bull Hairston was actually sentenced to fifteen years for the solicitation of murder for ordering the shooting of three men, one killed, who were selling heroin in Woodlawn. Right after Bull was locked up, the Italian and Irish mafias conspired with black drug kingpins like Lonnie Branch to flood the black community with heroin. With Bull gone, the will to prevent heroin from being sold was eliminated. It is believed by some that the El Rukns similarly prevented crack cocaine from being sold in Chicago in the early 1980s. However, from 1983 to 1989, the highest-ranking leaders of the El Rukn organization, including Jeff Fort, were all indicted and incarcerated. The Italian and Irish mafias again conspired with black drug kingpins like Flukey Stokes to flood the black community with crack cocaine.

Like most other Blackstone sets, the 8-Tray Stones got a visit from an outsider who made them an offer they couldn't refuse. One summer evening in 1992, they were hanging out about fifty deep, as usual, on the corner of 85th and Carpenter when they noticed an entourage of cars crawling in their direction from 83rd Street. The line stretched so long that they assumed it was a funeral procession. The first vehicle in the thirty-car entourage pulled directly alongside the 8-Tray Stones, who stared in a state of confusion. They were familiar with only some of the cars in the entourage, those belonging to a group of Foster Park Stones. None of the occupants of the cars exited until the last car made it onto Carpenter. At last, the car doors opened. Each car held four passengers. While bellowing "All well, Moe!" the visitors approached the 8-Tray Stones with the ritual Blackstone greeting: grasping each others' right hands with the index fingers extended to the wrist, the index fingers then sliding back to join each other in the formation of a pyramid (the organizational symbol) and the right hands each extending to represent the five fundamental principles of the Blackstone Nation. They then slapped them together, the original high five, to symbolize unity, and finally each Stone balled up his fist and pounded his chest over his heart to represent Stone love. The 8-Tray Stones were uncomfortable with this overwhelming display. They knew the visiting Stones hadn't come to pay them a visit more than one hundred deep just to show some Stone love.

And of course they were right.

Foster Park Stone Reno Wooldridge led the visiting Stones' caravan. The 8-Tray Stones knew Reno, but they knew him in his capacity as a big-time player in the crack game, not as a gang chief who rolled with goons and killers. Reno was known for his ability to move weight, not his rank in the Nation. But what the 8-Tray Stones would soon find out was that the new gang chiefs were guys who had enough money to buy their rank and the muscle to impose it.

Reno and some of his top guys pulled T-Bose and Loopy to the side to talk to them privately. From jump, they expressed that anything they said to them was a request and not a demand. They told them that Chief Malik had heard about the leadership they had provided to the Nation during a time when it had suffered under a great deal of duress. Given the circumstances of the Nation, they told T-Bose and Loopy that they had acted rightfully by providing leadership to 8-Tray. But they wanted to let them know that some changes had to be made to get the Nation back on track. They said that it had come down from Chief Malik that Reno would be holding the new title of the Kaaba. The Kaaba had the authority over all sets on the South Side and was only beholden to the Prince, also known as Watketa "Keeta" Valenzuela, Chief Malik's son, and Chief Malik himself. Reno and his men expressed to T-Bose and Loopy that for the Nation to get back on its feet, all sets needed to stop proclaiming themselves to be independent of the Nation. Reno pointed out that if T-Bose and Loopy brought 8-Tray back into the Nation and accepted Reno's authority, the chief would be forever in their debt and they would be provided with all of the rights and privileges of belonging to the Nation. To sweeten the deal, Reno promised them that under his leadership, he would provide T-Bose and Loopy with work at the best price so that they and the Stones of 8-Tray could eat well. He said if they didn't accept his offer there would be no hard feelings but the chief would appreciate it if they stopped using the name of Blackstone. Finally, Reno shared his personal vision with T-Bose and Loopy. As the new Kaaba, Reno envisioned uniting all Blackstone sets between Western and Commercial Streets from 71st Street to the south suburbs as one set called the Holy City of Mecca.

With all of Reno's assurances and the display of force he demonstrated, it seemed like a no-brainer for T-Bose and Loopy. They had no idea if all of this came from Chief Malik himself; they couldn't prove Reno right or wrong. But it really didn't matter. If Reno could orchestrate an elaborate show of one hundred members, he must indeed command the utmost respect and deference. They got in line with Reno, and, as promised, 8-Tray began to eat very well.

Through their new relationship with Reno, the 8-Tray Stones received "high-quality work at the best prices." According to them, Reno served as one of the middlemen between the Blackstone Nation and other street gangs, local mafias, and other organized crime groups that were plugged into a cocaine distribution network. The network comprised international drug cartels made up of financiers, producers, and transporters of cocaine. Facilitator Reno put the street gangs into play to move cocaine for local crime syndicates and international drug cartels that dealt in thousands of kilos, or bricks, at a time. Guys like Reno who had connections with the cartels usually dealt in hundreds of kilos at a time. Although what they made varied greatly from individual to individual, middlemen like Reno generally made millions for themselves. To move hundreds of bricks, drug kingpins like Reno hooked up with guys like T-Bose, Loopy, and others who were leaders of sets. The leaders of the sets usually worked with two to eight kilos at a time, and if they were decent managers they made hundreds of thousands of dollars for themselves. At the street level, the Moes were the ones who actually sold the drugs for the leaders of the sets or for other independent sellers for an agreed-upon percentage. From 1990 to 1995, fifteen to twenty Moes selling from a spot on 8-Tray could each average one hundred to two hundred dollars a day. The Moes at the top of the lower level who were bold enough to find an independent spot off the set—where two to three guys put up a thousand dollars to buy some work—had the potential to make as much as three thousand dollars a day to split among themselves. It seemed a surefire way to get robbed, but some Moes saw it as worth the risk because the money was so good. Keep in mind that these guys still lived at home with their parents or grandparents. Most of the money lined their pockets; they didn't have rent to pay or other household expenses. The money served as an incentive not to go to school or work a minimum-wage job. The risk of getting caught and being sent to jail seemed low at that time. The lower- to mid-level guys selling crack dealt with quantities called eight balls, or one-eighth of an ounce of crack cocaine. Anything less than an ounce was considered low level. Guys started moving up when they worked with more.

By the mid-1990s, the ability to earn extraordinary money selling crack had greatly declined after the violent turf wars and market demand lessened. By 1998, the same group of fifteen to twenty Moes would be lucky to share one or two thousand dollars per day selling crack. It got harder to find quality cocaine, which meant the hypes, or crack addicts, were not so eager to buy. Moreover, the federal welfare policy had changed so drastically by the mid-'90s that less money circulated to buy drugs. In addition, the drug laws got harsher; getting caught with five grams of crack could get an offender a five-year mandatory minimum sentence. Guys were beginning to get twenty-plus-year sentences for having less than a thousand dollars' worth of drugs. Selling drugs got too risky for the amount of money being made. On the other hand, illustrating racial disparities in sentencing, possessing the same amount of powdered cocaine—more prevalent in white communities—garnered a much lower penalty.

By 2000, the big moneymaking in the crack game had ended. However, throughout the Blackstone Nation, Stones who had become addicted to the 1990s money became desperate to get it back. They began to fight each other over drug spots, which led to rampant shootings and killings. Out of this desperation, the stickup era emerged. Those who could no longer eat by selling drugs began to rob those who had either drugs or drug money. It became common for crews to raid drug houses for their stashes. Guys who were still having success selling drugs were being kidnapped and held hostage until their families paid a ransom.

In the fall of 1993, twenty-four-year-old Reno was sitting in a parked car on the 8-Tray on 84th and May when someone shot him to death. Police never solved the murder. The rumor on the streets was that his Gangster Disciple cousin set him up. The GDs supposedly wanted him dead because he refused to provide them with "work." Many refute this theory because people who knew him say Reno sold to anybody who could pay his price—he was an equal opportunity distributor. His desire to make money far outweighed his loyalty to the Blackstone Nation. In 2001, his identical twin brother and successor, Deno, was murdered at the 50-Yard Line Lounge in south suburban Harvey, Illinois.

A couple of months after Reno's hit, Chicago police shot and killed Loopy. The news report of the shooting incident said Loopy was in his car on the corner of 63rd and Western Avenue when a confrontation occurred between him and the police. According to the police, Loopy refused to get out of the car when ordered and then tried to drive off. Claiming they feared for their lives, the police fired through the windshield of the car. A week after the shooting, a media report stated that Loopy had twenty bags of crack cocaine stashed inside one of his coat sleeves. Loopy's father reported to the media that the coroner's report said that Loopy had been shot several times around his armpits, which indicated that his arms were raised when he was shot. Loopy's father said that even if he had twenty bags on him, Loopy didn't deserve to be shot down on the street like a dog.

## Things Fall Apart on 8-Tray

LOOPY'S DEATH CAUSED a big rift on 8-Tray. One of the key reasons for T-Bose and Loopy's success as leaders was that they lived on different sides of the set, which was divided by Morgan Street. T-Bose lived on 85th and Carpenter, on the west side of the set, and Loopy lived on 83rd and Peoria, the east side. They complemented each other as leaders because they each had the respect of the soldiers on their respective sides, and through their leadership they brought the whole set together as one. When Loopy was killed, the Moes on the east side of the Tray felt that they didn't have equal representation on the set. Loopy's soldiers felt that T-Bose favored the Moes on the west side of the set. Some of Loopy's men, like his cousin Willie "Pooh" Thomas and his nephew Greedy, argued that since Loopy stood for being a renegade set, they would revert back to calling themselves Renegades. T-Bose didn't make a big deal about it because the only person who had challenged the renegade movement on 8-Tray was Reno, and he was dead. In addition, most of the money being made on 8-Tray was on T-Bose's side of the set, so he wasn't going to be affected by the Renegades. He decided to let them do their thing. However, some of the Moes on the west side of the set, T-Bose's side, took exception to the Stones on their set hollering renegade, and they began to distinguish themselves by calling themselves Vikings. 8-Tray was now officially divided, and a war between the two sides broke out. Several Vikings were shot as the Renegades ran nightly raids on the Vikings' territory. The Renegades tried to disrupt the Vikings' two drug spots on 83rd and 85th and Carpenter. The Renegades had always been jealous of their counterparts' ability to make money selling drugs. While the Moes on Carpenter, T-Bose's guys, were known for being moneymakers first and gladiators second, the Moes on the east side, Loopy's guys, were known for being gladiators first and moneymakers second. Loopy was the only person who could control the Moes on the east side of the Tray, but with him gone they began to push up on their own 8-Tray brothers. The beef ultimately turned into a war over who would control crack-selling spots. This type of internal beef became prevalent on most Blackstone sets. Although much has been made about gang violence in Chicago since the early 1990s, most of it hasn't been gang violence at all. Most of the so-called gang violence in Chicago has been inter-personal conflict and beefing between gang members over drug turf within the same set, like what erupted on 8-Tray.

From 1993 on, 8-Tray experienced a slow fracturing. There became less and less interaction between the two sides as the rift widened.

## The CHA Plan for Transformation

IN 1999, THE Chicago Housing Authority (CHA) began implemen-tation of its billion-dollar Plan for Transformation, considered to be the largest revitalization effort of public housing in the United States and an effort to dismantle concentrated poverty. Many of Chicago's high-rise projects came down, and mixed-income housing went up in some developments. Skeptics saw it as a way to kick black people off the prime land that many of Chicago's most notorious projects sat on. This gentrification had a traumatic impact on the public housing residents who were forced to leave their homes. Not everyone has been able to return to the new housing in the new neighborhoods. Many leaseholders have taken housing vouchers in poor, black, seg-regated neighborhoods.

Displaced CHA residents affected the 8-Tray Stones, along with each and every other Blackstone set. Some CHA residents who were displaced from the Madden Park Homes were relocated to the block of 86th and Sangamon in 8-Tray. The Madden Park Homes were a group of mid-rises clustered near the lake at 37th Street. In terms of street gangs, it was known as New Town, a Black Disciple (BD) set that operated one of the largest open-air drug markets in the city. Some say the New Town BDs made as much as one hundred thousand dollars a day selling crack. However, when the housing authority demolished Madden Park, the BDs had to find a new location to serve. The New Town BDs whose families were relocated close to the Tray came in and set up shop on Sangamon—putting them in direct competition with some of the Stones who of course were already serving the area. The BDs' new presence on 86th and Sangamon set off a war with the 8-Tray Stones that raged for a few years. During this time several BDs were killed in separate drive-by shootings, and countless others were wounded. The BDs weren't the only ones to suffer. Although no 8-Tray Stones were killed by the BDs, their retaliation made it clear to the Stones that they had no intention of being pushed off the new turf they claimed. Eventually the Stones left the BDs more or less alone; however, ongoing flare-ups continued over the years.

The influx of public-housing gangs out of the projects into other gang sets farther south in the city in the early 2000s exacerbated the chaos already taking place. The drug and crime problems that were once concentrated in Chicago public housing now merged with the drug and crime problems that already existed in traditional black communities on the South Side.

## Renaissance 2010

IN ADDITION TO the turmoil brought on by gentrification and new housing policies, Chicago Public Schools implemented a policy, Renaissance 2010, that had a devastating effect on the black community. CPS started the policy to increase the number of high-quality education options across Chicago, but some neighborhood high schools were simply reconstituted with new admissions standards. Calumet High School, the high school that students who lived on

8-Tray attended, was one of them. In 2007, Calumet became a new high school called Perspectives Charter School. Because admission was based on lottery, a large number of students couldn't enroll and were forced to go to other high schools that were dumping grounds for kids who couldn't qualify to go to schools close to their homes. This often meant they had to cross multiple gang turfs to get back and forth from school. In many cases, a different gang dominated the new school that they were assigned to. And in actuality, by this time in Chicago street gang history, it really didn't matter what gang you were in. If you were not from the neighborhood, regardless of whether you were in the gang that dominated that neighborhood, you were considered a potential target for violence.

Calumet High School once served fifteen hundred students; when it was reconstituted into Perspectives Charter School, it served fewer than seven hundred. And most of the students that enrolled in the new Calumet were not from the neighborhoods surrounding the school. The 8-Tray Stones were forced out. Most of them were sent to Hirsch High School. To get to Hirsch, the 8-Tray Moes had to catch the 79th Street bus and take it east through several Disciple sets to get to school. Moreover, the bus stops that they had to get off at to walk to Hirsch were right in the heart of one of the most active Gangster Disciple sets in the city. Going to school every day could be a journey through literal war zones. Clearly understanding this treacherous path, the most active Moes entering high school never even reported to school. Others started going, but their attendance became sporadic. Within a few months, they stopped going altogether.

Twenty years after starting his work on 8-Tray, Lance still works there helping them to mediate their problems, advises them on a collective level, and counsels them in their personal affairs.

WHAT IS LEFT of the Almighty Black P Stone Nation can be categorized into three groups: older Stones who never converted to El Rukn, El Rukns, and the new generation of Stones who claim

BPSN. Unless they were born into a family that had intergenera-
tional connections to the Blackstone Rangers, members in this third
group have probably never heard of Bull Hairston, the organization's
cofounder. Hairston, a one-time fierce opponent of dope, got strung
out on heroin. He was killed on 39th and Cottage Grove in the 1980s.

Most of the Stones who predate the El Rukn era have died or
suffer from severe health challenges. Those still alive don't have
the wherewithal to do the street thing anymore. Every year a group
meets at a Chicago park for a reunion. Their hard lives are evident in
the lines on their faces and the weariness of their bodies.

The El Rukns still claim a couple hundred loyal members. It is this
group of Stones that the sanctioned street leadership of the organization comes from. Many are practicing Muslims who aren't involved
in criminal activity. The leaders of this group are generally appointed
by Jeff Fort, and they have a direct line of communication to him via
his family. Because of their connection to the chief, they wield considerable figurehead power on the streets. However, they don't have
the type of power to implement any rules and regulations that the
young gangbangers feel they must adhere to. The young turks respect
the old heads, but they see them as throwbacks.

The largest group of Stones today consists of a hodgepodge of
sets dispersed through Chicago. Each of these sets has its own leader.
These sets have little interaction with one another and when they do
it often revolves around conflict.

By the 1990s, the Blackstone Nation, or the Moes, had reverted
back whence they came, a group of independent street gangs. In
2006, the Chicago Crime Commission estimated that the Black P
Stone Nation was the second largest street gang in Chicago, behind
the Gangster Disciples, but the Chicago Crime Commission has a
pro-law-enforcement perspective that exaggerates the gang problem
in Chicago. According to the CCC, BPSN is one organization that
functions as a loose group of independent sets. It estimated that the
Stones had twenty thousand members on the streets of Chicago and
another three thousand in prison systems throughout the United

States. This membership is probably the largest in the history of the organization. From the late 1980s to 2010, the decline of the El Rukns, the rise and fall of crack cocaine in Chicago, and Chicago public housing and school policies were powerful forces that shaped the last twenty years of the Blackstone Nation.

Jeff Fort is still the undisputed leader of the Black P Stone Nation, but he is really no more than a figurehead whose name is evoked on the streets only symbolically. He's scheduled for release in 2038. Over the past twenty years, it has been common to hear young Stones exclaim, "On chief, Moe," to one another. It's an homage to Chief Malik that's similar to someone saying, "I swear to God." The reality is that this evocation of Fort's name is mostly the empty bravado of a youth who wouldn't know the revered leader if he passed him on the street. This generation of Stones only knows the legend.

# Sources

## Introduction

*Almighty Black P Stone* newspaper, 1970.

## Chapter 1

Timuel Black. "The History of African American Gangs in Chicago." Address at the University of Illinois at Chicago, November 9, 2000.

Robin F. Bachin. *Building the South Side: Urban Space and Civic Culture in Chicago*. Chicago: University of Chicago Press, 2004, 250.

Woodlawn facts from *Local Community Fact Book*. Edited by Chicago Fact Book Consortium, 1990.

"Woodlawn." Encyclopedia of Chicago. http://encyclopedia.chicagohistory .org/pages/1378.html.

Andrew R. L. Claton, Richard Sisson, and Chris Zacher (editors). *The American Midwest: An Interpretive Encyclopedia*. Bloomington: Indiana University Press, 2006.

Robert L. Polk. *Tight Little Island: Chicago's West Woodlawn Neighborhood, 1900– 1950, in the Words of Its Inhabitants*. Bronx, NY: CNG Editions, 2008, 22.

Ron Chepesiuk. *Black Gangsters of Chicago.* Fort Lee, NJ: Barricade Books, 2007.

Nathan Thompson. *Kings: The True Story of Chicago's Policy Kings and Numbers Racketeers.* Chicago: Bronzeville Press, 1994–2003.

Saul Alinsky. *Rules for Radicals: A Pragmatic Primer for Realistic Radicals.* New York: Vintage Books, 1971, 130.

Nicholas Lemann. *The Promised Land: The Great Migration and How It Changed America.* New York: Vintage Books, 1991, 97.

John Fish Hall. *Black Power/White Control: The Struggle of the Woodlawn Organization in Chicago.* Princeton, N.J.: Princeton University Press, 1973.

"Teens Given Fresh Start." *Chicago Tribune,* April 1, 1965.

## Chapter 2

R. T. Sale. *The Blackstone Rangers: A Reporter's Account of Time Spent with Blackstone Rangers in Chicago's South Side.* New York: Random House, 1971.

"American Gangster," BET Television, 2007.

## Chapter 3

John Fry. *Fire and Blackstone.* Philadelphia: Lippincott, 1969, chapter 1.

Annual Report of First Presbyterian Church, 1967.

"Gang Chiefs' Crime Records Told." *Chicago Tribune,* June 26, 1968.

First Presbyterian archives, Newberry Library, Chicago.

Donald Mosey and Arnold Rosenweig. "Woodlawn Gang Joins Cops to Keep Peace." *Chicago Daily Defender,* July 20, 1966.

Donald Mosey and Arnold Rosenweig. "47 Woodlawn Youths Held in Gang Attack on Cops." *Chicago Daily Defender,* October 13, 1966.

G. Bensinger. "Chicago Youth Gangs: A New Old Problem." *Journal of Crime & Justice,* 1984.

"Report to the Presbytery of Chicago from Its Committee Investigating Allegations of Wrongdoing Made Against the Reverend John Fry, Mr. Charles LaPaglia and Miss Ann Schwalbach of the Staff of First Presbyterian Church." Presented to the Presbytery of Chicago, 1969.

Annual meeting notes, First Presbyterian Church of Chicago. January 18, 1967, and January 17, 1968.

"Report on the Black P Stone Legal Defense Project." Special Ministries Committee of the First Presbyterian Church, 1969.

Carol Marin. "Angel of Fear." Documentary by WMAQ-TV, 1988.

*Presbyterian Life* magazine, February 15, 1968.

"Millionaire Hit by Moore." *Chicago Daily Defender*, April 17, 1971.

"Organized Crime and Illicit Trafficking in Narcotics: Hearings Before the Permanent Subcommittee on Investigations of the Committee on Government Operations, United States Senate, Eighty-Eighth Congress, First and Second Sessions Pursuant to Senate Resolution 278, 88th Congress, Part 4." Senate hearing, July 30, 1964.

## Chapter 4

Sam Washington. "1,000 Rangers Make Promise to Pull for Peace in Area." *Chicago Daily Defender*, April 8, 1968.

"Youth Slain, 2d Is Wounded on S. Side." *Chicago Tribune*, January 1, 1968.

"Youth Shot in T.W.O. Center." *Chicago Tribune*, January 10, 1968.

"Tell Role of Teens in Youth Gang Killings." *Chicago Tribune*, January 13, 1968.

"Innocent in Gang Murder." *Chicago Tribune*, January 27, 1968.

FBI files. Memo. Mrs. Mildred Stegall, White House Personal Assistant to President Lyndon B. Johnson, to FBI Assistant Director and White House Liaison Cartha "Deke" DeLoach, February 13, 1968. "Blackstone Rangers Racial Matters—'interlocking directorates,'" Bureau file 157-9522-X2.

"Girl Killed, 2 Wounded in War of Gangs." *Chicago Tribune*, February 15, 1968.

"T.W.O. Teacher Is Charged in Death of Girl." *Chicago Tribune*, February 17, 1968.

FBI files. Teletype. Chicago to Director, FBI, March 6, 1968. Youth Gang Violence. Chicago, Illinois. Bureau file 157-1258.

FBI files. Airtel. Director of FBI to SAC [Special Agent in Charge], Chicago, March 28, 1968. Blackstone Rangers Youth Gang Violence, Chicago, Illinois, Racial Matters. Bureau files 157-1258; 157-1148.

James Gavin. "Argonne Lab Begins Hiring Gang Members." *Chicago Tribune*, March 31, 1968.

"Halt Disorders in Areas Near Jackson Park." *Chicago Tribune*, April 8, 1968.

Casey Banas. "Schools in West Riot Area Suffer Little Vandalism." *Chicago Tribune*, April 9, 1968.

Ronald Koziol and William Jones. "Police Probe Extortion by So. Side Gang." *Chicago Tribune*, April 13, 1968.

Ronald Koziol. "Two Business Leaders Defend Rangers, Deny Shakedowns." *Chicago Tribune*, April 17, 1968.

Ronald Koziol. "States Probes Alleged Extortion in Riots." *Chicago Tribune*, April 30, 1968.

"Gang Members Fight as Two Chiefs Parley." *Chicago Tribune*, May 9, 1968.

Bernard Judge. "Police See Blackstone Guns Blaze in Assassination Bid." *Chicago Tribune*, May 10, 1968.

Louise Hutchinson. "Share the Pain Set as a Goal of Poor March." *Chicago Tribune*, May 22, 1968.

James Yuenger. "Poor Appear at Capitol in Opening Rally." *Chicago Tribune*, May 22, 1968.

"Mutiny Breaks Out at Resurrection City." *Chicago Daily Defender*, May 23, 1968.

"March Leaders Are Hip to Gang Control." *Chicago Daily Defender*, May 23, 1968.

FBI files. Letterhead memorandum, FBI Chicago, May 13, 1968. Youth Gang Violence, Chicago, Illinois, Racial Matters. Bureau file 157-1258.

Bernard Judge. "Boy Tells of Killing by Rangers Gang." *Chicago Tribune*, May 22, 1968.

James Yuenger. "Street Gangs Create D.C. Camp Problem." *Chicago Tribune*, May 23, 1968.

"Witness Balks in Gang Killing." *Chicago Tribune*, May 25, 1968.

"Rangers Alibi in Murder: I Was in Church." *Chicago Tribune*, May 28, 1968.

"Gang Chief Convicted of Murder Bribe." *Chicago Tribune*, May 30, 1968.

Bob Hunter. "Should Branion's Lawyers Have Chosen Bench Trial?" *Chicago Daily Defender*, June 5, 1968.

Bob Hunter. "Sentencing of Rangers Postponed to July 18." *Chicago Daily Defender*, June 19, 1968.

FBI files. Airtel. SAC, Chicago, to Director of FBI, June 17, 1968. Youth Gang Violence, Chicago, Illinois, Pleasant Valley Farm. Bureau files 157-1258; 157-1148.

"Man Convicted of Illegally Shipping Guns." *Chicago Tribune*, June 12, 1968.

"Police Plotting to Put Down Rangers, Fort Says." *Chicago Daily Defender*, June 13, 1968.

FBI files. Teletype. SAC, Chicago, to Director of FBI, June 29, 1968. Blackstone Rangers; Youth Gang Violence NCIC RM, CPD report busting Stones with weapons to FBI. Bureau files 157-1258; 157-1148.

FBI files. Letterhead memorandum. FBI Chicago, July 2, 1968. Blackstone Rangers, Youth Gang Violence, Chicago. Bureau file 157-1258.

Paul McGrath. "Open Hearing Today on Street Gang Aid." *Chicago Tribune*, June 20, 1968.

Aldo Beckman. "4 Charge Is Made by Warden of County Jail." *Chicago Tribune*, June 21, 1968.

William Jones. "Ex-Blackstone Ranger to Tell of Gang Killings, Drug Traffic." *Chicago Tribune*, June 21, 1968.

Betty Washington. "T.W.O. Denies Gang Charge." *Chicago Daily Defender*, June 22, 1968.

"Ex-Leader of Gang Testifies on a Plan for Negro Uprising." *New York Times*, June 22, 1968.

"U. of C. Unable to Trace $64,000 Federal Gift." *Chicago Tribune*, June 23, 1968.

FBI files. Airtel. SAC, Chicago, to Director of FBI, July 23, 1968. Youth Gang Violence, Chicago, Illinois. Blackstone Rangers involved in militant activity in rural areas south of Chicago. Bureau file 157-1258.

FBI files. Teletype. SAC, Chicago, to Director and Springfield of FBI, August 2, 1968. Youth Gang Violence, Chicago, Illinois. Blackstone Rangers accused of possessing explosives. Bureau files 157-1258; 157-1148.

FBI files. Letterhead memorandum. FBI Chicago, August 14, 1968. Racial Matters, Warning of Blackstone Rangers planned Demonstrations at the National Democratic Convention (NDC), August 1968, Youth Gang Violence Chicago. Bureau files 157-1148; 157-2410.

FBI files. Airtel. SAC, Chicago, to Director of FBI, August 14, 15, 16, 1968. Racial Situation warning of Stones Plans to cause a militant attack on Chicago Heights, Illinois, 1968. Bureau file 157-1132.

FBI files. Letterhead memorandum. FBI Mobile, Alabama, September 4, 1968, Blackstone Rangers Chicago, Illinois. Bureau file 157-1148.

Chicago Reader. "Gang Green." November 17. Volume 27, number 7.

## Chapter 5

"Riots, Civil and Criminal Disorders." Hearings before the Permanent Sub-committee on Investigations of the Committee on Government Operations, U.S. Senate, Ninetieth Congress, Second Session, 1968. Includes testimony of Fry, Griffin, Cook County State's Attorney, mother of Stone members.

"Rangers' Leader Walks Out on Probers." *Chicago Tribune*, July 10, 1968.

Aldo Beckman. "Gang Hearings Draw Full House; Best Capitol Hill Show in Years." *Chicago Tribune*, July 7, 1968.

Paul McGrath. "Open Hearing Today on Street Gang Aid." *Chicago Tribune*, June 20, 1968.

Aldo Beckman. "4 Charge Is Made by Warden of County Jail." *Chicago Tribune*, June 21, 1968.

William Jones. "Police to Tell Senators of Gang Bribe Bid." *Chicago Tribune*, June 25, 1968.

Aldo Beckman. "Mother Tells Sons' Gang Killing Role." *Chicago Tribune*, June 27, 1968.

Bob Hunter. "Democratic Candidate Raps McClellan Probe." *Chicago Daily Defender*, July 18, 1968.

"Report to the Presbytery of Chicago from Its Committee Investigating Allegations of Wrongdoing Made Against the Reverend John Fry, Mr. Charles LaPaglia and Miss Ann Schwalbach of the Staff of First Presbyterian Church, Chicago—1969." Presented to the Presbytery of Chicago.

Aldo Beckman. "Senate Cites Gang Chief." *Chicago Tribune*, July 20, 1968.

"OEO Cuts Off Federal Funds for South Side Negro Gangs." *Chicago Tribune*, August 1, 1968.

Nicholas Lemann. *The Promised Land: The Great Migration and How It Changed America.* New York: Vintage Books, 1991, 97.

Patricia Leeds. "Conlisk Tells Plans to Enlarge Gang Unit." *Chicago Tribune*, November 8, 1968.

Arthur Siddon. "$9,000 Youth Job Goes to Gang Leader." *Chicago Tribune*, November 9, 1968.

William Jones. "Kenwood Leader Is Ex-Convict." *Chicago Tribune*, November 13, 1968.

"Fort Quits $9,000 Job with Kenwood Group." *Chicago Tribune*, December 3, 1968.

"Arrest Fort, Three Others in High School." *Chicago Tribune*, February 12, 1969.

"Viet Veterans Cut Ties with Ranger Gang." *Chicago Tribune*, March 28, 1969.

William Jones. "Ranger Jeff Fort Fears for Life." *Chicago Tribune*, May 29, 1969.

"Jeff Fort Is Sentenced to 6-Month Term." *Chicago Tribune*, June 4, 1969.

"Unit Forms to Battle Crime." *Chicago Daily Defender*, January 17, 1970.

Donald Mosby. "Indict Jeff Fort, 17 Other Stones." *Chicago Daily Defender*, January 31, 1970.

"Fort a Preacher?" *Chicago Daily Defender*, August 22, 1970.

"Stones Take Political Aim." *Chicago Daily Defender*, September 29, 1971.

William Jones. "Reveal Rangers Asked $150,000 of Sammy Davis." *Chicago Tribune*, March 7, 1970.

Harold Remy. "Gang Leader Jeff Fort Arrested in N.Y." *Chicago Tribune*, October 30, 1970.

William Jones. "Black P Stone Nation Empire Totters." *Chicago Tribune*, December 27, 1970.

Rudolph Unger. "23 in P Stone Gang Indicted for Role in U.S. Poverty Fraud." *Chicago Tribune*, April 8, 1971.

"Rangers Chief Found Guilty of Battery." *Chicago Tribune*, May 17, 1969.

"Rangers, Mob Link Told." *Chicago Tribune,* March 6, 1970.

"The Black Mafia." *Chicago Tribune,* March 7, 1970.

"Say Sammy Davis Lost Loot in Gang Deal." *Chicago Daily Defender,* March 7, 1970.

Robert Wiedrich. "Tower Ticker." *Chicago Tribune,* March 19, 1970.

"Gang Leader Arrested in Two Slayings." *Chicago Tribune,* June 13, 1970.

"Bar Bail for Two Gang Cheiftains." *Chicago Daily Defender,* June 16, 1970.

"Gang Leader Seized in Alfano Murder." *Chicago Tribune,* September 3, 1970.

"7 Stones Indicted in Cop Death." *Chicago Tribune,* September 4, 1970.

"Hunt 2 for Shooting Alfano Trial Witness." *Chicago Tribune,* March 10, 1971.

"Two Gang Members Sought in Shootings." *Chicago Tribune,* August 1, 1971.

"Drop Charges Against 2 in Gang Shooting." *Chicago Tribune,* October 19, 1971.

Steven Pratt. "Fort Guilty in Gang Fraud." *Chicago Tribune,* March 30, 1972.

"Probe Bey 'Hit Orders'." *Chicago Daily Defender,* March 13, 1973.

Thomas Powers. "Police, Gang Look for Bey's Assailant." *Chicago Tribune,* March 13, 1973.

"Bey Names 3d Man in Shooting." *Chicago Tribune,* March 16, 1973.

"3 Still Sought in Bey Shooting." *Chicago Tribune,* March 18, 1973.

"2d Suspect Identified in Bey Case." *Chicago Daily Defender,* March 17, 1973.

"Carey: Exhume Body of Lucas." *Chicago Daily Defender,* March 20, 1973.

"3 Charged in Shooting of Charles Bey." *Chicago Tribune,* March 27, 1973.

"3 Suspects Freed on Bail." *Chicago Daily Defender*, March 28, 1973.

Ronald Yates. "Weapons Sold to Gangs." *Chicago Daily Defender*, April 23, 1973.

"Two Gang Leaders Guilty in Murders." *Chicago Tribune*, June 15, 1973.

Charles Mount. "Saw Slayings." *Chicago Tribune*, June 13, 1973.

"Drop Charges Against 2 in Gang Shooting." *Chicago Tribune*, October 19, 1971.

"Doing a Number on the Mob." *Chicago Tribune*, April 21, 1974.

"P Stone Nation Hit by Power Struggle." *Chicago Tribune*, April 22, 1974.

"Slaying in Temple Probed by Police." *Chicago Daily Defender,* September 21, 1974.

Bob Wiedrich. "Two Punks Who Made Crime Pay." *Chicago Tribune*, October 30, 1971.

Bob Wiedrich. "Ex-Gang Goons Busy—As Union Organizers." *Chicago Tribune*, November 3, 1974.

"Judge Cuts Jeff Fort's Prison Sentence; To Get Out 3 Months Earlier." *Chicago Tribune*, April 25, 1975.

Vernon Jarrett. "A Leaderless Folk Just Waiting It Out." *Chicago Tribune*, July 13, 1975.

Harry Kelly. "Rangers vs. Panthers." *Chicago Tribune*, November 20, 1975.

Bob Wiedrich. "Perspective." *Chicago Tribune*, November 26, 1975.

John O'Brien and Richard Phillips. "26 Are Named." *Chicago Tribune*, November 27, 1975.

Henry Wood. "Ex-gang Leader Is Ambushed." *Chicago Tribune*, December 16, 1975.

## Chapter 6

F. Richard Ciccone. "Jeff Fort's 'Nation': Allah Gets a Chief Priest." *Chicago Tribune*, April 11, 1976.

Lynn Emmerman. "Jeff Fort: 'Criminal Genius' or a Punk?" *Chicago Tribune*, October 18, 1981.

Robert Enstad. "FBI OKd Ranger Threat: Ex-official." *Chicago Tribune*, February 11, 1976.

Richard Philbrick and Lee Strobel. "Jeff Fort Appears in Trial Audience; Judge Halts Case." *Chicago Tribune*, April 8, 1976.

Richard Phillips. "P Stone Figures' Appearance in Court Leads to Mistrial." *Chicago Tribune*, April 9, 1976.

F. Richard Ciccone. "Moore Calls Fort 'Punk,' Not Builder of New Faith." *Chicago Tribune*, April 11, 1976.

"A Problem with the P Stones." *Chicago Tribune*, April 13, 1976.

Robert Enstad. "Gang's Display of Arms Revealed." *Chicago Tribune*, May 7, 1976.

"'Vacuum Cleaner' Spies Costly to FBI." *Chicago Tribune*, May 7, 1976.

Lee Strobel. "Charge Moore Lets Killers Roam." *Chicago Tribune*, September 24, 1976.

Jerry Thornton and Philip Wattley. "Black Gang Chief Slain Near Home." *Chicago Tribune*, February 26, 1977.

Wallace Turner. "Search Grows for Nevada Unionist; Dispute on Pension Fund Reported." *New York Times*, March 1, 1977.

James Coates. "Documents Bare FBI's Role in Fatal Panther Raid." *Chicago Tribune*, November 22, 1977.

"Movie Typecasting in Stateville Is Real Thing for New TV Film." *Chicago Tribune*, May 11, 1978.

Bob Greene. "Rangers Redux? A 'Grad' Shudders." *Chicago Tribune*, June 12, 1979.

"Police Nab 2 in Raid on Jeff Fort Mosque." *Chicago Tribune*, July 14, 1979.

Jerry Crimmins. No title. *Chicago Tribune*, December 2, 1979.

Monroe Anderson. "City Street Gangs: Ember Flares Anew." *Chicago Tribune*, October 13, 1980.

"Two More Suspects Held in City Drug Crackdown." *Chicago Tribune*, October 16, 1980.

Jerry Thornton. "Gang Leader, 6 Fur-Clad Followers Are Arrested After High-Speed Chase." *Chicago Tribune*, December 13, 1980.

Philip Wattley and Sam Smith. "Jeff Fort Back in Gang Business; Cops Fear a War." *Chicago Tribune*, December 21, 1980.

"Jeff Fort Brings Minions to Court." *Chicago Tribune*, December 25, 1980.

Photo. *Chicago Tribune*, February 27, 1981.

Lynn Emmerman. "T's and Blues: Cheap 'Heroin' in Chicago." *Chicago Tribune*, March 1, 1981.

Henry Wood. "Two in Gangs Held in Slayings." *Chicago Tribune*, March 19, 1981.

Lynn Emmerman. "Guns, Gangs, and Terror . . . A Way of Life at Cabrini." *Chicago Tribune*, March 22, 1981.

Bonita Brodt. "Three Jailed in Street Gang Crackdown." *Chicago Tribune*, April 7, 1981.

"Courts." *Chicago Tribune*, June 25, 1981.

Patricia Leeds. "Column 1." *Chicago Tribune*, August 17, 1981.

"Gang Leader Fort Hid Fugitive, Police Charge." *Chicago Tribune*, October 11, 1981.

"City Report." *Chicago Tribune*, October 12, 1981.

Lynn Emmerman and Thomas Powers. "Drug Ring Broken; 26 Seized." *Chicago Tribune*, March 22, 1981.

Lynn Emmerman. "Smiles Follow Drug Sweep." *Chicago Tribune*, October 15, 1981.

Photo. *Chicago Tribune*, October 15, 1981.

Lynn Emmerman. "Calm Follows South Side Drug Sweep." *Chicago Tribune*, October 15, 1981.

"City Report." *Chicago Tribune*, October 24, 1981.

"Gang Member's Purchase of Building Investigated." *Chicago Tribune*, December 27, 1981.

"Trial Postponed for Gang Leader" (photo). *Chicago Tribune*, January 6, 1982.

Lynn Emmerman. "Dope, Guns, Gang Leader Seized." *Chicago Tribune*, February 7, 1982.

Kenan Heise. "Substitute Teachers Optimistic Despite Frustrations." *Chicago Tribune*, March 5, 1982.

"Lawyers Face Fines or Jail." *Chicago Tribune*, March 8, 1982.

Philip Wattley. "Drugs, Guns Seized in El Rukn Raid." *Chicago Tribune*, June 15, 1982.

"Jeff Fort and 16 Others Are Arrested." *Chicago Tribune*, July 19, 1982.

Bonita Brodt and Philip Wattley. "Brother of Gang Chief Is Indicted in Murder." *Chicago Tribune*, June 15, 1982.

Lynn Emmerman. "Dixon Hopes New Prison Might Ease Its Pain." *Chicago Tribune*, June 21, 1982.

Bonita Brodt. "Will Daley Run? Wait Till Fall." *Chicago Tribune*, June 21, 1982.

"Multiplier End Sought." *Chicago Tribune*, July 19, 1982.

"Daley Sets Date for His Decision." *Chicago Tribune*, December 21, 1982.

"7 Gang Members Held." *Chicago Tribune*, July 22, 1982.

Robert Davis. "El Rukn Street Gang Joins Drive to Register Voters." *Chicago Tribune*, August 25, 1982.

"Making the Black Vote Count." *Chicago Tribune*, September 24, 1982.

"Two Indicted on Charge of Intimidating Witness." *Chicago Tribune*, December 2, 1982.

Marianne Taylor. "Murder Suspect May Be Freed for Ruling Appeal." *Chicago Tribune*, December 30, 1982.

Lynn Emmerman. "The Most Dangerous Game." *Chicago Tribune*, January 9, 1983.

David Axelrod and Lynn Emmerman. "Gang Members Campaigning for the Byrne." *Chicago Tribune*, February 4, 1983.

"City's New Attorney a Loyal 'Hired G'." *Chicago Tribune*, June 5, 1983.

"City Report." *Chicago Tribune*, June 9, 1983.

"Fort's Brother Is Convicted." *Chicago Tribune*, June 12, 1983.

John O'Brien. "Ex-gang Figure Is Indicted on Arson Charge." *Chicago Tribune*, August 5, 1983.

"Jeff Fort, 2 Aides Indicted." *Chicago Tribune*, August 13, 1983.

"Gang Leader Pleads Innocent in Drug Case." *Chicago Tribune*, September 1, 1983.

"Gang Reportedly Got $10,000 Meant for Ex-Chicago Mayor." *Chicago Tribune*, December 30, 1983.

"Democrat Disavows Gang Pay." *Chicago Tribune*, September 11, 1983.

"City Report." *Chicago Tribune*, September 16, 1983.

Charles Mount. "El Rukn Sale of Building Is Challenged." *Chicago Tribune*, October 13, 1983.

Michael Arndt. "Fight Brews over Rort Drug Trial Site." *Chicago Tribune*, November 8, 1983.

"Fort Misses Dope Trial; Now Sought." *Chicago Tribune*, November 30, 1983.

Marianne Taylor. "Jeff Fort Pleads Guilty in Drug Case." *Chicago Tribune*, November 10, 1983.

"Gang Leader Jeff Fort on U.S. Most-Wanted List." *Chicago Tribune*, December 1, 1983.

Marianne Taylor. "Jeff Fort Gets 13-Year Term in Mississippi." *Chicago Tribune*, December 17, 1983.

William Recktenwald and Howard Witt. "Prison No Bar to Fort's Leadership." *Chicago Tribune*, December 19, 1983.

Nathaniel Sheppard Jr. and William Recktenwald. "New Upsurge in Street Gangs." *Chicago Tribune*, January 8, 1984.

William Recktenwald. "On the Wall." *Chicago Tribune*, January 10, 1984.

"The Evolution of Street Gangs." *Chicago Tribune*, January 13, 1984.

"Rukn 'General' Gets 10 Years." *Chicago Tribune*, February 4, 1984.

Bill Granger. "I Tell Ya It's Criminal, All of This Ingratitude." *Chicago Tribune*, February 15, 1984.

Leanita McClain. "Jeff Fort Can't Be 'Rewritten'." *Chicago Tribune*, April 29, 1984.

"Grand Jury Investigating Alleged Property Tax Sale Abuse." *Chicago Tribune*, May 13, 1984.

"City Trains First Workers Since End of Hiring Ban." *Chicago Tribune*, May 25, 1984.

"1 of 2 Extortion Counts Against Lawyer Dropped." *Chicago Tribune*, May 25, 1984.

Andy Knott. "Paroled Murderer Gets Life Prison Sentence." *Chicago Tribune*, June 21, 1984.

Maurice Possley. "Panther Infiltrator Still in Hiding." *Chicago Tribune*, July 22, 1984.

"Again, a War on Gangs." *Chicago Tribune*, November 29, 1984.

Manuel Galvan and Hanke Gratteau. "Mayor Aims at 5 Gang Hot Spots." *Chicago Tribune*, December 6, 1984.

Maurice Possley. "State Parole Policy Voided by Judge." *Chicago Tribune*, December 27, 1984.

## Chapter 7

"Louis Farrakhan: Gets $5 Million Loan Interest-Free from Libyan Leader Muammar Qadafi." *JET*, May 20, 1985.

Tape. Nation of Islam Saviour's Day speech, 1982.

"Farrakhan Continues Hon. Elijah Muhammad's Mission." *Final Call*, March 10, 2000. http://www.finalcall.com/national/savioursday2k/farrakhan.htm.

George Curry. "Farrakhan Reveals Loan from Libya." *Chicago Tribune*, May 3, 1985.

Douglas Frantz and George de Lama. "Farrakhan Probed on Libya Visit." *Chicago Tribune*, April 13, 1986.

Michael Arndt. "Clements Rejects Libya Pitch to Black Soldiers." *Chicago Tribune*, March 4, 1985.

Jerry Thornton. "Gang Leader, 6 Fur-Clad Followers Are Arrested After High-Speed Chase." *Chicago Tribune*, December 13, 1980.

Philip Wattley and Sam Smith. "Jeff Fort Back in Gang Business." *Chicago Tribune*, December 21, 1980.

George Lewis. *A Power Stronger than Itself: The AACM and American Experimental Music.* Chicago: University of Chicago Press, 2008.

Emma McDaniel in Mary Pattillo. *Black on the Block: The Politics of Race and Class in the City.* Chicago: University of Chicago Press, 2007, 272.

Lynn Emmerman. "Dope, Guns, Gang Leader Seized." *Chicago Tribune*, February 7, 1982.

Phillip Wattley. "Drugs, Guns Seized in El Rukn Raid." *Chicago Tribune*, June 15, 1982.

Robert Davis. "El Rukn Street Gang Joins Drive to Register Voters." *Chicago Tribune*, August 25, 1982.

"'Unjailable' Jeff Fort Surrenders." *Chicago Tribune*, June 9, 1983.

"Jeff Fort, 2 Aides Indicted." *Chicago Tribune*, August 13, 1983.

Dick Mitchell. "Democrats Gave Gang $10,000." *Chicago Sun-Times*, September 11, 1983.

Dick Mitchell. "El Rukns Concede Vote Role." *Chicago Sun-Times*, September 17, 1983.

Ron Chepesiuk. *Black Gangsters of Chicago.* Fort Lee, NJ: Barricade Books, 2007.

"Street Gang Faces 4 Additional Suits." *Chicago Tribune*, September 16, 1983.

"El Rukn Sale of Building Is Challenged." *Chicago Tribune*, October 13, 1983.

Marianne Taylor. "Jeff Fort Pleads Guilty in Drug Case." *Chicago Tribune*, November 10, 1983.

Douglas Frantz. "Fort Misses Dope Trial; Now Sought." *Chicago Tribune*, November 30, 1983.

"Gang Leader Jeff Fort on U.S. Most-Wanted List." *Chicago Tribune*, December 1, 1983.

Marianne Taylor. "Jeff Fort Gets 13-Year Term in Mississippi." *Chicago Tribune*, December 17, 1983.

Ron Chepesiuk, *Black Gangsters of Chicago*. Fort Lee, NJ: Barricade Books, 2007.

William Recktenwald and Howard Witt. "Prison No Bar to Fort's Leadership: Crafty El Rukns Chief Still Pulled Strings on Street." *Chicago Tribune*, December 19, 1983.

Jean Davidson. "Informant Turns Heat on Rukns." *Chicago Tribune*, August 9, 1985.

William Recktenwald. "Gangs Battle Renegades for City Drug Trade." *Chicago Tribune*, May 28, 1985.

William Recktenwald. "8 Members of S. Side Gang Indicted in 9 Slayings." *Chicago Tribune*, June 5, 1985.

Maurice Possley. "El Rukn Tells Court Prison Prayer Denied." *Chicago Tribune*, November 19, 1985.

Maurice Possley. "El Rukn Win One on Jail Religion." *Chicago Tribune*, November 20, 1985.

Maurice Possley. "Witness El Rukns 'Like a Frat'." *Chicago Tribune*, November 21, 1985.

"When Gangs Get Religion." *Chicago Tribune*, November 22, 1985.

Maurice Possley. "Warden Says Rukns Would Intimidate." *Chicago Tribune*, December 5, 1985.

E. R. Shipp. "Chicago Gang Sues to Be Recognized as Religion." *Chicago Tribune*, December 27, 1985.

"Brother of Gang Leader Fort Charged in Slaying of Defector." *Chicago Tribune*, February 19, 1986.

Linnet Myers. "Gang 'General' Found Guilty in 3 Murders." *Chicago Tribune*, February 5, 1986.

Linnet Myers. "Reputed Gang Leader's Brother Granted Bond." *Chicago Tribune*, February 21, 1986.

Jerry Crimmins. "Gang's Religion Label Rejected." *Chicago Tribune*, June 2, 1986.

Rudolph Unger. "Rukn Security Service Gets Stung." *Chicago Tribune*, June 20, 1986.

John O'Brien and Jack Houston. "El Rukn Arsenal Raided." *Chicago Tribune*, August 6, 1986.

Dean Baquet. "El Rukns Say Raid Stemmed from Bet." *Chicago Tribune*, August 9, 1986.

"A Gang That Won't Go Away." *Chicago Tribune*, August 10, 1986.

"Why We're Losing War on Gangs." *Chicago Tribune*, August 17, 1986.

Linnet Myers. "Jury Approves Death Sentence for 2 El Rukns." *Chicago Tribune*, August 23, 1986.

Maurice Possley and William B. Crawford Jr. "El Rukns Indicted in Libya Scheme." *Chicago Tribune*, October 31, 1986.

Rick Hornung and Thomas M. Burton. "City Feels Heat to Cut Datacom." *Chicago Tribune*, November 1, 1986.

"The Nation." *New York Times*, November 2, 1986.

Maurice Possley. "More Inquiries Target El Rukns." *Chicago Tribune*, November 7, 1986.

No title. *Chicago Tribune*, November 7, 1986.

"Visitor to Jailed Fort Faces Trial in Texas." *Chicago Tribune*, November 15, 1986.

William B. Crawford Jr. "Fort Pleads Innocent in Libya Plot." *Chicago Tribune*, November 18, 1986.

Maurice Possley. "Prosecutors Ask Judge to Bar Fort Phone Calls." *Chicago Tribune*, November 19, 1986.

"Jailed Gang Leader Loses Phone Rights." *Chicago Tribune*, November 20, 1986.

Linnet Myers. "Jeff Fort's Brother Is Convicted." *Chicago Tribune*, November 22, 1986.

"Charge Street Gang with Libyan Link." *Chicago Tribune*, November 22, 1986.

Maurice Possley. "Police Crack Secret El Rukn Crime Code." *Chicago Tribune*, December 14, 1986.

Maurice Possley. "El Rukn Probe Fed on Wiretaps." *Chicago Tribune*, December 15, 1986.

"Gangster Ordered Death of Man Tied to Jesse Jackson." *Chicago Tribune*, November 5, 1987.

William E. Schmidt. "U.S. Squares Off Against Tough Gang." *New York Times*, November 5, 1987.

"Sammy Davis Jr. Did Agree to Help Gang." *Los Angeles Sentinel*, November 19, 1987.

"5 Are Convicted in Terror Scheme." *New York Times*, November 25, 1987.

"Five Draw Long Sentence for Terrorism Scheme." *New York Times*, December 31, 1987.

## Chapter 8

*United States of America v. Jeff Fort, Leon McAnderson, Roosevelt Hawkins, Alan Knox, Reico Cranshaw, and Melvin Mayes*. No. 86CR572.

Yahia H. Zoubier. "Libya in US Foreign Policy: From Rogue State to Good Fellow." *Third World Quarterly*, vol. 23, no. 1, 2002, 31–53.

Jonathan B. Schwartz. "Dealing with a 'Rogue State': The Libya Precedent." *American Journal of International Law*, vol. 101: 553, 2007.

*Economic and Political Weekly*, vol. 21, no. 4, January 25, 1986.

Mansour O. El-Kikhia. *Libya's Qaddafi: The Politics of Contradiction.* Gainesville: University of Florida Press, 1997, 109.

U.S. State Department Web site, Libyan jets shot: www.state.gov/r/pa/ei/bgn/5425.htm#foreign.

Adrienne Dell. "Trial Cost Estimated at $500,000." *Chicago Sun-Times*, November 25, 1987.

Michael Cordts and Adrienne Dell. "Fort Trial Hard on Gallery." *Chicago Sun-Times*, November 1, 1987.

Adrienne Dell and Phillip J. O'Connor. "'Rocket' Signals 2 El Rukn Arrests." *Chicago Sun-Times*, August 8, 1986.

Adrienne Dell. "El Rukn Jury Locked Up After 'Ominous' Calls." *Chicago Sun-Times*, October 21, 1987.

Thomas Frisbie. "DuPage Inmates Fear Trial Fallout." *Chicago Sun-Times*, October 28, 1987.

Adrienne Dell. "Tapes Tell Rukns' Suspicion." *Chicago Sun-Times*, November 3, 1987.

Adrienne Dell. "Fort Gets 80-Year Term, Fine." *Chicago Sun-Times*, December 30, 1987.

Tim Berber. "Ex-Rukn Nabbed in Libya Terror Case." *Chicago Sun-Times*, March 15, 1995.

## Chapter 9

Rosalind Rossi and Adrienne Drell. "Fort, 4 Rukns Found Guilty." *Chicago Sun-Times*, October 19, 1988.

Rosalind Rossi. "75 More Years for Fort." *Chicago Sun-Times*, November 15, 1988.

"Bennie Fort, 38, Brother of El Rukn Chief, Is Slain." *Chicago Sun-Times*, June 12, 1988.

Adrienne Dell. "Threat by El Rukn Charged." *Chicago Sun-Times*, June 23, 1988.

"Rukns Found Guilty in Threat Shooting." *Chicago Sun-Times*, October 28, 1988.

Michael Gillis. "'Fort' Raided, 64 Rukns Indicted." *Chicago Sun-Times*, October 28, 1989.

Rosalind Rossi. "Court Told of Rukn Drug 'Chalk Talk'." *Chicago Sun-Times*, May 1, 1991.

Rosalind Rossi. "$330,000 Heroin Payoff Thrilled Robinson: Witness." *Chicago Sun-Times*, July 16, 1991.

Daniel J. Lehman. "Ex-Rukn Convicted of Murders in Retrial." *Chicago Sun-Times*, March 23, 1995.

"Jury Convicts 10 Members of Notorious Gang." *New York Times*, August 11, 1991.

"Mayor Will Not Run for Governor." *Los Angeles Sentinel*, November 11, 1993.

Case No. 89 CR 908. Lexis Nexis.

Robert Blau and William Rectenwald. "El Rukn Razing Doesn't End Gangs." *Chicago Tribune*, June 7, 1990.

"Jackson's Relative Is Charged in Killing Former Employee." *New York Times*, September 22, 1988.

"Briefing the News." *Los Angeles Sentinel*, September 29, 1988.

"Authorities Tense as Jury Selection Begins in Robinson Trial." *Atlanta Daily World*, January 19, 1989.

Eric N. Berg. "Jackson's Half Brother Is Indicted in Hiring of Killers and Skimming." *New York Times*, October 28, 1989.

"Indict 65 Members of Chicago Gang; Case Involves 3 Half-Bros. of Jackson." *Atlanta Daily World*, October 31, 1989.

"Noah Robinson Busted in El Rukn Crackdown." *Los Angeles Sentinel*, November 2, 1989.

"Jesse Jackson's Half-Brother Ordered Held Without Bond." *Atlanta Daily World*, November 2, 1989.

Stephen Wade. "Jackson Relatives Named in Indictment." *New Pittsburgh Courier*, November 11, 1989.

Jesse H. Walker. "Jesse's Brother Charged in Murder for Hire Case." *New York Amsterdam News*, November 11, 1989.

Andrew H. Malcolm. "Modern Communications Muddy Rights of Criminal Defendants." *New York Times*, November 10, 1990.

Don Terry. "In Chicago Courtroom, Nation's First Super Gang Fights for Life." *New York Times*, May 19, 1991.

"Jury Convicts 10 Members of Notorious Gang." *New York Times*, August 11, 1991.

Alex S. Jones. "Despite Correcting Its Error, Newspaper Loses Libel Case." *New York Times*, May 24, 1991.

Lawrence I. Shulruff. "Can Nameless Jurors Be Impartial?" *New York Times*, May 24, 1991.

Katherine Bishop. "New Front in Marijuana War: Business Records." *New York Times*, May 24, 1991.

David Margolick. "At the Bar." *New York Times*, May 24, 1991.

"Life Term for Jesse Jackson's Half-Brother." *New York Times*, August 23, 1992.

"Prosecutors in Gang Cases Accused of Misconduct." *New York Times*, December 20, 1992.

"El Rukns Get New Trial." *Los Angeles Sentinel*, July 1, 1993.

"Gang Conviction Overturned." *New York Times*, September 21, 1993.

"Mayor Will Not Run for Governor." *Los Angeles Sentinel*, November 11, 1993.

## Chapter 10

FBI transcript. File number 315N-MM-106989. December 16, 2005. DVD number 22. Case agent: Special Agents John P. Stewart and Dana Brager. Reviewed and edited by Special Agent John P. Stewart.

FBI transcript. File number 315N-MM-106989. December 21, 2005. DVD number 22. Case agent: Special Agents John P. Stewart and Dana Brager. Reviewed and edited by Special Agent John P. Stewart.

United States District Court, Southern District of Florida, Case No. 06-20373-CR-LENARD. *United States of America v. Narseal Batiste et al.* Outline of expert witness testimony. Document 1199, FLSD Docket 03/05/2009.

Rod Emery. *The Blueprint: From Gangster Disciple to Growth & Development.* Elgin, IL: Morris, 1996.

Vanessa Blum. "5 of Liberty City 6 Guilty—In 3rd Trial, Men Convicted in Plot to Fell Sears Tower." *Chicago Tribune,* May 13, 2009.

Michelle Garcia. "N.Y. Using Terrorism Law to Prosecute Street Gang." *Washington Post,* February 1, 2005.

Ron Scherer and Alexandra Marks. "Gangs, Prison: Al Qaeda Breeding Grounds?" *Christian Science Monitor,* June 14, 2002.

James Oliphant. "Padilla Guilty in Terror Case—U.S. Wins Key Conviction of Chicago Man Ted to Al Qaeda." *Chicago Tribune,* August 17, 2007.

Angela Rozas and Margaret Ramirez. "Religious Group Denies Link to

Alleged Terrorist Plotters." *Chicago Tribune*, June 28, 2006.

Angela Rozas. "Alleged Plotter No Jihadist, Mom Says." *Chicago Tribune*, June 25, 2006.

James Janega, Ray Quintanilla, and David Kidwell. "Sears Tower Plot: Chicago-Raised 'Good Son' Found Trouble as Adult." *Chicago Tribune*, June 24, 2006.

## Additional Reading

R. Lincoln Keiser. *The Vice Lords: Warriors of the Streets*. New York: Holt, Rinehart and Winston, 1969.

# Index

40; open housing, campaign for in, 41; public housing in, 9–10, 15, 255–56; public schools in, 16, 256–57; racial covenants in, 10–12; rioting in, 18, 81; segregation in, 10, 16; youth violence in, 4–5
Chicago Crime Commission, 227, 229, 258
*Chicago Defender* (newspaper), 9, 11
Chicago Freedom Movement, 39–42
Chicago Heights (Illinois), 91
Chicago Housing Authority (CHA): public housing, dismantling of, 255–56
Chicago Land Clearance Commission, 15
Chicago Police Department (CPD), 227; and Gang Intelligence Unit (GIU), 61, 65, 92, 107, 113, 127, 141, 157
Chicago Public Schools (CPS): and Renaissance 2010 policy, 256–57
Chicago Urban League, 58
Chief Malik, 3. *See also* Jeff Fort
Childress, Maurice, 140
Christianity, 134, 148, 194
Christmas, Allen, 64
Cicero (Illinois), 42
Cincinnati (Ohio), 175
Civil Rights Act, 81
civil rights movement, 3, 39–40, 55, 83, 229
Clarke, John Henrik, 162
Clark, Mark, 120
Clark, Sidney, 84–85
Clark, Theotis "Thee," 37, 207
Clay, Nate, 153–54, 188–89, 207
Clements, George, 163–66, 212
Cleveland (Ohio), 92, 175
Coalition for United Community Action (CUCA), 114
Cobra Stones, 23, 36, 95–96, 124, 143. *See also* Mickey Cobras
cocaine, 173–75, 248–49, 251–53
Codwell, Edwin "Caboo," 33
Cogwell, Henry "Mickey," 5, 36, 57, 95, 114, 124, 128, 133, 140–43, 228
Cogwell, Jerome "Pony Soldier," 95–96, 124
Cohran, Kelan Phil, 43, 45–46, 164, 174
Collins, Tom, 90
Commission on Human Relations, 18
Community Renewal Society (CRS), 90, 112, 117
Conference on Third World Countries, 46
Conlisk, James, 114
Conlon, Suzanne B., 210
Conservative Rangers, 34, 50, 73, 88. *See also* Blackstone Rangers
Coons (gang), 20
Coordinating Council of Community Organizations (CCCO), 39–40
Cosey, Pete, 45
Cranshaw, Charles "Reico," 35, 47, 133, 141, 143, 180, 189–91, 195–97, 201
Cross, James, 179–80
Crowder, Bob, 45

Crowder, Lawrence, 205

Daylie, Daddy-O, 117, 119
Daley, Richard J., 9, 10, 15–16, 18, 57–58, 80, 94, 107, 111–12, 114–15, 123, 169
Daley, Richard M., 169, 212–13
Davis, Floyd, 212
Davis, Miles, 43
Davis, Terry "T-Bose," 241–42, 245, 250–51, 254
Davis, Sammy Jr., 46, 91, 116, 200
Davis, Tramell, 180–81, 183–84, 189, 191–93, 196, 200–201
Deacons (gang), 20
Dell Vikings, 2
DeLoach, Cartha D. "Deke," 75
Democratic National Convention, 70, 79, 90–91, 93–94
Destroyers (gang), 20
Detroit (Michigan), 79, 81, 104, 136
Devil Disciples. *See* Disciples
Dillard, Samuel "Two Mac," 36
Dinkins, Edward, 85
Dirty Sheiks (gang), 20
Disciples, 2–3, 5, 35, 39, 57, 61, 63, 69–70, 92, 94, 103, 113–14, 128, 159; Blackstone Rangers, rivalry between, 31–33, 50–51, 56, 71–72, 77, 84–85, 95–96, 115–16, 228; "dirty folks," as term, 32; turf of, 32. *See also* East Side Disciples
DiVarco, Joseph "Little Caesar," 141
Doane, Jeff, 129–30
Dodd, Aaron, 45
Dorenzo, Nick, 76
Dorsey, Thomas, 13
Downers Grove (Illinois), 118
Downie, Paul, 209
Doyle, William, 172, 212
Drexel Casanovas, 34. *See also* Nova Stones
Drug Enforcement Agency (DEA), 160, 169–70, 204
Duck Town set, 242
Dunbar-Bey, Susan Russell, 225
DuSable High School, 96

East, Ray, 206
East, Robert, 206
East Side Disciples, 32, 56, 58, 76. *See also* Disciples
Egyptian Cobras, 20, 97. *See also* Imperial Chaplins; Black P Stone Nation; Vice Lords
8-Tray Stones, 236, 238–39, 243–45; alakhbar, claiming of, 245–46; and drugs, 247–49, 252; history of, 240–42; public housing, dismantling of, 255; rift in, 254–55; turf wars, 256. *See also* Blackstone Rangers
Ellison, Douglas, 206
Ellis Rebel Stones, 34, 36, 84–85
El Rukns, 1, 132–33, 136–38, 142, 147, 160, 174, 188–89, 193–95, 203, 217, 229, 233, 235, 240–41,